DAVID ECCLES

DAVID ECCLES
Pioneer Western Industrialist

Leonard J. Arrington

Utah State University
Logan, Utah
1975

Copyright © Utah State University

Cataloging in Publication Data

Arrington, Leonard J.
   David Eccles: pioneer western industrialist.

   Bibliography:
   1. Eccles, David, 1849-1912.
HC102.5.E2A77   338'.092'4 [B]   75-2093
ISBN 0-87421-078-X

Published in cooperation with
Festival of the American West

*To Nora, Lila
and the
Memory of Cleone*

Royal Eccles Collection. Dry Gate, Glasgow, Scotland. With Children about the age of David when he was there with his family.

Preface

THIS BIOGRAPHY of Utah's first multi-millionaire was made possible by grants to the Utah State University Development Fund by Mrs. Nora Eccles Treadwell Harrison, a daughter of David Eccles. These grants were designed to assist with the development of a quality ceramics program, and to encourage scholarship in Western American history. In gratitude to Mrs. Harrison for the generosity of her contributions, and in celebration of Utah's greatest businessman and financier and his illustrious family, the University commissioned me as part of my teaching and research function in Western American history to write this biography.

Fortunately, Mrs. Cleone Rich Eccles, a daughter-in-law of David Eccles, allowed me to use a large number of manuscripts and documents relating to David Eccles that had been collected and prepared by her late husband, Royal Eccles. In this sense, Royal Eccles has been a collaborator in this work, and we can all be grateful for his prescience in collecting the material during the 1920s and 1930s when some of the individuals who had been associated with David Eccles were still alive. A substantial number of manuscripts, photographs, and family history were also made available by Nora Eccles Harrison and her brothers and sisters.

I am grateful to Nora and Richard Harrison, to Cleone and Justin Eccles, to Mrs. Lila Eccles Brimhall, to Marriner and George Eccles, to Mrs. Marie Caine, to Mr. and Mrs. S. J. Quinney, and, in fact, to all members of the David Eccles family who have furnished me materials relating to the life and character of David Eccles; to Stewart Eccles, a nephew of David Eccles, for similar information and help; and to N. D. Salisbury, Reed Bullen, Julia Eccles Johnson, Richard and Pat Bennett, and Richard Jensen. None of these persons, of course, is to be held responsible for what I have written.

In order to facilitate the research for this biography, the Utah State University Development Fund generously provided me with the assistance of my former secretary, JoAnn Woodruff Bair, and a number of bright undergraduate students at Utah State University. They include Newell George Daines III, Christine Rigby, Annette Randall Haws, Brad Morris, Richard Daines, RaNae Allen, and Ron Pedersen. These students (and Mrs. Bair) prepared task papers, wrote histories of the various Eccles enterprises, and helped me with the organization and writing of the first draft. Their contributions have been substantial, and I wish it were practical to list them as collaborators.

I am particularly grateful for the suggestions of Wallace Stegner, a friend of Utah State University and of the Eccles family, who generously read portions of this biography in an early draft. Dr. Stegner's critique was a miniature manual on the writing of good biography. Because of my own preoccupation with some administrative challenges during the revision process, I was fortunate to have the assistance of Maureen Ursenbach, a talented writer and editor of publications of the Historical Department of The Church of Jesus Christ of Latter-day Saints. Dr. Ursenbach's creative revision of the manuscript gave it a quality that is beyond my own abilities. I am grateful to Christine Croft, Pat Jarvis, and Beva Ott, who did the final typing. The index was prepared by Jill Mulvay.

Salt Lake City, Utah
July 2, 1974

L.J.A.

The five-state area of David Eccles' business operations, showing the location of most of his enterprises

Contents

1	Prologue: Boyhood in Scotland	1
2	Hope of Prosperity and Promise of Glory	11
3	The Emigrants	17
4	Ogden to Oregon: The Early Trek	27
5	Independence and Ambition	41
6	The First Business ... and Marriage	47
7	Bold and Cautious Venturer	57
8	Interlude in Politics	67
9	Lumber and Railroads in Oregon	83
10	David Eccles and the Development of Utah: The 1890s	99
11	Frontier Capitalist	115
12	The Man David Eccles	125

13	The Ogden Family	141
14	The Logan Family	153
15	David Eccles, Paterfamilias	163
16	Death and Burial	171
17	Settlement of the David Eccles Estate	181
18	Epilogue: Reasons for Eccles' Success	191

Appendix I: Chronological List of Companies Founded by David Eccles and Associates		205
Appendix II: Brief Histories of the Business Enterprises with Which David Eccles was Associated		207
	A Lumber Companies	211
	B Railroads	228
	C Beet Sugar Refineries	240
	D Food Processing Establishments	247
	E Construction	251
	F Banks and Insurance Company	256
	G Land and Livestock Projects	263
	H Other Enterprises	267
Bibliography		275
Index		281

Illustrations

David Eccles	Frontispiece
The Five-State Area of David Eccles' Business Operations	vi
Dry Gate, Glasgow, Scotland	xv
The Family of William and Sarah Hutchinson Eccles	10
William Eccles	40
Sarah Hutchinson Eccles	40
Bertha Marie Jensen Eccles	46
Logo of Oregon Lumber Company	80
Logging Teams, Chenowith, Washington	80
Loading Logs in Sumpter Valley, Oregon	81
Early Eccles Sawmill, Baker, Oregon	81
Eccles Sawmill at Chenowith, Washington	82
Steamer "Pearl" and Lumber Rafts, Viento, Oregon	82

Oregon Lumber Company Plant at Dee, Oregon	96
Oregon Lumber Company Plant at Baker, Oregon	96
Sketch of Plant of Grande Ronde Lumber Company	97
Eccles Employees at First Mill at Baker, Oregon	97
Oregon Lumber Plant and Related Enterprises	98
David Eccles and Charles W. Nibley	98
Eccles: Utah's First Tycoon	112
One of Nevada Ranches of Utah Construction Co.	113
Deseret National Bank Building	114
Ogden First National Bank Building	114
President Heber J. Grant	139
President Joseph F. Smith	139
David Eccles in 1900	140
David Eccles and Bertha Eccles	148
David Eccles about 1873	149
The Six Eldest Children in the Ogden Family	150
The Six Youngest Children in the Ogden Family	151
David Eccles in 1878.	152
David Eccles' Logan Family in 1909	159
David Eccles, Prosperous Businessman	160
Ellen Stoddard Eccles	161
David Eccles in 1883	161
Salt Lake Valley, Ogden Valley, and Cache Valley	162
Arnold D. Quantrell	191
Matthew Sandefur Browning	192
Judge Thomas D. Dee	192

1

Prologue: Boyhood in Scotland

On December 10, 1912, in cold morning light, persons in five Western states raised their flags and then somberly lowered them to half-mast. Later a temporary pause interrupted the daily routine in Utah, Idaho, Oregon, Nevada, and Washington. In Ogden, Utah streetcars stopped on their tracks, automobiles halted, and in several Ogden and Salt Lake City banks workers momentarily paused. Employees in Logan, Utah, and Burley, Idaho, businesses interrupted the task of the moment, and workmen in beet sugar factories in three states stood beside motionless machines. In Oregon, employees on two railroad lines ceased work; trains were halted. For five minutes everyone silently paid tribute as a funeral began. David Eccles was dead.

On December 6, below the headline "David Eccles, Wealthiest Citizen of Utah, Drops Dead," the front page of the *Ogden Standard-Examiner* carried four solid columns of type, relating the story of the life, accomplishments, and death of David Eccles. Newspapers throughout the state carried tributes from respected citizens, expressing sorrow and disbelief. His death was news throughout the United States.

It is not without reason that such widespread honor should be paid this man. The number of people who owed their livelihood to one or more of the fifty-four separate enterprises David Eccles had founded in the American West would alone justify such observance. Several banks, the Oregon Lumber Company, Amalgamated Sugar Company, Sumpter Valley and Mt. Hood Railways, and the world's largest mining and construction firm, the Utah Construction Company, all owed their existence to the enterprise of this man. Within his Church and the vast western area, predominantly Mormon, he was known, but even more, among non-Mormons he was respected as a loyal Latter-day Saint who functioned successfully among Gentile businessmen; he pioneered the desacralization or secularization of business in the Mormon cultural setting. To the opening and industrialization of the vast intermountain and northwest he contributed his vision, his energy, his prudent management. The West, vast and growing when David Eccles found it, was even fuller of promise when he departed it.

This was the man to match the land; America's opportunities and Eccles' abilities were well met. David Eccles' beginnings were not here, however, but in the Scotland of the bleak years following the industrial revolution. Beneath the bright facade of clans, kilts, and tartan plaids, the real life in nineteenth century Scotland was drab and commonplace. Its people were not dancing in village streets to the shrill excitement of the bagpipes, but rather toiling inside dingy mills, spinning and weaving the linen, cotton, and wool which made the country a world leader in manufacture of textiles.

Scotland's world prominence was bought at high cost to her working people, David Eccles' ancestors among them. The new factories deprived townspeople of the tasks for which they had been trained, and unskilled laborers were often thrown out of work by the unpredictable rhythm of over- and under-production. The unemployed received little help from authorities. When they once secured jobs, low wages forced them to recruit all available members of their families to supplement their scanty incomes. With the introduction of lighter machines more women and children were sent to the factories. Gas lighting lengthened the normal working day to thirteen or fourteen hours through a six-day week. Lack of fresh air, and a rigid routine requiring continual concentration of both physical and mental strength contributed to the heavy incidence of sickness among the children.[1] Punishments were severe if young workers slowed down or allowed their attention to wander. The appalling conditions are reflected in the "improvements" required by the 1833 Factory Act: children under nine were prohibited from working, and children under twelve could not be worked more than twelve hours per day.[2]

Despite the widespread Knox Doctrine that everyone be educated in order to be of use to the Church and the Commonwealth, and despite the national system of free graded education, most people could not afford the loss of income occasioned by school. In Paisley, where the Eccles family was living, in the early years of the century only one child in fifteen had attended school. By mid-century, twenty years after the Factory Act, a law requiring that children be released from the factories for half-time education was generally evaded.[3]

With the shifting from the fields to the factories came the move from the country to the town and the growth of town into

---

[1] Janet R. Glover, *The Story of Scotland* (London, 1960), pp. 317-19.
[2] T. C. Smout, *A History of the Scottish People, 1560-1830* (New York, 1969), pp. 415-17.
[3] Smout, pp. 261, 471; Elizabeth S. Haldane, *The Scotland of Our Fathers: A Study of Scottish Life in the Nineteenth Century* (New York, 1934), pp. 152-53.

city. Towns originally made compact for defense became even more concentrated. Tall stone tenements crowded each other in narrow streets. At times "up to fifteen . . . lived in one [one-room] house, where they cooked, ate, slept, washed, when they did wash, bore and begot their children."[4] Water for all purposes had to be fetched from public wells or bought in stoups (buckets) from vendors, then carried up precipitous lanes and stairways to upper floors. The usual daily diet of the working people included oatmeal porridge morning and night, with potatoes, bannocks (loaves of unleavened oat or barley bread), and salt herring for dinner.[5]

Filth and stench accompanied the crowds which swarmed in the straining cities. Slaughterhouses and tanneries increased with the population, and the small space around each building was filled by pigsties, stables, and dairies. Burgh councils made some effort to keep the streets clean, but they felt no responsibility for the staircases in the tenements. Since the narrow, smelly passageways were no one's particular domain, the dwellings continued to accumulate more dirt and vermin. Nearby farmers came with their carts to buy the accumulated midden (sewage and animal waste) for use on their fields.[6]

The ordure in which they lived, coupled with the Scots' farinaceous diet, beckoned disease to the cities. Cholera, breaking out in Glasgow in 1831, waxed and waned through four decades. Virulent epidemics wracked whole tenements with smallpox, typhus, and typhoid. Tuberculosis and rickets were common. In 1843 one in every eight of the total Glasgow population was attacked by the louse-borne typhus with its resulting high fever, rash, headache, and alternate periods of stupor and

---

[4] Agnes Mure Mackenzie, *Scotland in Modern Times* (London and Edinburgh, 1942), p. 171.
[5] Glover, *Story of Scotland,* p. 315; Haldane, *The Scotland of Our Fathers,* p. 260.
[6] Glover, *Story of Scotland,* pp. 315-16.

delirum. Half the city's children died before they were five years of age.⁷

Those who survived the childhood illnesses and rampant adult diseases had another "plague" to contend with: drunkenness. The problem was serious throughout Britain, but Scots' consumption of liquor, the ill-considered balm to poverty, sickness, and misfortune, far outranked that of other Britons. In 1840, when yearly consumption of "spirits" was seven pints per head in England and thirteen in Ireland, the per capita intake in Scotland was twenty-three pints.⁸

In two of Scotland's overcrowded mill towns, Glasgow and Paisley, the Eccles family sought its living, moving from one to the other as the economic situation fluctuated. Paisley had gone through several phases in its history. Up to the mid-eighteenth century it had been a small regional marketplace, with a growing weaving industry becoming an important part of the economic life of the small city. Toward the end of the century the textile industry had become prominent, and this largest shawl-manufacturing center in Great Britain expanded to meet the demand for its products. Its high quality cotton and the famous Paisley shawls were popular early in the century, but by the late 1830s increased competition for Paisley threads and a decline in the demand for the shawls brought an economic slump with the accompanying unemployment — half the town's people worked at the looms, and others were employed at related trades — and the inevitable poverty and filth blighted the once prosperous town.

Here in Paisley William Eccles, the man who became father of David Eccles, plied his woodturner's trade, making spools for the city's spinners and weavers. William, who had been born in Old Kilpatrick, in Dumbartonshire, in 1825, was

---

⁷Mackenzie, *Scotland in Modern Times*, p. 172.
⁸Glover, *Story of Scotland*, p. 321.

a young man working in Paisley when he became afflicted with the most trying of handicaps: the mistiness of his vision developed into double cataracts which left him almost blind. How could a craftsman earn a living without his vision? William persisted, and learned to feel his way with the wood on his lathe. He continued to work at his trade, as long as there was work to be done.

William Eccles was "a rugged Scotsman, patient, pious, and good humored," wont to make light of his troubles. He could carry on; one trouble could not be allowed to spoil a lifetime. As he observed later of his lost sight, "If the Lord has so decreed that some men on earth must be blind, why then should it not be my lot to be one of them?"[9]

It was in 1843, on May 5, that the young William, just eighteen years old, married an Irish immigrant, Sarah Hutchinson, in a humble ceremony in Paisley. Life was not kind to the young couple and to the children who arrived in due time: the vagaries of the town's economy compounded with William's failing vision, forced them to struggle for mere subsistence. They lived in the crowded Milliston tenement, just a block from the huge J. & P. Coates mill, established earlier in the century. The sympathetic Mr. Coates often gave William such temporary employment as he could in his Coates and Clark mills, but the mainstay of the family was the money he could earn from the production of his lathe, which he set up in the home of his wife Sarah's sister, Elizabeth Hutchinson Moyes. Still, there was not always a market for spools, or even for the kitchen tools and other wooden items the lathe could produce. Forced to look elsewhere, William Eccles moved his family, permanently, the six miles to Glasgow, then Scotland's biggest

---

[9]Marriner S. Eccles, *Beckoning Frontiers: Public and Personal Recollections* (New York, 1951), p. 5; William Eccles File, HDC. Most of the biographical materials about William Eccles, his conversion to Mormonism, and his emigration to Utah, are from this file.

city.[10] It was 1855, and the sightless woodturner and his Irish wife had by then four children. William and Sarah and their little flock were few among the hordes who found their way into the squalor of Glasgow's Dry Gate, latecomers in a migration from the surrounding countryside which doubled the city's population from 200,000 in 1830 to 400,000 in 1860. Here David Eccles, the second son of the family, born May 12, 1849, and now just six years old, learned what it is to have to work, and to work hard, merely to stay alive.

Here in Glasgow there was little demand for the spools which had supported the family in Paisley. Wood was scarce in the city and most people heated their homes with coal. Resin sticks could ignite a coal fire, so the family set to work manufacturing and selling them. David and his older brother John would gather kindling wood and, often with help from their cousins John and Robert Moyes from Paisley, would saw it into ten-inch lengths, tie the small sticks into bundles of one hundred, and tip one end into a pot of hot resin. One or two sticks could set a coal fire blazing.

Young David soon became the family merchant, peddling the resin sticks, along with the kitchen utensils which his father made at his lathe, through the streets of Glasgow. He quickly acquired a frugality and a cleverness beyond his years, and by the time he was eleven he and his small burro were distributing their wares in neighboring towns, gone from home for days at a time.

There was little thought of school for David or any of the other children of William and Sarah Eccles. Like the children in the factories, they were more needed to bring food to the

---

[10]Glasgow Branch, Scotland-British Mission Records, HDC. The records show that in late May 1848 William and Sarah Eccles left the Glasgow Branch, and that in April 1851 they moved from Paisley back to Glasgow. Apparently, William followed employment opportunities in either city during those trying years.

family than to "be of use to Church and Commonwealth" by going to school, even the half time that the education act prescribed. By the time he was fourteen, David had had only six months of formal education, probably acquired in two winter sessions of three months each.[11] In succeeding years he would speak with regret of his lack of schooling.

With no school, and no respite from the arduous responsibility of caring for the needs of a blind father and a continually growing family, David learned early to hunt out ways of earning money. There were the peddling trips, but there were also things to do right in Glasgow: one could always carry luggage for the travelers who came and went at the railroad stations and hotels in the city. David was so scrawny and undernourished, though, that sometimes sympathetic tourists would hand him a penny and carry the bags themselves! Wherever there was a bit to be earned, David would be on hand.

And there were the peddling trips. With each venture David would wander farther and farther from home, one time causing his parents extreme worry when he stayed away three weeks. He had been in Edinburgh, forty-five miles distant. With his wider travels came bigger ideas: rather than just returning home with the cash intake from the resin sticks or kitchen utensils he was hawking, he would barter with his customers, or with his cash receipts buy other goods. These he would add to his stock, and then sell further on for a profit. Every penny was needed, and clever merchandising often multiplied the income. Clever as one might be, there was still not enough; a hungry family waited at home. The poverty around David in his journeys reminded him of the circumstances of his family in Glasgow; even the price of a bed was too much to pay from his earnings, so he slept in doorways or the hall-

---

[11]*Goodwin's Weekly* (Salt Lake City) May 6, 1916. The 1861 Glasgow Census lists David, 12; Stewart, 8; and Sarah, 6, as attending school.

ways of buildings. There seemed not much improvement, though, for all his diligence and enterprise. Day to day the family barely managed to stay together and stay alive. It was a life without a hope. Except one.

The family of William and Sarah Hutchinson Eccles. Front row left to right: Stewart Eccles, Sarah Eccles Baird, William Eccles (father), Sarah Hutchinson Eccles (mother), John Hutchinson Eccles. Back row left to right: Samuel Hutchinson Eccles, William Hutchinson Eccles, David Eccles, Margaret Hutchinson Eccles Hiatt Swinger.

2

Hope of Prosperity
And Promise of Glory

THERE WAS ONE HOPE in the heart of William Eccles, a hope that had been planted there many years earlier, in 1842, when he was living with his widowed mother in Paisley. The hope was a double one of worldly betterment and heavenly glory, and it was brought by missionaries of the American-founded Church of Jesus Christ of Latter-day Saints, the Mormons. Revivalist and orthodox practitioners had long preached of the better life in the world to come. The Mormons promised that, and more: an earthly salvation from the grime and hunger of the overcrowded cities of Europe — emigration. America, the golden dream of the poor, was painted with the even brighter gleam of pure religion: by emigrating one could build God's earthly kingdom at the same time as he was preparing his own heavenly mansion.

The first Mormon converts in Scotland had been baptized little more than two years before Elder Andrew Sprowl knocked at the door of the cottage in Paisley where Margaret Miller Eccles and her son were living. William was not yet seventeen, but had carried the responsibility for the care of his mother since the death of his father on a trip in England the year before. Both mother and son listened receptively as Elder Sprowl taught of restored religion, the ancient Church of Christ reintroduced to the earth through a living prophet. Joseph Smith, the chosen one in our time, had seen the Savior in vision, had been instructed by the Lord in the reestablishment of His Church, and had been given, for doctrine as well as for proof of his divine calling a book of metal plates long buried in the earth. These Joseph Smith had translated as the Book of Mormon, a sacred record of ancient inhabitants of the Americas. Elder Sprowl gave to William Eccles and his mother a copy of the book, taught them of its coming forth, told of the gathering of the new chosen Israel to the new Zion under the direction of the new prophet. The Kingdom of God was assembling in the promised land of midwestern United States. Missionaries all over Great Britain were actively spreading the restoration message; William and his mother could help. And did, by offering their humble cottage as a meeting place of the growing congregation. Andrew Sprowl recorded in his journal:

> Saturday, Febr. 5th 1842 — Margaret Eccles & William Eccles was baptised for a remission of thar sins in Miclerigs burn by A Sprowl. This is the woman who has given us hir hous to meet in at Charleston. Lord bless hir & him.[1]

It was not without risk that the group of the faithful in Paisley submitted to baptism at the hands of the Mormon elders. From the introduction of the gospel there by Orson Pratt in 1840 public reception had been varied: where some, like the Eccleses, were receptive, others were resentful or even vindictive. Reuben Hedlock reported:

> The spirit of inquiry was very general in this place [Paisley] and the adjoining villages. Many came to hear. Some of the preach-

---
[1]Diary of Andrew Sprowl, HDC, February 5, 1842.

ers said we were not worth minding when we first began to preach. But soon their hearers began to leave them; they then began to sound the tocsin of war; the people were exhorted not to come and hear us. A master in a cotton mill threatened to turn out of his employment any of his workpeople who went to hear us, but the truth fastened on the hearts of the people with such power that many were determined to sacrifice all things for the sake of it.[2]

William Eccles' convictions were strong, and his enthusiasm for the newly restored gospel contagious. A young man from Glasgow appeared one day at his lathe with a piece of wood to be turned. In broad dialect, the blind Scotsman invited him in: "Man, Robert, come and sit down, and I'll tell ye something far mair to your guid than a' the turnin' in the world."[3] With the same conviction William taught the gospel to his bride, Sarah Hutchinson, and baptized her himself the same year they were married.

About a year after her conversion to the faith, Margaret Eccles emigrated to America to be with the body of the Church. Serving as a midwife aboard the ship *Metoka* from Liverpool, she arrived in New Orleans on October 27, 1843, and traveled up the Mississippi River to Nauvoo, Illinois, by boat. From this City of the Saints, Margaret wrote to her children of the new Zion, and exhorted them to be faithful to the gospel they had espoused. Margaret Eccles never lived to see her children join the "gathering"; she died in Nauvoo in 1845, the year after the martyrdom of the Prophet Joseph Smith and his brother Hyrum.[4]

---

[2] *Latter-day Saint's Millennial Star* (Liverpool), II (October 10, 1841), 92.
[3] Andrew Jenson, *Latter-day Saint Biographical Encyclopedia* (4 vols., 1899-1936), I, 666.
[4] On Margaret Miller Eccles see Frank Esshom, *Pioneers and Prominent Men of Utah* (Salt Lake City, 1913), p. 854; Early Church Records: Nauvoo Baptisms, D-52-53; Journal of John McEwan, HDC, entries for September 1, October 27, 1843.

Mother Margaret's exhortations did not go unheeded. William and Sarah and their growing family remained true to their covenants in Scotland and hoped for the day of the better life in Zion. Their young family was expanding, and the move to Glasgow did little to improve the family's economic situation. Their condition was little better than that of their missionary friend, Andrew Sprowl, who could not afford to travel the few miles from Paisley to Glasgow when Church official Orson Hyde spoke there in 1847:

> Sunday, Jeneuary 31, 1847 . . . I could not possibly get to hear him, poverty is in upon us like a fiend. Scarcity of labour, idleness for fore & five weeks together, nothing to depend upon for my famely but my own labour, dearth of food, part of the last & this year has reduced us to want . . . all our clothes pledged except our every day appearal to purchase a little food, up to the mouth in debt . . . to keep the house . . . thinley clad & wether long, cold & frosty & all of us suffering a degree of ill helth our little boy in particular . . . .[5]

So they remained in Scotland, where the membership of the Church continued to grow, sometimes seemingly more in quantity than in quality. During the 1850s, when Ezra T. Benson pointed out the need for a reformation "to awaken, arouse, stir and shake them [the wayward Church members], and if necessary, to kick and thump, hammer and pound them, until we are satisfied with the results," Eccles remained the "faithful and energetic Church worker" that he would be all his life.[6] Around him entire congregations were being disfellowshipped, and men were called before Church councils for opening their shops on the Sabbath, for arguing with presiding officers in Church meetings, and for objecting to the Church doctrine of plural marriage. In the reformation fervor, even William Eccles himself was excommunicated for a short period

---

[5] Andrew Sprowl Diary, January 13, 1847.

for not tithing his income. He was soon reinstated, however, when Church authorities came to realize the dire economic condition of his family.

Always in the hazy future there was the promise of the gathering to Zion. By 1860 William and Sarah Eccles had had seven children; where would a blind woodturner find enough money to carry them all across an ocean, half a continent, and a great plains, since by now the main body of the Saints, driven out of Illinois by hostile mobs, had found their final refuge in the Valley of the Great Salt Lake. Where would that kind of money come from?

The plight of the Eccleses was the plight of most of the converts to the new faith. In response to the need, the Church had in 1849 inaugurated the Perpetual Emigration Fund, initially to assist those already en route, but later to bring European Saints to Utah. From members already in the valley contributions of cash, commodities, and equipment were collected to enable the poor to emigrate. John Lyon, a Scottish Mormon poet, expressed it:

> Come on, ye rich, with all your gifted store;
> Give to the poor, and God will give you more![7]

The poor, nevertheless, were expected to contribute as much as they had to their own expenses, and as soon as they could after their establishment in Salt Lake City, they were to reimburse the fund in labor or goods. Sloth was not to be tolerated; those who made no initial effort to help themselves seldom made the journey. Rather than aid they received from their Church leaders only rebuke, similar to that expressed to members in Paisley:

---

[6] William Eccles File, HDC.
[7] Frederick S. Buchanan, "The Emigration of Scottish Mormons to Utah, 1849-1900" (Master's thesis, University of Utah, 1961), p. 66.

> There are some old Saints here yet, who entered the Church when it was first organized in this country; they are firm in the faith, still waiting, hoping and praying for something to turn up, instead of taking hold and turning up something for themselves, and thereby effect their own emigration.[8]

But the Eccleses had not been slothful. Those who could had helped in supporting the family — David's merchandising journeys must have brought quite a little into the family coffers. Still, there were all those children to be fed and clothed. To contemplate paying passage for that large a group across the ocean and on to Zion must have caused William and Sarah many a restless night.

Eight years they had struggled in Glasgow, and still there was far from enough money to buy passage. Then the first real ray of light for the blind woodturner: in April 1863 the Perpetual Emigration Fund confirmed the advance to him of £75 ($375). Enough, with what they had saved from their meager earnings, to take them to Utah. They would arrive with nothing but themselves and their hopes, but what matter—it would be Zion, America, the Kingdom of God on earth!

---

[8] Conference president David M. Stuart to Paisley members, cited in Buchanan p. 68.

3

The Emigrants

IT TOOK ONLY two days after the money from the Perpetual Emigration Fund was advanced for the whole Eccles family, and one nephew, James Moyes, eldest son of William's sister Elizabeth, to arrive in Liverpool. They surveyed the hundreds of Mormon emigrants on the dock, the people who would be their traveling companions on the ocean voyage and the land trek. There were glassblowers, butchers, locksmiths, shoemakers, farmers — tradesmen and artisans of many sorts they could see in the mass waiting on the dock.

The hour came, and the Eccleses carried their few belongings aboard the sailing vessel *Cynosure* in Liverpool harbor. The excitement was electrifying. The Mormon emigrants had heard from friends and missionaries about the voyage, and fear must have mingled with the bright hope which filled their souls.

They knew what to expect on the ship: accommodations in steerage would be not so very different from the conditions of the squalid Scottish tenements. Beds in steerage sections of emigrant ships, they knew, were filthy and never aired; the floor was not washed or scraped; the stench was intolerable. Privacy was impossible, and mere proximity threatened moral standards. Strangers would be thrown together, people with varied customs, varied standards of living, levels of education, even languages.[1]

By contrast, Mormon travelers were kept together under close supervision. Following the counsel of Church leaders, most traveled as entire families. The typical emigrant, even before he set foot upon the gangplank in Liverpool, was assured of a welcome to direct his settlement at journey's end. All details had been prearranged. Through the Liverpool periodical, the *Latter-day Saints' Millennial Star,* and the guidance of Church leaders, the Mormon emigrant had been advised as to cost of the journey, sailing dates, regulations on baggage, type of clothing, method of packing, and baggage labeling. If he was among a large group from one area he usually had been accompanied to the city of departure by an experienced Church official. Whenever possible Mormons chartered whole ships, or at least the steerage, in order to keep their people united and under Church leadership.[2] Because of the organization and discipline which prevailed, Mormon ships quickly gained the distinction of being among the best on the Atlantic run between Liverpool and American ports, and a Select Committee of the House of Commons on emigrant ships commended Mormon-directed vessels for superior safety and comfort. Charles Dickens, who observed the Mormon emigration of 1863 and devoted a whole chapter of *The Uncommercial Traveler* to their story, wrote: "The Mormon ship is

---

[1] P. A. M. Taylor, *Expectations Westward: The Mormons and the Emigration of Their British Converts in the Nineteenth Century* (Edinburgh, 1965), p. 184.

[2] Taylor, p. 189. Also Frederick S. Buchanan, "The Emigration of Scottish Mormons to Utah, 1849-1900" (Master's thesis, University of Utah, 1961), pp. 80-81.

a Family under strong and accepted discipline, with every provision for comfort, decorum, and internal peace." He cited with approval a London writer who testified: "There is one thing which they [the Mormons] can do, viz. — teach Christian shipowners how to send poor people decently, cheaply, and healthfully across the Atlantic."[3]

The *Cynosure* was no exception. Order would prevail; the travelers would feel a discipline controlling their behavior; problems would be properly dealt with. Before the ship weighed anchor that morning, May 30, 1863, the president of the European Mission of the Mormon Church went aboard to appoint David Stuart, a returning missionary, president of the company.

On the shoulders of Elder Stuart fell the responsibility for the deportment of the Saints aboard, and, more significantly, for their spiritual well-being. But it is not the way with Mormons to put such a load of responsibility on one such minister; hardly a few days out to sea the new president chose two counselors and organized the people into wards, each in turn headed by a president. These ward presidents, who reported daily to Stuart, kept lists of names, supervised the work of cleaning, watched over the emigrants' conduct, and took charge of lost property. Other appointments included a captain of the guard to keep watch at night, a clerk or secretary to keep a journal, and a chorister to lead members in their hymns. On some ships a committee planned recreation, including the publication of a ship newspaper. A small band provided music.[4]

The prescribed daily routine included rising at the sound of a bell at five or six in the morning, cleaning their living quarters and the deck, and assembling for prayer and breakfast. After breakfast all had their allotted tasks, including the mak-

---

[3]Charles Dickens, *The Uncommercial Traveler*, Vol. VI of *The Works of Charles Dickens* (New York, n. d.), pp. 635-38.
[4]Taylor, *Expectations Westward*, p. 188. In general, descriptions of conditions and activities aboard the emigrant ship are from this source.

ing of tents to be used in crossing the Great Plains.[5] Often wards rotated cooking under supervision of the president. Regular religious services, evening prayers, and Sunday meetings of prayer and preaching were an integral part of the schedule. On some ships daily schools for children was provided, as well as evening classes for adults who sat on the deck floor around the lecturer and learned of geography, astronomy, agricultural innovations, history, and literature. Children often devised games for themselves — Little Margaret Eccles at the time was only six, and young Sarah not yet ten. The baby Samuel was just four months old, and so must have occupied much of his mother's time, leaving three-year-old William to be tended by his sisters. The older boys probably helped the sailors with the ropes, as much for amusement as for assistance. And father William most likely found work for his hands to do where his eyes would not be needed.

Although nineteenth-century concepts of hygiene did not yet include the benefits of fresh air, the sick and the babies were taken on deck "whether willing or not," as often as weather permitted. All activities were carried out under the observant eye of Elder Stuart, who visited every part of the ship several times a day. The enforced spirit of industry and order was calculated to be a good preventive against grumbling, as it "kept the minds of the people actively engaged in the better things of the kingdom." When dissension arose, the matter was handled by the ship's council, consisting of the ship president and his counselors. A brother would be requested to appear before the ship's council, confess that he had given way to a wrong spirit, and ask forgiveness. Tension was often alleviated by leaders who retained a sense of humor. (On the *Charlie Buck* in 1854 when discontent with the provisions led to excessive grumbling, Richard Ballantyne had called a meeting and an-

---

[5]Buchanan, "The Emigration of Scottish Mormons to Utah," p. 83.

nounced that the next one to be heard complaining would be "appointed . . . to grumble for the company, and as many as unite with him we shall appoint to be his counsellors.")⁶

While the *Cynosure* was still in the estuary, before the pilot ship returned to land, President Stuart had time to write the following report to the mission president who had seen them off in Liverpool:

President George Q. Cannon.

> Dear Brother, — as the tug will soon leave us, before its doing so I hasten to send you a few lines to inform you of our well-doing. We left the Mersey this morning about five o'clock, in charge of a pilot, who left us about 7:30. We now have a light, air breeze, and the captain says he will not keep the tug over an hour longer.
>
> The people are all feeling fine; a good, contented, quiet spirit prevails in their midst, and the songs of Zion and Israel are reverberating from stem to stern of the ship. Grumblers and discontented ones do not appear to have embarked on this vessel, such is the spirit of unity amongst them. They do not seem to fear seasickness, but look forward to it as a natural consequence which they will endeavor to endure with fortitude and forbearance one to another. Your remarks and instructions to them at the organization on Friday last seem to have sunk deep into their hearts, and they are already practising the same. Yesterday, after you left us, was spent in counselling and instructing them relative to little matters which they found themselves at a loss to proceed in, and in the evening we went round the ship and organized the people into six wards, the first to be presided over by Elder Wm. H. Pitts, the second by Elder James Watson, the third by Elder Edward Cliff, the fourth, or bachelors' hall by Elder Lewis Bowen, the fifth by Elder Wm. Hopwood, the sixth by Elder John Gibbs, with from two to four teachers in each ward, and have desired them to see that prayers are held in each ward at eight A.M. and eight P.M. each day, and that cleanliness

---

⁶*Ibid.*, pp. 84-85; Taylor, *Expectations Westward*, pp. 190, 200.

and good order predominate, and that no iniquity of any nature exists in their several wards. . . . [7]

Organization kept order, and work projects made time pass less slowly. Still, the passage was slow, the days dreary, and the nights stormy. Lookouts were posted for many nights as the ship was blown far into the North Atlantic iceberg region. The Saints aboard the *Cynosure* might have expected an average crossing — the usual voyage lasted five weeks — but it was July 1 when the weary voyagers arrived at Castle Garden, New York.

Four weeks and three days, must have seemed an eternity for the travelers eager to begin their new lives in a new land. And the land which they finally sighted was doubly thrilling to the Mormons because of their conviction that it was the chosen land, the land of promise, Zion. One such emigrant a few years earlier expressed what these travelers must have felt:

> How well I remember the first step that I took on American soil! How thrilled I was to be in the land of the free — the land of promise! I had been taught to believe it was the land of promise blessed above all other lands, and although only a boy of fifteen years, I felt like thanking God for the blessings I then enjoyed.[8]

Castle Garden would have held less anxiety for the Saints aboard the *Cynosure* than for most immigrants. At the depot where the immigrants were processed, Church agents tended to the Mormons' needs and acted as guardians against the "sharpsters, apostates and the curious enquirers" waiting outside. There too were facilities for the new arrivals to rest and buy meals, receive and write letters, buy rail tickets, change money, and obtain information about work and lodgings in the city. The

---

[7]David M. Stuart to President George Q. Cannon, May 31, 1863, aboard the ship *Cynosure,* thirty miles from Liverpool. From Manuscript History of the British Mission, 1863, HDC.
[8]Buchanan, "The Emigration of Scottish Mormons to Utah," p. 87.

usual immigrant groups disbanded at Castle Garden, but the Mormons remained together for their westward pilgrimage; their journey was less than half over, and the hardest part was yet to come.

They traveled first by rail, in cattle cars along the route from Castle Garden toward the Missouri River, which marked the outer reach of the railroad — the iron rails would not cross the continent for another six years. They crossed Roebling's bridge at Niagara into Canada, seeing the famous falls on the way. A stretch of the route passed through Canada, then they re-entered the United States at Detroit, continued to Chicago, then onward toward the railhead. All around them the Civil War was raging. Roaring cannon added to the din of the railroad cars, and burned-out bridges delayed their progress.

Along the journey the train pulled into Hannibal, Missouri. There, as usual when the train stopped, the travelers piled out of the car for a walk and some food. John and David Eccles and their friend Thomas Cunningham were among the group on the platform. People milled about them. Suddenly the train began to pull out. In alarm the boys ran after it, but were told it was simply moving to a siding. Mollified, the boys waited and watched. But the train kept on going, down the track and out of sight. There were the three youths, John, just barely seventeen, David, fourteen, and Thomas — alone in a strange land, without food or money.

A boy who can make his way peddling goods for weeks at a time through big cities of Scotland is not going to be cowed by the big spaces of Missouri. David must have felt challenge and excitement along with anxiety and concern at their predicament. The adventure was one to be savored — their chance to try themselves against this new land.

It was not long before they were on a train — and who knows under what circumstances, for they had no money —

bound for St. Joseph, Missouri.

There in St. Joseph John parted from his brother and Thomas and made his way, working as a shipper, back to Scotland, not to return to America for several years. But David and Thomas were able adventurers, and soon found themselves on a river boat up the Mississippi and to Florence, the fitting-out place where their families were waiting. There must have been an anxious blend of emotions among the Eccleses as David greeted them in Florence on his arrival. His explanation of the mishap in Hannibal, their journey to St. Joseph, and mostly his announcement of John's departure for the East; all must have created turmoil in the minds of the elder Eccleses. At the same time the new circumstances placed a new responsibility on the shoulders of David Eccles: he would have to take the responsibility of two sons now. But he could. His safe arrival in Florence had proved that he could take care of himself; he could extend his capability to others as well.

The outfitting continued, preparation for the long trek west. The company was met at Florence by Horton D. Haight, one of several Mormon teamsters who made round trips between Salt Lake City and the Missouri River freighting converts and supplies. The companies were again organized as they had been on board the *Cynosure,* this time with Elder Haight as captain. Order and unity would be essential for survival on this journey, as they had been for peace on the ocean voyage.[9]

The wagons were ready, the companies formed, and the long walk began. Everyone, blind William included, must walk; only the provisions and some goods belonging to the immigrants could be loaded into the wagons. One can picture the Eccleses, trudging between the wagons along the dirt trail, the two girls

---

[9] William Eccles File, and Record of 1863 Emigration, HDC; Interview, Royal Eccles with Thomas Cunningham, September 18, 1929, REC.

chattering to each other as they went, three-year-old William between them. The older boys might spell off the wagon drivers. Or walk with their new-found friends along the way. Perhaps David would walk along with his father, guiding the older man's steps and describing to him the scenes as they changed — the grassy plains of Nebraska, the brown hills of Wyoming. The land was new and strange — how does one evoke the vastness of the Great Plains to a man whose last sights were of tenemented streets in Scotland? The swallows overhead, the snakes along the trail, the rabbits in the fields alongside: all these David might have described to his father along the way.

Sarah would have had other concerns: the baby must be cared for and carried, or bundled carefully onto a wagon among the supplies. The children must be watched — accidents were frequent, and Mother Sarah would be overly cautious lest one of her young ones clamber onto one of the slow-moving wagons only to topple off under the wheels.

Each day was much like every other day. A raucous horn blast awoke the travelers each morning. Prayers, and breakfast, then the preparation for the day's journey. David, increasingly practiced at the routines, would soon have become proficient at making and breaking camp.

Like every other day, that is, except for the rain which sometimes held up the company at rivers too swollen to ford. Or the buffalo herds which occasionally appeared and had to be headed off lest the Mormon cattle mingle with the wilder herd and wander off. Or the Indians who occasionally appropriated some few head of cattle. They never seriously menaced the Saints, but the Scottish families must have been apprehensive at every evidence of the "savage redskins" of whom they would have read such fearful accounts.

There were the ordinary distresses of the trail: the pesky mosquitoes, the sudden thunderstorms, the wagons which pitched forward over a broken wheel, the frequent sickness. And the howling wolves. For the Eccles children, and perhaps even for the parents, those wild cries in the black prairie nights must have been more terrifying than all the city noises of crowded Glasgow.

There were the pleasures, too. Each evening there would be singing, and maybe dancing around the campfire. There was always the dream coming closer and closer as the mountains came into nearer view. How would David describe those towering Rockies to his weary father? But why would that be necessary, when they were simply the physical metaphor for William's hopes and plans for his family, dreams William had cherished these many years.

The hardest part was the last part, up mountain inclines and through narrow canyons, but even that passed. On October 5, 1863, four months after leaving Scotland, William and Sarah Eccles and their young family stood on the east bench over Great Salt Lake City. They had endured sickness, hunger, and weariness to reach their promised land. There it lay, spread out before them. How David expressed to his father the wide sweep of flat valley floor, the settlements spotted along the few streams, the business center forming to the north of the canyon mouth would have revealed the youth's feeling — excitement? disappointment? eagerness? challenge? Probably not fear or anxiety, for David seldom approached new experiences otherwise than confidently. More likely high hope and impatient anticipation. Taking his young sister by the hand, David Eccles began the last section of the trek.

4

Ogden to Oregon: The Early Trek

THIS FIRST ZION the Eccleses saw, however, was not to be *their* Zion; they stayed only briefly in Salt Lake City before moving thirty-five miles northward to Ogden. No streets paved with gold, no mansion awaited them there. In fact, the shack in which they spent their first winter in the new land was probably less than what they had left behind in Scotland; certainly no better. Their countryman William Fife provided for them a lean-to behind the Ogden Council House, probably a one-room affair, and certainly little insulation from cold canyon winds and blowing snow.[1] Seeing his family's condition little improved physically and none economically, David must have wondered that first winter about the promises of the promised land.

Spring came, and the family moved up Ogden Valley to Liberty and the shelter of a one-room cabin. Later they moved to Eden, still in Ogden Valley, where they operated a small homestead. William returned to his lathe, making small wood-

---

[1] Interview, Royal Eccles with John H. Moyes, November 11, 1934, REC.

en articles for sale. Adapting his business to the needs of his neighbors in the new frontier, he included in his stock a variety of kitchen tools which he fashioned from the maple saplings to be found in the mountain canyons.

David was the main support of the family in their new home. As he had done in Scotland, he helped to sell his father's wares or trade them for other needed items. He was often seen walking the road between Ogden and Brigham City with a peddler's pack on his back. Again he must have wondered about this new land, where one had to walk so much farther between customers than he had in Scotland. And no burro to carry the pack. Sometimes the selling was fruitless, and even bartering among the coin-poor neighbors netted too little to feed the family. Still, he could sell his own strength, and his neighbors would pay him in cash or foodstuffs to cut their wood and do other odd jobs.

The new Zion was not an Eden of self-generating prosperity, nor had the Eccleses or their immigrant neighbors expected that. They had been well-warned that hard work lay ahead. As the hymn suggested they must

> Think not when ye gather to Zion
> Your troubles and trials are through,
> That nothing but comfort and pleasure
> Are waiting in Zion for you.[2]

Even when prepared for a settlement which would be less than paradise, the Eccleses found things more difficult than they had anticipated. The Mormon communities were built on an agrarian economy — the Eccleses were not farmers. The prevailing economic doctrine encouraged the Saints to be self-sufficient — William Eccles' skill was in creating a product

---

[2]Eliza R. Snow, "Think Not When Ye Gather to Zion," *Hymns: Church of Jesus Christ of Latter-day Saints* (Salt Lake City, 1950), p. 21.

which had no market elsewhere but in a large factory community. Merchandising was David Eccles' greatest skill — his neighbors had little or no money with which to buy anything that he might offer for sale. There were great influxes of immigrants, but they required more of their neighbors than they at first could contribute to the general good. All in all, the going in those early days was tough, and for the Eccleses it seemed especially difficult.

For Father William Eccles it was enough just to be among the Saints in the Zion of the Lord's appointing, but a growing family needs more than just spiritual food. Physical sustenance was still minimal, even after two or three years in this new land of opportunity. The family passed the time more in hope of a less strenuous life in the future than in satisfaction with the meager comforts of the present.

It will be recalled that David's cousin, James Moyes, had originally traveled to Utah with the Eccleses. In 1866 James was joined by his mother and three of his brothers and sisters, Stewart, John, and Margaret. They also brought along William Hamilton who had been raised by the family but was not actually their child.

Upon arriving in Utah in October of 1886, the Moyeses stayed for two or three months with the Eccles family in Liberty. Later, they too moved to Eden, three miles to the north.[3] James and his brother at first employed themselves in weaving, the trade they had brought with them from Scotland, but their enterprise did not bring the prosperity they hoped for. The whole valley was having hard times those years. First, there was severe drought. Then there were grasshoppers (Rocky Mountain locusts) driven by the drought-caused shortage of the desert foilage on which they customarily fed to

---

[3]Moyes interview.

migrate toward the green fields of the farmers. In 1865, 1866, and 1867, grasshoppers destroyed as much as half of the crops.

The prospect for the settlers was discouraging. The Moyes brothers, James, John, and Stewart, seriously discussed the desirability of returning to New England to work in the mills. There, they were sure, would be market for their skills. They urged William to leave his homestead and the hard life it represented. William Eccles was loathe to give up the Zion for which he had already sacrificed so much. Perhaps, though, if they could "get a stake" somewhere, and then come back, perhaps the drought would be over when they returned. Perhaps if they went away for a while, but not too far away . . . And his thoughts turned to the tales he'd heard of the Pacific Northwest.

Tales he'd first heard from friends like David Stuart, the Mormon president on the *Cynosure,* the ship which had brought the Eccleses to America. Stuart had been sent by the Church on a preaching mission to Oregon in 1857, and had spent several months there proselyting, holding meetings, and spying out the country. He made enthusiastic reports on what he saw. Then there was the word of Joseph Tracy, a Mormon who owned an orchard in Oregon City. He visited Ogden Valley in 1867, and his telling of the resources and beauties of the area persuaded the Eccleses and their cousins. They would relocate in Oregon for two years — long enough to earn their pile in the woolen mill which, according to Tracy, was being constructed in Oregon City. There would be jobs for the Moyes cousins, weavers by trade, and a market for William's spools.[4] It shouldn't take long, William figured, before they could return to Utah, the settlements of the Saints. If one must venture out into Babylon, one could always gather again to Jerusalem. Two years would not be long in passing.

---
[4] Moyes interview.

The Eccleses and the Moyeses set out together in April 1867. The great highway for those headed into the Northwest was, of course, the Oregon Trail, and the two families, the Eccleses with "a cart with a yoke of cattle," the Moyeses with another team and a wagon, started off towards Soda Springs, near Cache Valley on the present Utah-Idaho border. It was early April, and the journey would take, they considered, three months. Sarah, David Eccles' younger sister, was about fourteen at the time, but her description, written later in her life, is replete with details about the trip.[5] She tells how the travelers moved from station to station of the pony express, each time happy to see another human face, especially when it was white, not red. Brigham Young had promised William Eccles, Sarah reports, that they would never see an Indian. Even so they must have worried: so small a party would have little protection. Indian raids were a common experience along the Oregon Trail in parts of Idaho and Oregon, and they were sufficiently troublesome during the 1860s that military units made occasional forays into the region. From 1866 to 1868 the Shoshone Indians in Idaho were antagonists in a campaign called the Snake Indian War. All during this period small bands of Indians would attack travelers; massacres were not uncommon. By 1868 most of the Shoshone had been placed on reservations; still there was enough threat in the air in 1867 to worry the little company of William Eccles.

Sarah records in her reminiscence that during the early part of the trip, probably still in Idaho, they were told that a family of travelers had been murdered by a band of Indians just three days earlier. The fear of the Eccles group can be felt through Sarah's words:

---

[5]The account provided in the typewritten "Memoirs of Sarah Eccles Baird," REC, is detailed in its description of this trip. There is now a copy of the memoirs in the writer's file, HDC.

Their graves had been covered and we shuddered to think this terrible thing might have happened to us. As we slept that night and the coyotes howled from the darkness, we felt a great sympathy for the unfortunate family that had met such a terrible fate. We would have been grateful for a campfire but this we could not have, because the light might attract the Indians again. There was only a small group of us and the Indians would not have very much trouble with us. The dawn was a welcome sight the next day, although it meant hours of walking over the trail with the sun shining down upon us.

There were the usual, less dramatic problems of the trail: the tire that came off one of the wagons when they were nearly to Five Points, near present day Pocatello; the Snake River, where they would have had to pay a steep toll to cross at the ford (so they traveled along the river until they found their own crossing place); and the sore feet which the cattle developed, forcing the group to lay over two weeks in Boise.

Along the trail the Eccles group would be joined from time to time by fellow journeyers. One such proved most providential: he was a stone mason, and along the way, a couple of hundred miles beyond Boise, they were approached by a settler who needed men to build a wall on his ranch. The fellow-traveler with the Eccles group did the engineering and supervised the labor, and the Moyes and Eccles boys were able to earn some much-needed cash to aid them along the remainder of the trek. The habit was a usual one among the wayfarers; the earlier Mormons had often stopped along the way to render some service to settlers and were paid in money or goods.

The wall completed, the route led onward, out of what is now Idaho and into the eastern mountains of Oregon. After Fort Hall on the Snake, described by one account as a "wild, rocky, barren wilderness, of wrecked and ruined Nature; a vast field of volcanic desolation,"⁶ and the steep mountain roads where sharp rocks cut the oxen's feet, the view of the Grand Ronde, hundreds of feet below them must have seemed like paradise. The descent into the idyllic valley, however, must have been pure torture, even after thirty-odd years of travelers had worn the road deep into the mountainside. But what luxuries were there: fodder for the animals, streams where Sarah and Elizabeth could wash their travel-stained clothes, rest for all before they must turn to face the last barrier, the Blue Mountains.

Struggling upward through a rocky canyon out of Grand Ronde the group would have emerged on a high plateau which sloped gradually downward toward the Columbia River; from here on the way would be smoother, at least until the Cascade Mountains which would come after the long smooth trek across the Oregon plain and along the Columbia.

Sarah remembered two incidents which occurred in the mountains along the way. A forest fire was a terrifying sight; she describes the "great cloud of smoke rolling up," and the fear of the animals. There was nothing for the little band of travelers to do but keep moving alongside; eventually they were passing over hot earth, feeling as well as hearing the thunderous rolls of the trees as they fell. Hot rocks and tree trunks burned the shoes from their feet, and cattle bellowed from the pain in their already tender hooves.

The second mountain experience which remained stark in the young girl's memory was the sharp decline down which they had to drive the wagons. Carved on a rock at the beginning of the decline were the words "The straight way to hell," and the men glancing down the precipice must have agreed.

---

⁶Overton Johnson and W. H. Winter, *Route Across the Rocky Mountains* 1932), p. 31, as cited in Ray Allen Billington, *The Far Western Frontier* (New York, 1956), p. 104.

But the experience of crossing mountains with the companies of Saints into Utah had taught David and his cousins how to cope with rough terrain. Tying logs behind the wagons, they locked the wheels and, edging the teams onto the decline, they eased the wagons down the slope.

Another few days of rest, and the party moved onward. So the trek continued, interrupted by whatever opportunities there came for work along the way, until they had stretched the trip from the three months they had anticipated to the seven months which it took.

It was December 1, 1867, that the Eccleses and the Moyeses reached the Oregon community that was their destination, Oregon City at the foot of the falls on the Willamette River. The city had all the growing pains of a developing industrial town, but it must surely have looked more like paradise to the work-seeking Scots than had the agricultural Eden of Ogden Valley. The woolen mill of which Brother Tracy had spoken had indeed been built — the sight of the factory buildings must have welcomed the young men as much as if they had come home to jobs and a place they knew. Quickly they found a spot about a mile outside the city and erected a crude house out of log slabs.

Things did work out better for the Mormon emigrants in this Gentile world. William soon obtained a contract to furnish the Jacons Brothers mill with wood at three dollars a cord. He hired a man to help with the larger trees, and David, now eighteen, and sixteen-year-old Stewart felled the smaller ones. They learned quickly, though, how to bring down the big ones, the ones three feet or more through the trunk. John Moyes describes the process:

> They would drill a hole up about eight inches from the bottom and down through the middle with an auger, just one hole up and down for the draft. They would saw off the burned part.

They would chop one side of the tree where they wanted it to fall. There were 18 cord of wood in one tree at $3 per cord. To cut it up they would chop in about a foot and a half for the saw to work. Uncle Eccles did the sawing of the wood in four-foot lengths, and all of the felling was done by David, Stewart, and the hired man.[7]

Soon the Moyes boys were working in the mill as weavers, and being paid $2.50 for forty yards. That gave them about fifty dollars each per month, and within four months they had saved $200 to send to Scotland to pay the passage to America for other members of their families. Their money, supplemented by additional from the Perpetual Emigration Fund, brought Robert, Alec, and William Moyes to Utah in 1868.

Things went well; here among the industries they knew the Eccleses and the Moyeses could be at home. William could even investigate one of his imaginings: he had an idea about making cloth with a mangle. So with his hired man he made a boat trip to San Francisco to visit some Scottish friends there in hopes of raising backing for his invention. His friends could not support his project, but they did give the two men fare back to Oregon City.

That was not the end of William's imaginative ventures. One idea did prove successful: he ran a profitable little distillery. A two dollar keg of beer, about four gallons, would yield two pints of whiskey in his still, three miles above the city. Paradoxical as it seems for this ardent proselyte to the Mormon faith, with its "Word of Wisdom" forbidding the consumption of intoxicants, to be selling whiskey to his neighbors, it was a neat little money-making business. But then the interdict against liquor was not so firmly established in Mormondom at that time, and the good man more than likely found sufficient justification for his moonlighting in the fact that the more

---

[7] John Moyes interview.

money he earned, the sooner he could take his family back to Utah and the Church.

Meanwhile, David had found work which was more lucrative than the mill provided. He went to Puget Sound with the great lumber merchants of the Pacific coast, Pope and Talbot. They paid him $75 per month, much of which he could turn over to the family. During these months the Eccles family lived in Salem down the Willamette from Oregon City, where they sold cordwood for fuel, apparently to individual customers.

Life among the Gentiles made more than just economic differences to the small group of Mormons. The Moyes cousins were young adults, of an age to marry. The Church's indictment against marrying out of the faith could have little meaning in this place where there were none but non-Mormons outside of one's own family. William's proselytizing had borne some fruit; some one or two of his neighbors had joined the Church. James Moyes chose a bride among the family of Charles Larson, a convert to William's persuasion. Later, as the group was returning to Utah, James's sister Margaret married Charles himself, and the two of them remained behind in Oregon. It must have been consoling to William that his David, who was also of marriageable age, kept himself free of such entanglements. William's insistence that the family return when they did may have been partly motivated by just that fear — after all, Stewart was approaching manhood, and young Sarah would soon be of an age.

The two years passed. The Moyeses and the Eccleses had agreed that their stay would last just that long, so in the spring of 1869, William and Sarah drove from Salem to Oregon City to plan with their sister and nephew for their return. Their reception was far from what they had expected. The Moyes boys wanted to stay in Oregon where the work was plentiful and the living was easier than in the Zion of the Saints. William argued; the boys countered. He preached; they rebelled, finally telling their uncle to stay away from them with his preaching, and punctuating their words with derogatory comments about Brigham Young. Concerned and hurt, William and Sarah returned to Salem.

Not two weeks had passed, however, before a telegram arrived. Mrs. Moyes, Elizabeth, was seriously ill with typhoid fever, and the doctors did not expect her to live. Once again William and Sarah drove to Oregon City. The Moyes sons begged their Uncle William to save her. The pious man replied in the only vein he knew: the sons must kneel down and ask the Lord to forgive them for the things they had said about the Church and Brigham Young. Chastened, they knelt and prayed while William anointed their mother with oil and blessed her after the Mormon manner of administering to the sick. Sarah later recalled that "after the blessing a peaceful sleep came to auntie, and she slept soundly all the night, . . . the first night's sleep she had been able to have for many nights."

Humbled by the experience, the Moyes sons agreed to return to Utah. As soon as he was sure of Elizabeth Moyes's recovery, William went back to Salem to prepare for the journey, leaving Sarah to nurse her sister back to health.

Preparations were made for the trip. Two men, converted by William's preaching, were to accompany the group. Each of the two families bought a wagon and a yoke of oxen, bringing the total equipment to two wagons and four yoke of oxen. Better equipped than they had been for the journey to Oregon, the group set out for their return to Utah.

The Indian threat had since been alleviated, and there were no forest fires along the way, but the journey was not without incident. Again, Sarah recounts the events, and tells of a strange incident which occurred while the two families were camped for the night. She and David were washing up after the evening meal, she tells, when two men approached the family. Though they were dressed much like her father, Sarah recounts, they spoke no English. Their pantomime indicated to Mother Sarah that they were hungry. Aware of the simplicity of their fare, Sarah turned to David questioningly. "We can share what we have," he responded, so a simple meal of cooked apples, bread, and crust coffee was set before the strangers.

Sarah continues:

> When they had finished they came over to Mother, and one of them handed [her] some money out of his pocket. Mother would not take it though, and tried to show them that they were welcome to the food they had eaten, and to more of it if they wished. . . . When they understood they came close to Mother and one put his hand on her head and they both gave Mother a blessing in a foreign tongue. We were all awed by this action, and when they left, my Sister Margaret and I ran up a little incline to see which way they had gone. Although the country was flat and barren, [and] we could see for miles, neither of us could see them. . . . We expected that our Aunt and the boys would have seen the men, as they passed right by their wagon when I saw them, but none of our cousins had seen them.[8]

In later years, Sarah records, her mother was told by Eliza R. Snow, a prominent spiritual leader of women in early Utah, that the two men were two of the legendary Three Nephites, immortals often recorded as appearing to bless the Saints in their times of need.

The route of the group took them through Canyon City. It was here that Margaret Moyes married Charles Larson, the young man William had converted, and remained with him there in Oregon. Other than that, the remainder of the trip seemed without incident; in just three months the two families

---

[8] "Memoirs of Sarah Eccles Baird."

were back in Eden, ready to make another start.[9]

William had hoped that two years would make a difference; it is doubtful that he dreamed *what* a difference the time would make, or that the difference would be even more pronounced in the economic condition of the Ogden Valley settlements than in the financial status of the Eccleses. But such was indeed the case. The transcontinental railroad had been completed, the rails joined just west of Ogden. Ogden had become a railhead where the two big companies' lines met, and the business the railways brought had made the economy of the town boom. Money was circulating; markets were opening up; there were abundant job opportunities. David and Stewart hired themselves out to cut and haul hay through the summer, and to cut and haul wood throughout the winter, and the neighbors helped the Eccleses build a two-room log house on their homestead. The new beginning augured well for the returning emigrants.

---

[9]David's father, William, remained loyal to the Church, was ordained a High Priest in 1883, visited Scotland in 1890 as a missionary. He and his wife, in 1896, were recommended by their bishop and stake president, to receive their "second endowments"—the highest spiritual ordinance in which a Latter-day Saint may participate. Letter of Bishop James Taylor, Mound Fort Ward and L. W. Shurtliff, President of Weber Stake, to Wilford Woodruff, President of the Church, January 7, 1896. In the Wilford Woodruff Papers, Church Archives.

Royal Eccles Collection. William Eccles, father of David Eccles.

Royal Eccles Collection. Sarah Hutchinson Eccles, mother of David Eccles.

5

Independence and Ambition

EVEN BEFORE THE LAST BLOW secured the golden spike into place at Promontory, a period of transition had begun in Utah. Although they welcomed the advent of the "Iron Horse," Mormon leaders felt that the railroad threatened both their theocratic control and the economic autonomy of Utah. With the coming of eastern and midwestern enterprisers, it was inevitable that Mormons would increasingly become involved in worldly trade and exchange. Former close ties would be broken as the Saints emerged into conflicting segments. Thus, Brigham Young and his supporters inaugurated a program of cooperative protection, including independent railroad branches and centralized trade, to preserve group loyalty and strengthen community institutions. A new test of faithfulness was the founding in 1868 of ZCMI ("Zion's Cooperative Mercantile Institution"), a cooperative wholesale house, and a network of cooperative retail department stores. Independent Mormon merchants learned that they were expected to close out their stocks and merge with the church cooperative. Disapproving of the tendency of the increasingly stronger Gentile merchants to take wealth out of the territory, Brigham Young made it clear that trading with Gentiles was bad behavior, and further suggested that the Mormon people not trade with a man "who does not pay his tithing and help gather the poor, and pray in his family." The School of the Prophets, a policy-making organization of the priesthood, then voted that "those who dealt with outsiders should be cut off from the Church," though this was a last resort. Men of most occupations responded obediently to the edict.[1]

Although completely loyal to his adopted faith, David Eccles had no experience with corporate Mormonism. Independent and enterprising like his Scottish ancestors, he was too ambitious, too energetic, too impatient to mesh with others whose work might be slower or less exacting. Cooperative enterprise under priesthood rule would have been a strain on him. After spending most of 1869 helping on his father's homestead and cutting and hauling load after load of wood to Ogden, David struck out alone.

It was inevitable that he would; the experience in Oregon, the job in Puget Sound, had taught him that in this new land as much as in Scotland, one fared better on one's own, using his own initiative, enterprise, skill, and ingenuity. One took the land as it was and turned it to his profit. This was not the Mormon way; this was not cooperation. But it was Eccles' way: independent, uninhibited, and unafraid. The almost unprotected resources of the frontier lay before David Eccles, and he chose to attack them, alone.

It was in Gentile Wyoming that David found his next employment, freighting with an ox team from the newly constructed line of the Union Pacific to the mines at South Pass.

---

[1] Leonard J. Arrington, *Great Basin Kingdom: An Economic History of the Latter-day Saints, 1830-1900* (Cambridge, Mass., 1958), pp. 234, 296-98.

The cold blasts of winter winds, the snow on the high passes, belly-deep drifts to tromp through, rude shelters to sleep in — these insured that David's money would be painfully earned. Years later he would recall that cold winter he spent freighting the 170 miles from Aspen to South Pass.[2]

David had in his own mind determined on the limits of his financial obligation to his family: he had set age twenty-one as the point at which he would turn his profits to his own interests rather than automatically contributing everything to his family for the common good. The first $200 he earned after he turned twenty-one he left in the care of his mother, while he went back to Wyoming. Sarah, David's sister, was being married, and their mother, with or without David's permission, used the money at the marriage.[3] David's reaction to the news on his return is a matter for conjecture, juxtaposing as the situation did two of his strongest motives: love of family and material ambition. David cared for his sister Sarah, but justice must also have her voice, and certainly, having contributed so energetically to the family's security already, David had some rights to his own "stake."

In any case, early spring of 1871 found him back in Eden, helping on the homestead. But David was not born a helper, and soon he had taken a contract with the Wheeler sawmill, located at the confluence of Wheeler Creek and the Ogden River, to cut and haul logs in Ogden Canyon. His remaining stake, the dollars scrupulously hoarded during the frozen winter in Wyoming, he spent on the first property he ever owned outright: a yoke of oxen. With his own team he could multiply his efforts, cutting and hauling both, delivering his logs to the sawmill, and keeping the full profit from the operation. How David must have exulted in his near self-sufficiency! Never-

---

[2]"Dates and Data Concerning the Life of David Eccles," REC, p. 8.
[3]Memoirs of Bertha Marie Eccles, REC, pp. 16-17.

theless, his joy was short-lived. As he drove his two prized animals down the damp ground of the steep mountainside the turf gave way, the oxen slid, and the solid wooden yoke broke their necks. Both were killed. His investment lost and his savings gone, David was forced to seek employment again for the rest of the spring and the summer.[4]

Fall of the year, 1871, found him in Wyoming again, this time working in the Almy coal mine of the Union Pacific Railroad. Through the winter he earned $2.50 for a ten-hour day, turning a windlass which pulled loaded mine cars up the incline to the portal. Jealous of every minute which was not helping him rebuild his stake, David put in as many as fourteen hours daily; that February, for example, he had worked the equivalent of thirty-five ten-hour days, including Sundays, before the foreman, concerned about that breakneck pace, sent him off to the bunkhouse. So impressed was he with the industry of the young Eccles that he advanced him to the responsibility of weighing and totaling the weights of the loaded mine cars. Whether the advancement brought with it more salary or not, it did mean progress and the chance to carry greater responsibility. David must have felt exonerated to have his potential thus recognized. Unfortunately, though, because he had spent more years with a peddler's pack on his back than with a book in his hand, David had not learned to cope with figures in the way the new job demanded. So slow was he, in fact, that within a few days he was once more turning the windlass. The pain of shame must have been excruciating. The irony of the circumstance would not have been then apparent to soften the hurt, but it must have brought a smile to the lips of the mature Eccles when a colleague years hence would remark the speed with which David could cope with huge sums. With the coming of spring came one more humiliation: Chinese workers were

---

[4]"Dates and Data," p. 8.

brought to Almy to work the mine for lower wages, and David lost his job.[5]

Still smarting from the memory of his demotion, David returned to the logging operations back in Ogden Valley, soon becoming his own foreman. Then, though there was no longer any need to satisfy an employer, David determined to add academic skills to the practical ones he had so thoroughly mastered. He set aside the drive for money, the rush to rebuild his capital, long enough to attend the school of Professor Louis F. Moench in Ogden during the winter of 1872-73, and again a later winter. These two terms, together with the few months' schooling he had had in Scotland, constituted the whole of David Eccles' formal education.

Professor Moench's school gave David Eccles something even more significant, perhaps, than books and pencils. There were young people in the school, young ladies, and David became aware of one in particular. Bertha Jensen was just fifteen years old when David began at the school, but there was time for her to grow up, and for David to establish himself in the business world that was becoming so important to him. The spark could stay a small fire for a year or two while David and Bertha both caught up with life.

---

[5]"Dates and Data," p. 8-9.

Royal Eccles Collection. Bertha Marie Jensen as a bride.

6

The First Business ... And Marriage

DAVID ECCLES was barely twenty-three when he made the change from hired hand to enterpriser. Four undertakings introduced David to the hazards of self-employment, and at the same time provided the foundation for future investments that earned him a fortune.

The story of the first of these enterprises begins in the summer of 1872 when, after leaving the Almy coal mine, he signed a contract to supply white pine logs to a portable sawmill located forty-five miles east of Ogden on the Bear Lake Divide of the Monte Cristo Mountains. This mill was managed by Henry E. Gibson and W. T. VanNoy, on behalf of David James, who owned a retail lumber yard in Ogden. According to the terms of his contract, Eccles was to fell the trees, split them, and haul them to the mill with his oxen. He needed to hire help in the project, but although he was experienced and capable, he had as yet no reputation in the locality. Only four men would hire with him, so he, as he later remarked, did the work of two men that season, and often slept beside his work. The results were gratifying. The mill had to wait no more than one half-hour for his logs that summer, and David never again had difficulty hiring men to work for him.[1]

David's profit was $1,500. Impressed both with David and the prospects of the sawmill, Gibson and VanNoy joined with David in the purchase of a portable sawmill for operation during the summer of 1873.

David expected that the $1,500 he had earned would serve as his portion of the capital investment. During the winter, however, his mother persuaded him to lend his earnings to his brother John, who had now come from Scotland and needed the money to finance a furniture business he was opening. John was unable to repay the debt, leaving David without his share for the proposed sawmill.

Not one to be put down by reverses or disappointments, David sought a quick way to recoup, and, in partnership with his cousin, John Inglis (sometimes spelled Ingles), took a contract to freight goods to newly opened mines in Pioche, Nevada. Since their payment was calculated on the basis of the poundage of the loads, David and John piled the freight as high as they could. They later found that the large boxes they hauled contained coffins. Arriving at Dog Valley (near Cove Fort, Utah), David and John were overtaken by a snowstorm that lasted for eight or ten days, forcing them to turn the cattle out to feed and wait for the weather to clear. At the end of the storm when they went to round up the cattle, they found one dead and one crippled. Misfortune seemed to heap upon itself, and this one was the last straw — replacing the two head of cattle would take more than the profit from the whole venture. David became so disheartened at this last discovery that, as Inglis recorded it, he "sat right down and cried."[2] Nevertheless, he

---

[1] "Dates and Data Concerning the Life of David Eccles," REC, p. 10.
[2] "Memoirs of John E. Inglis," REC, p. 8.

continued to inquire and scheme, and soon found that some other freighters in the same valley had cattle they didn't need for that trip. David "rented" two head to replace the ones he'd lost, hitched them to his wagon, and set out once again.

At the border between Utah and Nevada came the next challenge to David's ingenuity: a customs duty was levied on goods passed from one state to the other. There was a loophole, however; once a driver had crossed once, he could cross again without paying tax on the second load. Desperate to show profit on his enterprise, David managed to avoid paying the tax by hiring a driver who had already crossed the line to take his freight the remaining distance to Pioche.

The goods delivered, David collected his share of the money and headed back to Ogden to join his partnership with Gibson and VanNoy. There had not been enough profit from the freighting trip to make the full $1,500, but David was able to raise the remainder through a loan from Warren Childs, an Ogden merchant.[3]

Locating their mill near the David James mill at which they had worked the year before, Gibson, VanNoy and Eccles prepared for operation in the summer of 1873. The logs which they processed during that first year of operation they sold to Barnard White, an Ogden lumber dealer. When the first year's operation proved profitable, though, the three partners decided it would be to their advantage to retail their own lumber, so in the fall they purchased a yard in Ogden. Gibson and Van-Noy managed the retail business, and David had primary responsibility for the sawmill in the canyon.

With all his involvement in the growing business, David had not lost contact with the social life of the Ogden and Ogden Valley community. Nor with the young Bertha Jensen, the girl from Professor Moench's school. Coming down from

---

[3] "Memoirs of Bertha Marie Eccles," REC, p. 11.

the sawmill for a dance in Huntsville, he made an impression on the girl, by now seventeen. "His hair was long," she later recalled, "and he had a red bandana handkerchief around his neck."[4] She must have seen under his shaggy mountaineer appearance something of the knight of her young girl's dreams, for she met him again at a dance in Ogden, and after that again, and again, over a two-year courtship.

During that time, David learned about the girl he was falling in love with. Comparing their early lives they must have been struck by the contrasts. David had been born to a blind woodturner; Bertha was the daughter of a wealthy landowner. David was one of seven children; of her mother's four children, Bertha was the only one who survived childhood. From the time he was eight, he had to work to help feed his family; she went to school four or five months out of each year. Emigrating to America, David's family assisted by the Perpetual Emigration Fund, tossed four weeks on the ocean; Bertha's family aboard a steamship crossed the Atlantic in less than two weeks and financially aided twenty-one other Church converts in making the journey. The contrasts were marked. But as the two continued to discover each other's lives they must have discovered more and more similarities: both were foreign-born; both had had to walk across the plains; both had lived with their families in log cabins in Ogden Valley. They knew the pioneer life.

Bertha Marie Jensen had been born in Pannerup, Aarhus, Denmark on January 30, 1857, daughter of Christian (or Christen) and Maren Anderson Jensen. When Bertha was only two years old her mother died, leaving Bertha and her brother Jens. Two previous children, a boy and a girl, had died in infancy. When her father remarried in 1861, Bertha was thrilled: "I remember my brother Jens and I on a small

---

[4]"Memoirs of Bertha Marie Eccles."

hill, dancing for joy waiting for our new mother to come."⁵ Thus Bertha was reared by her stepmother, Karen Peterson. When Jens died of diphtheria at the age of five, Bertha remained the only surviving child.

After the death of his first wife, Christian Jensen began to investigate the teachings of the Mormon missionaries proselytizing in Denmark. A serious inner struggle ensued, as he considered popular opinion against the Mormons and his own position of respect in the community. Studying long and diligently the teachings of Mormonism, he had converted four of his tenants long before he himself made the decision to affiliate with the Church. At length he was baptized in 1864.

As a part of a large group of Mormon emigrants, in June 1867 Christian and Karen Jensen, with ten-year-old Bertha and her little half-sister Mary, age two, departed Liverpool aboard the steamship *Manhattan,* quite possibly the first Mormons to cross the Atlantic in anything other than a sailing vessel. The voyage was short and, with the exception of two days of rough sea, pleasant. Bertha later recorded her childish impressions of the voyage, including her surprise when one stormy morning she awoke to find her clothing and shoes gone from their place. In a heap at one end of their quarters she found her belongings; they had been tossed out of her bunk and down the aisle by the pitching of the ship. During the thirteen days a child died, and the awed young Bertha witnessed a funeral at sea.

The *Manhattan* docked in New York harbor to the booming of cannon and the waving of flags on July Fourth, 1867, and ten-year-old Bertha passed with her family through the Castle Garden immigrant reception depot exactly four years

---

[5]"Bertha Marie Jensen Eccles: The Wife of David Eccles Relates Her Story," prepared by Cleone R. Eccles, p. 1, REC. The early experiences of Bertha Jensen are based primarily on this source.

and three days after fourteen-year-old David and his family had entered the United States. Bertha recorded later the sharpest image which remained with her: that of her first American pie — cherry, and "full of seeds"!

The remainder of their journey to North Platte, Nebraska, where the ox-team trek would begin, was filled with both good times and disappointments. Traveling aboard a steamer up the Hudson River to Albany, Bertha and her father stood on the deck "most all day . . . watching the beautiful scenery and marveling at the fine homes and gardens in the pleasant green hills and countryside along the river." Buffalo followed Albany, and with other families they made temporary quarters in a large warehouse. Nearby were the famed Niagara Falls, but since Bertha was only ten, she had to go to bed early while the grownups went to see the falls. That night she cried herself to sleep.

After taking a train to St. Joseph, Missouri, the family traveled up the Missouri River aboard a steamer to Council Bluffs, Iowa, where Christian Jensen purchased his "outfit" for the journey to Utah and again assisted members of the emigrant company to obtain needed supplies. Bertha recalled "how proud we were of the fine Charter Oak stove" which he bought her. For ten dollars each, the Jensens rode from Omaha on the newly completed Union Pacific railway to the end of the line at North Platte. The railroad cars had no spring, and the family rattled and jolted along on straight, backless benches. Uncomfortable and tired, Bertha fell asleep on the floor under the seats, only to be awakened when the conductor walking past kicked her feet which had sprawled into the aisle.

Although the Mormon Church formerly had sent wagons, teams, and supplies east to aid companies of converts, no assistance was forthcoming that year. And to further trouble their journey, the wagon outfits they had purchased at St. Joseph were delayed because of Indian raids which had destroyed some of the railroad lines.

After waiting almost a month for the goods to arrive at North Platte, the collection of six or seven hundred persons, the first large independent company of converts to travel to Utah, finally embarked under the direction of Captain Leonard G. Rice.

Although Bertha's father had purchased a fine outfit of three wagons with four oxen yoked to each wagon, unscrupulous dealers had taken advantage of his inexperience in the new country. Not knowing that the buyer should inspect the teeth of the animals, he had bought a brindle ox that was healthy but had poor teeth. Unable to graze the tough grass, the poor ox could not get sufficient food, so one of Bertha's daily chores was to care for him. Green herbs, volunteer corn — whatever tender forage Bertha could find — and bread made from damaged flour constituted the diet of the weak-toothed ox. Whenever the wagon train stopped, she fetched the animal a piece of bread and fed him in the evening at the wagon before turning him out with the others. When they reached the Salt Lake Valley, the ox was in as good a condition as any of the stock and had worked as many days.

Unlike earlier parties burdened with hardships and want, the Rice company traveled in relative ease. The weather was generally good, and food was plentiful. Several cows among the livestock provided a constant supply of milk and butter. Bertha would always remember gathering dried buffalo chips for fuel, camping in "those sticky yellow headed weeds that infest much of the West," and being presented with a generous bag of stick candy by a soldier at one of the forts they passed. Ten miles a day was average for the party, but she must have run an extra five miles gathering feed for the ox and fuel for campfires. In the evenings, the older people played games and danced, but again Bertha suffered the fate of an early bedtime after helping her mother with cooking and cleanup.

On a rainy day in early October of 1867, the travelers descended Emigration Canyon into the Salt Lake Valley. Their well-worn wagon wheels left narrow tracks in the muddy streets as they entered the city for a brief stay. It was time for the LDS semi-annual conference, and as they attended services, the first ever held in the newly completed Salt Lake Tabernacle, young Bertha was attracted by the massive pipe organ. Continuing with his family over the rough Ogden Canyon road to Huntsville, Christian Jensen sold his outfit and bought a farm occupied by a single log house.

The small dwelling with its dirt roof and six panes of glass was an extreme departure from the fine white homes with green shutters Karen Jensen had admired in the eastern states, but after the trek across the plains she was glad to have even a log house to shelter them from the cold Ogden Valley winters. In January Bertha's half-brother Peter M. Jensen was born in the little cabin. That year Bertha, now eleven years old, helped her parents mix mortar and whitewash to plaster the inside of the cabin, that year the dirt roof was replaced with shingles. Three years later Christian built a brick house, his wife's home for the rest of her life. During those first years Bertha often went hungry, fought swarms of grasshoppers "so thick they darkened the sun," and curiously watched the Indians that camped on the south side of the Ogden River.

During a part of each year Bertha attended school. She had had some previous schooling in Denmark, in Elev, a village about a mile from the family's home; in Utah she first attended a school conducted by William Hall, and later "Aunt Mandy" Bingham's school. With her father's consent, at thirteen Bertha moved to Ogden, where she earned one dollar a week working for Mrs. D. H. Peery. For the next two winters she worked for board and room for Mrs. Samuel Higginbotham while attending the school of Professor Moench in the old city hall, the same school to which David came after his Wyoming winter.

The people who settled Ogden were as divided by language differences as people anywhere, and as a rule the young people who spoke a language other than English found themselves excluded from the social life of the larger English-speaking group. Bertha Jensen too might have found herself an outsider among her peers, but she soon spoke excellent English and so was invited to their parties and dances. It was at one of these that she met again the rough "mountaineer" who had attracted her at the dance in Huntsville, and the two-year courtship began.

The courtship was spasmodic — David had his responsibilities at the mill on the Monte Cristo and Bertha was still at school in Ogden — but persistent. In May of 1875 she was called home to attend her very sick father. There she told him of David's proposal and of her decision to marry him. Christian Jensen's reply was encouraging: "I don't know much about him," he said, "but I rather like his looks and I know he is a good worker." That night Brother Jensen worsened, and the next day he died, but Bertha had had the assurance she wanted and so committed herself to David.

Letters and visits were exchanged; in fact, Bertha was criticized by the townsfolk for having visited David on one occasion. People were talking, she must have complained to him in a letter, to which he characteristically replied, "Let them say what they have a mind to. Who cares? I don't think it will hurt you."[6] Apparently it didn't, for that winter, on December 27, 1875, Bertha married him in the Endowment

---

[6]David Eccles to Bertha Jensen, September 5, 1875, REC.

House in Salt Lake City, fulfilling her promise to her parents that she would marry a man who belonged to the Church, did not drink, and was "a worker." She lacked one month of being nineteen years old; David was past twenty-six.

They moved into their first home, significantly a small adobe house on Ogden's Lincoln Avenue adjacent to the lumber yard David and his partner owned. Bertha learned to share his business interests, and was willing to participate in the work, no matter where. David felt strongly that women should be present in the lumber camps where they could exercise "their good influence on the men," so Bertha accompanied him to Monte Cristo.[7] For the first three summers of their marriage she lived with him there and cooked for the men at the sawmill camp. It was a good beginning, and augured well for a good marriage, as the successful continuation of the mill and the lumber yard augured well for a good business career. David Eccles was well on his way.

---

[7]"Your father regarded it necessary that women should be in the cookhouse because it kept the men more respectful. In camp as well as elsewhere your father showed his respect for the Gospel. He always said grace at the table in the camp. He did this himself when he was there, and when he was not there he expected grace to be said just the same. Your father never permitted any work on Sunday, except that which was necessary to operate the mill the next day." "Memoirs of Bertha Marie Eccles," p. 17.

7

Bold and Cautious Venturer

THE NEXT DECADE of David Eccles' life established patterns which would typify his business practices for the remainder of his life. Moving fearlessly from shared responsibility to sole proprietorship, from single venture to diversified interests, and from young businessman to established entrepreneur, he solidified his financial position and expanded his commercial influence. The reputation which in the decade following would push him into politics, and in the decade after that would make him a millionaire, was founded in the years 1875-1885.

At the time of his marriage to Bertha Jensen, David was partner in the three-man enterprise of the sawmill in the Monte Cristo region and in the retail outlet in Ogden. Two years later, in 1877, after four years of profitable partnership, one of the three, W. T. VanNoy, sold his interest to Eccles and Henry Gibson. Part of the settlement was that VanNoy kept the sawmill which had operated in Monte Cristo. Removing VanNoy's name from the title of the company, Gibson and Eccles purchased a new portable sawmill which they located in the same area and continued as before.

Business continued to thrive, but the two remaining partners had difficulty getting along. The last straw of the many disagreements, according to Eccles' wife Bertha, came in 1881 when Gibson traded two of Eccles' horses for two yoke of old worn-out cattle. The partnership dissolved, with Gibson retaining the yard in Ogden and Eccles the mill at Monte Cristo. The division left each of the partners with a profit of $15,000.[1]

Older heads, aware of Eccles' capital at hand, warned him. Be cautious, they would say, against rash investments. Leave well enough alone, they seemed to imply, alluding to his still profitable milling operation in the Monte Cristo. Eccles could well have heeded their advice and contented himself with his now sole ownership of one successful enterprise. Such was not his nature, though, and their cautions turned to challenges in his ears: he would turn their predictions of bankruptcy into proofs of success.[2]

The first investment from the profits of the Gibson-Eccles partnership was another lumber yard — Eccles was still convinced of the sound practice of retailing his own goods. David Eccles & Company in Ogden was the first enterprise in which Eccles could be considered the sole originator. That he was independently capable found proof in the continually rising profits — by 1888 they would reach $100,000 yearly.[3] That he felt personally involved in this first sole venture is indicated by the fact that, despite the diversity of businesses in which he would become involved in the future, he would retain his principal offices throughout his life at this first business, and promi-

---

[1] "Memoirs of Bertha Jensen Eccles," REC, pp. 13-14; Dictation of David Eccles, May 15, 1888, Utah Manuscripts, PF 81:49, Bancroft Library, Berkeley, California.
[2] "Memoirs of Bertha Jensen Eccles," p. 12.
[3] Dictation of David Eccles.

nent people seeking out David Eccles would always be instructed to call on him at the Eccles Lumber Company.

Eccles always considered himself a lumberman. And rightly so, for had he not worked in every aspect of the business, from logger to owner? His second independent venture was again into sawmill operations, this time at Scofield, a coal mining district important to the Rio Grande Western Railroad then pushing through eastern Utah toward Salt Lake City. Moving his Monte Cristo sawmill to the site, 180 miles southeast of Salt Lake City, Eccles began an operation which by 1883 involved three portable mills in the area. Eccles' cousin John Inglis directed the operation, the production of which averaged about 12,000 feet daily from each of the steam-powered mills with their crosscut saws. Workers signed on by contract and were paid one dollar per thousand feet for each ten-hour day.

In the Scofield venture David Eccles joined with his brother Stewart, who, with John Gibson, had purchased a shingle mill from the Gibson-Eccles partnership in 1880. The whole enterprise at its peak consisted of the three sawmills, the shingle mill, a lumber yard, and a general store — all in Scofield.

Stewart's share of the enterprise was thriving some years later when he received a call from his Church to serve a two-year proselyting mission abroad. Disappointed at the impending absence of the brother closest to him, David cajoled him: "You're a fool if you go; we're just getting ready to make money." Nevertheless Stewart sold his interest to David, arranged his affairs, and prepared to spend his twenty-six months proselytizing in Scotland. Arriving at the depot to purchase his rail and ocean ticket, he was astonished when the agent handed him the ticket — already paid for by David.

David Eccles' personal life was thriving along with his business enterprises. At home in Ogden, he was seeing his family grow. David Junior was a six-year-old in 1883 when the Scofield operation was peaking, and LeRoy was four. Vida had just been born, and the next year, 1884, Royal would be born. Their father was not just building a financial estate which they would inherit; he was establishing for them the name which they bore.

The name Eccles would, for example, represent unlimited credit in Utah businesses. The experience is related of Eccles' dealings with John Watson, manager of the Ogden ZCMI (Mormon-owned cooperative wholesale and retail department store) in the early 1880s. Eccles needed a roll of leather belting for one of the Scofield mills. As yet unknown to the salespeople at the ZCMI parent store in Salt Lake City, he had to wait patiently while a clerk telephoned Watson and asked if Eccles' credit was good. Watson's reply, "Why, yes, for anything he [wants] to buy," satisfied the clerk fully.[4] It may have been the last time anybody in Utah had to check Eccles' credit rating.

At the same time that the Scofield mills were thriving Eccles was building a third enterprise, a sawmill at Gray's Gulch, four miles west of Hailey on Idaho's Wood River. The discovery of rich veins of galena ores in the area in 1879 had turned this lonely section of Idaho into a rowdy series of mining camps, all marked by the need for lumber. Eccles somehow learned of the boom at Galena and in 1881 made a trip to Wood River which confirmed his plans for a lumbering business that would supply smelters and businesses as well as townspeople. Not willing to tie himself to one enterprise, especially one so far from home, he found as a partner A.D. Quantrell, a Swiss immigrant who was already on the spot.

Success was inevitable, at least for a while: timber prospects were good and demand for lumber was high. The portable sawmill Eccles brought in produced profits as fast as it

---

[4]Interview, Royal Eccles with John Watson, REC, September 20, 1929.

did lumber, despite competition from other mills which soon established themselves in the area. As the supply of timber in the vicinity of Gray's Gulch neared depletion, Eccles and Quantrell moved their sawmill to Elk Creek, on the head of Kelly's Gulch, three miles east of Bullion, Idaho,[5] improving their original equipment by the addition of new planing and moulding machines and a 56-inch circular saw that would cut 10,000 feet of lumber per day. By May of 1883 the partners had brought in a larger steam sawmill, encouraged in their expansion by the 1882 decision of Union Pacific investors backing the Oregon Short Line to construct a Wood River Branch to Hailey and Ketchum.[6]

But the boom was short-lived; three years of operation and $50,000 of profit later, it played out, and the partners dissolved their business. Quantrell turned to cattle ranching in the Idaho Falls district, lamenting later that he had not continued in the lumber business with Eccles.

Well might he lament, for Eccles went on to still another venture in lumbering which also proved profitable. This was the establishment of a complex of mills and store in Beaver Canyon, Idaho, close to the Montana border. In 1884, the same year he and Quantrell closed at Bullion, Eccles suggested to H. H. Spencer, an associate in Ogden, that the completion of the narrow gauge Utah and Northern Railroad to that area would open up the whole Upper Snake River region to extensive settlement and commerce, previously undeveloped because of the difficulty of transporting goods into or out of the area through the narrow canyon. Even after the railroad was completed Beaver Canyon was referred to, because of the harsh blustery winter winds, as the "tie yourself down" place.

[5]*Wood River Times* (Hailey, Idaho), November 16, 1882. These are in the library of the Idaho State Historical Society, Boise, Idaho. I am grateful to Dr. Gwynn Barrett, Boise State University, for some of this research.
[6]Memoirs of H. H. Spencer, REC.

VanNoy, the Stoddard brothers, and William F. Rigby had been involved in the area after the main tie-cutting operations had been set up, and it seemed natural that Eccles would find himself involved as well. The existence of a railroad on which to ship the lumber the 275 miles to Ogden made the prospect especially inviting to him. So it was that under Eccles' direction Spencer established a sawmill and a large merchandising store, as well as a ranch with several thousand acres of land and vast herds of cattle. He sold some lumber in Idaho, but most of it was shipped to the Eccles Lumber Company in Ogden.[7] Things looked good for the Beaver Canyon enterprise.

Not all Eccles' successes in this enterprising decade were commercial; nor were his personal satisfactions all connected with his growing family in Ogden. During these years, he came into contact with John Stoddard, a Scot like himself, from circumstances similar to his own. Stoddard was a faithful Mormon who, during the early 1880s, served a mission in Great Britain, leaving his wives and their families in Wellsville, Utah. It was probably on his return in 1883 that the event occurred which connected David with the Stoddards in more than just business dealings.

It seems that David, driving to Logan on business, thought to stop on the way and visit his associate Stoddard. He went first to the home of a Stoddard relative where some of the cousins, among them Stoddard's daughters, were getting ready for a Church function. One of the girls seemed to stand out from the rest; "a quick snip," David thought her, and remembered his impression long afterwards. She was spunky and independent, qualities David liked in people. This was Ellen, Stoddard's daughter, and she retained an impression of her father's associate as strong as David's of her.

---

[7]Interview, Royal Eccles with Joseph B. Evans, August 16, 1929, REC; *Idaho Falls Post-Register,* June 9, 1971.

Plural marriage was still being practiced among faithful Mormons, and Eccles would have found encouragement from Church officials in his growing affection for this eldest daughter of his Scottish friend and his English wife, Emma Eckersley Stoddard. Eccles would have known already of Ellen's family background and have learned later of her own life.

He would have known Stoddard, most likely, because of their mutual involvement in lumbering, the proximity of locales — both lived and worked in Ogden and Logan — but most significantly because of their shared Scottish origins. Stoddard had come to Utah from Scotland, probably in 1850, and had lived for a time in Cedar City. His first marriage was to Emily Kershaw in 1857, and their first child was born while they were still in that Southern Utah town.[8] By the time their third child arrived, in late 1860, however, the Stoddards had settled in Wellsville, a Cache Valley community near Logan.

An intriguing question arises in connection with Ellen's mother, Emma Eckersley, John Stoddard's second wife. On April 30, 1863, just thirty days before the *Cynosure* sailed out of Liverpool carrying fourteen-year-old David Eccles with his family to the new world, the *John J. Boyd* left England for America, carrying Joseph and Alice Eckersley, Mormon converts from Lancashire, and their children, among them their seventeen-year-old daughter Emma. Both groups would have passed through the Castle Garden immigration depot; both would have taken rail transportation to Florence, Nebraska, the fitting-out point for the crossing of the plains; both would have arrived in the Salt Lake Valley in the fall of that year. The fascinating conjecture concerns the possibility of the Scottish Eccleses having known the English Eckersleys, of David's having

---

[8]Information on the Stoddard family has been gleaned piecemeal from genealogical records in the Genealogical Society, LDS Church, Salt Lake City, and from emigration and ward records, HDC.

known Emma, the girl who would be mother to his wife Ellen.

But that is all supposing. There are more facts to indicate Emma Eckersley's activities once she arrived in Utah. She was married to John Stoddard in the Endowment House in Salt Lake City on July 2, 1864, the summer following her arrival in Utah, and became part of his growing family in Wellsville. By the time Ellen, their second child and first daughter, was born, that family consisted of the two mothers, three children of Emily (two had died as babies), the two of Emma, and the father. And the family continued to grow: Emily bore one more child, but died shortly thereafter, so the responsibility for her children fell upon Emma, who raised them along with the twelve of her own. In 1871 John Stoddard married yet another two wives, sisters, Sarah and Elizabeth Yates, who may have been cousins of his other living wife Emma. They gave birth to three and eight children respectively, all but the last three arriving in the family before Ellen was of an age to marry. In later years Ellen recalled to her daughter Nora some thirty-two siblings, all growing up as members of one family. Throughout her years at home, then, brothers and half-sisters, most of whom were younger than she. The ingenuity she later demonstrated, and the efficiency and thrift she practiced all her life had a sound foundation in the responsibility she had always had to bear.

Ellen, and the other Stoddard children, had the advantage of what elementary schooling was available in Wellsville. A school attendance record still extant shows four of them in the class taught in 1878, the year Ellen was eleven, by Joseph Howell, who later served seven terms (1903-1917) as Congressman from Utah. Ellen's name was the first on the list of a class of eighteen. Marriner Eccles later recorded that his mother Ellen "advanced in her schooling as far as the Fourth Reader," which could have been her status in Mr. Howell's 1878 class.[9]

Marriner also tells of Ellen's experiences in Aspen, Wyoming, where she apparently worked for a time with her sister in the sawmill and logging camp their father managed, cooking for the sawyers and the lumberjacks. In that remote forest, Marriner relates the two girls worked "from early dawn to late at night."[10]

This was the "quick snip" David Eccles found himself attracted to. And she to him. As she later recalled to her daughter, "I cared a lot for him before I ever heard his name even."[11] Polygamy was "legal" in Ellen's eyes, because it was condoned by the Church, and so she welcomed David's advances. But federal officials in the Territory were actively searching out men who entered into plural marriage and arresting them on charges of unlawful cohabitation. David was extremely circumspect in his courting of Ellen. She later recalled that he would stop at the Stoddard's "to see my father, or me through father, or father through me, or something." In 1884 John Stoddard moved his family to Ogden; there Ellen and David were able to be together a few times, always taking precautions against arousing the suspicions of their families and neighbors.

When David finally proposed to Ellen, her first answer was no. For whatever reason, she soon relented, and they were married secretly in the Logan Temple early the following January, 1885.

David, who more than once took care of John Stoddard's family, had moved them, with Ellen, to a farm where he would

---

[9]Marriner Eccles, *Beckoning Frontiers: Public and Personal Recollections* (New York, 1951), p. 21.
[10]Marriner Eccles.
[11]Recorded interview, Nora Eccles Treadwell with Ellen Stoddard Eccles, typescript in possession of the writer. Many of the details of the courtship and marriage of Ellen and David Eccles are taken from this interview.

visit on occasion. Their marriage still secret to everyone but Ellen's mother (and probably Bertha), they would sit with the rest of the family "and visit, and eat apples" until time for Ellen to walk David to the gate.

Ellen it was who most feared the consequences of discovery by the legal authorities, and well she might. Her father, husband to four wives, had lived under the threat of arrest, and would later spend nine months in Europe, possibly sent there to escape arrest, and be arrested immediately on his return. (He spent the months from November 1886 to May 1887 in the penitentiary, during which time David helped to support his father-in-law's large family.) The spectre of David's possible arrest hung menacingly over Ellen and made her cautious in the extreme. But her vigilance was rewarded: David Eccles was never imprisoned for unlawful cohabitation, in spite of the prominent public position in which he found himself in the next few years of his life, a position he assumed just five weeks after entering his second marriage.

8

Interlude in Politics

DAVID ECCLES' POLITICAL CAREER was a four-year interlude, 1885-1889, during which he served as alderman and then as mayor of Ogden. The events of his political participation and public administration interweave themselves into the existing pattern of the divergence not of political parties but of religious factions. As the political history of Utah Territory is one of struggle between Mormons and non-Mormons, so the chronicle of David Eccles' career in public life is one of attempted resolutions of their differences, in the interest of the universal well-being.

Nationally Eccles, as most Mormons, found himself initially in sympathy with the Democratic Party, favoring local sovereignty and "states' rights." Later, as befit his increasing responsibility as banker and industrialist, he switched to the more compatible Republican Party when Bryan and Free Silver came on the scene.[1] But national politics caused little stir in Utah where the principal issue was whether the territory would be controlled by Mormons or by Gentiles.

---

[1]Memoirs of Bertha Jensen Eccles, REC, p. 33.

Utah, of course, had been settled almost exclusively by the Latter-day Saints. As late as 1869, when the transcontinental railroad was completed, about the time that the Eccles family returned to Utah from Oregon, non-Mormons constituted hardly five percent of the population. Mormon authorities provided direction in political matters in the interest of their members and "the Kingdom of God." Support of Church nominees by all Mormons was almost automatic — equivalent to religious adherence.

After the joining of the rails, non-Mormons, hopeful of creating a center of economic power of their own, established a tent town on the Bear River at Corinne. Here, in 1870, they were joined by a group of apostate Mormons and organized the Liberal Party. Their announced intention was to place control of the territory in the hands of "loyal Americans." Mormon officials responded to this action by forming the People's Party, essentially an ecclesiastically-directed party — a political mechanism of the Church.

The People's Party managed to control every seat in the territorial legislature until the election of 1887. In almost every election, Mormons voted as a bloc and People's Party candidates won by large majorities. In the 1880 election of the delegate to Congress from Utah Territory, for example, George Q. Cannon, the "Church candidate," received 18,568 votes, as compared with 1,357 votes cast for A. G. Campbell, the Liberal candidate.[2]

On the local level, though, Ogden was prefiguring political directions other Utah communities would move; its Gentile population was enlarging ahead of that of other areas. Two

---

[2]G. Homer Durham, "The Development of Political Parties in Utah: The First Phase," *Utah Humanities Review* (April 1947), I, p. 133; Nels Anderson, *Desert Saints: The Mormon Frontier in Utah* (Chicago, 1942), p. 133.

main railroads met there, and the increased commerce introduced into the territory through Ogden was accompanied by increased non-Mormon influences. Ogden politics during the 1880s became increasingly volatile as the numbers of non-Mormon businessmen and laborers continued to grow. One of the moves made by the Church to solidify its position there was the 1869 election of Apostle Franklin D. Richards as county probate judge. David Eccles would have been content, along with his fellow Church appointees and nominees. But the build-up of the non-Mormon population of the city, together with the insistence of that group, a very vocal minority, on eliminating "Mormon rule," forced prominent figures in the community to choose sides and contribute active support.

On December 23, 1884 the five Mormon bishops of Ogden met to discuss the upcoming election. Two weeks later the Central Committee of the People's Party announced that primary elections would be held in the ecclesiastical wards of Ogden on Monday, January 26. At these primaries forty delegates were elected to attend the party's city convention on January 30. There, David H. Peery, the incumbent, was nominated as mayor, and David Eccles and Thomas D. Dee were nominated as new aldermen. Concurrently, the Liberal Party convention nominated Fred J. Kiesel for the office of mayor, and W. M. Rank to oppose Eccles as alderman for the third ward.[3] Whether pushed or persuaded, David Eccles took his step into the political arena.

The February 9, 1885 election was held in the Central School House. It was a snowy day, and a variety of buggies, sleighs, and bobsleds brought voters to the polls. Each party had a brass band, and the carriages they used to transport voters were decorated with their campaign mottoes. Through-

---

[3]*Ogden Daily Herald,* January 22, 1885; Journal of Charles F. Middleton, HDC, December 23, 28, 1884, January 19, 26, 30, 1885.

out the day the Liberals challenged some of the voters of the People's Party to present their full citizenship papers, and some who could not were not permitted to vote. Presumably the People's Party retaliated. There were several arrests for disorderly conduct during the day as tempers flared and tensions ran high.

The final tabulation was closer than many had anticipated; certainly it justified the anxiety demonstrated during the polling. The People's Party took all the individual races, but each count was close enough to indicate the growing strength of the Liberal position. In the race for mayor, Peery, the Mormon candidate, received 1,129 votes to 946 for the Liberal Kiesel. All four of the People's Party's aldermanic candidates were elected: A. T. Wright, Robert McQuarrie, Thomas D. Dee, and David Eccles, as well as the five councilmen, the recorder, the treasurer, the assessor and collector, and the marshal. A clean sweep for the Mormons, but just barely in most cases. David Eccles received 1,144 votes against 918 votes for his opponent W. M. Rank, and that was a larger margin than that secured by either the mayor or any of the other three aldermen.[4]

The city council met regularly on Fridays at four o'clock, and dealt typically with citizens' petitions for action on various problems . These petitions would be referred to the appropriate committee for consideration, and the committee would report its findings the following week, making its recommendations for vote by the rest of the council. In that context, where the business of the council would in fact be carried on in committee, it seems natural that David Eccles would find himself strategically placed. His skills in organizing and his financial acuity seem to have been immediately recognized, for in the council meeting of February 27, immediately following the

---

[4] *Ogden Daily Herald,* February 10, 1885.

election, he was appointed to the Committee on Public Buildings, the Committee on Water Supply, the Committee on Laws, and the Committee on Finance. He made his first report to the council, as spokesman for the Committee on Water Supply, just a week after his appointment.

The Finance Committee, in which Eccles was particularly active, was concerned with the need to borrow money at a rate of interest lower than the 10 and 12 percent it had been paying. Through his intervention the city was able to borrow $20,000 from the Deseret National Bank and from the First National Bank of Ogden at 8 percent interest.

Council meeting minutes reporting on Eccles' activities are too close to the event to record in any perspective the contribution he was making to the administration of the city; the following excerpt from the Ogden *Herald* reporting on the meeting of May 1, 1885, is representative of the day-by-day business of running a city:

> Alderman Eccles of the Committee on Water Supply and the committee had employed Mr. D. Moore to construct the pipe bridge at the mouth of the canyon, and the work is going along first rate. They had received some correspondence in regard to pipe, but had no report to make on the subject. They had investigated the question of allowing Mrs. Nielson to use Mr. Wilson's hydrant and had instructed the Superintendent to do what he thought proper under the circumstances.[5]

Two years passed, David Eccles alternating his public duties with his private concerns. Bertha presented him with a fifth child, Bertha Olivia, in January of 1887, and Ellen secreted in Scofield, ran the general store there for him for a time, after which Eccles moved her with her parents to Oregon. Never during the political career of Eccles did his opponents accuse him publicly of the paradox of Mormon patriotism:

---

[5] *Ogden Daily Herald,* May 2, 1885.

that he was creating and administering municipal laws at the same time as he was living outside of federal laws. Only once during Eccles' life as husband to more than one wife was he brought before the courts for unlawful cohabitation, and that was not until 1893, when the charges against most "cohabs," Eccles among them, were dropped because of a presidential amnesty for those who had entered plural marriages prior to 1890. Existing statutes would have forbidden his voting, much less holding office, had the truth of his second marriage been known.

By the expiration of his aldermanic term Eccles had so proven his worth to his constituents, as well as to the body of delegates to the People's Party convention in 1887, that they nominated him in his absence — he was "in Oregon on lumber business" — as their candidate for mayor, a nomination which he would have declined, he later said, had he been present.[6] The Ogden *Herald,* which was a pro-Mormon paper managed by Edward H. Anderson, reported the nomination this way:

> The election of candidates then being in order, the following gentlemen were placed in nomination for Mayor: David Eccles, John A. Boyle, and David H. Peery. The latter gentleman's name was subsequently withdrawn at his own request. A vote was taken, which resulted in Mr. David Eccles receiving an overwhelming majority, and he was duly declared the People's Party nominee for Mayor.[7]

Typical of the close alignment of politics and religion among Mormon electoral bodies, the delegates closed their meeting with a hymn, "Praise God from Whom All Blessings Flow," and a prayer, offered by the chairman of the convention.

On his return from Oregon, Eccles was informed of his

---

[6]Dictation of David Eccles, May 15, 1888, Utah Manuscripts, PF 81:49, Bancroft Library, Berkeley, California.

[7]*Ogden Daily Herald,* February 8, 1887.

nomination. His wife Bertha later recounted that "he became very troubled and subsequently spent a sleepless night." Eccles did not consider himself a politician at that time, any more than later when he looked back at the political interlude in his life. But there was really no way out: he had the support of the People's Party, obviously. Even more significantly, that support represented the confidence of his Church. He could hardly refuse.

The Liberal Party convention nominated Fred J. Kiesel as Eccles' opponent. The vote would be close, everyone recognized, and election day activities were frenzied. The Liberals "captured every livery stable team, job wagon, and other vehicle" available to transport the electorate. Again there was a succession of challenges on voter eligibility, with the final tally about evening up: the Liberals were able to force rejection of about the same number of People's voters as People's Party supporters were of the Liberal supporters.

Victory went again to the People's party, but with an even slimmer majority than two years previous. Eccles won the mayoralty by a narrow 110 votes, 1,364 to Kiesel's 1,254.[8] The handwriting was on the wall; astute political predicators might have seen even then that the next election would turn the tables. But for two more years at least city administration would rest in the hands of the Church-favored administrators.

The Ogden city council under David Eccles followed his lead in directions which might have been predicted, given Eccles' standing, influence, and business acumen. The administration stressed sound fiscal and business management, an emphasis Eccles outlined in his inaugural address to the newly elected council. The council would, he hoped, provide for public improvement in accordance with available finances, and would work to decrease the city's indebtedness, and in general

---
[8]*Ogden Daily Herald*, February 15, 1887.

carry on a wise and economical management of city affairs. The Ogden *Herald* applauded Mayor Eccles' objectives, but at the same time pleaded for municipal improvements:

> Public improvements are respectfully demanded by the citizens of Ogden. The voice calls for a city hall, a gas franchise, beautiful parks, and a cemetery relieved from its present external horrors; this is the Voice of the People.
>
> Ogden has at this time a municipal administration, consisting of men who, without exception, are enterprising and successful in their individual business affairs. These men are doubtless inclined to carry into public policy the same energy and liberality which have been fruitful of good in their personal ventures — if they can feel that such a course will meet with the approval of the community.[9]

David Eccles' most significant contribution as mayor was the organization of the Ogden Chamber of Commerce. This represented an attempt to get bi-party support for a program of business improvement and economic development. In the economic arena, as in politics, relationships between Mormons and non-Mormons were polarized. Mormons had organized Zion's Central Board of Trade, an organization concerned primarily with Mormon goals. Non-Mormons, on the other hand, had formed a territorial board of trade which was primarily concerned with unseating Mormons from power. Friendly with both Mormon and non-Mormon businessmen, David Eccles was able to obtain the support of both groups in a joint endeavor to build Ogden and Weber County. The first bi-faith organization in Utah Territory, the Ogden Chamber of Commerce started a precedent which saw the formation of similar organizations in Salt Lake City and other bi-polarized communities in the region. The Chamber also rallied support for some of the programs of civic improvement advocated by

---

[9]*Ogden Daily Herald*, February 25, April 7, 1887.

Mayor Eccles. Having been established while the Mormons were still in power in Ogden, it could carry Church support even into subsequent periods when city administration had passed into Gentile hands. David H. Peery, Mormon and ex-mayor, was president of the Chamber during its first year, and Judge P. H. Emerson, non-Mormon and Liberal, succeeded him the second year.[10]

Other accomplishments of the city council during Mayor Eccles' term, though not so strikingly reflective of his personal viewpoint as the merging of Mormons and Gentiles in a common enterprise, still represent his concerns for the city and the citizens. They include the completion of the improvements to Liberty Square, the granting of the gas franchise to the Cincinnati firm of McDonough and Company for the creation of The Ogden Gas Light Company, substantial street improvement, an augmented water supply, and the building of a new city hall. The mayor also lobbied successfully for the establishment of the territorial reform school in Ogden for which he and the council donated the required thirty-seven acres of land.[11] Under Eccles' urging the council sold $100,000 worth of bonds for city improvement. Of this action, Joseph A. West, a member of the council, wrote:

> In those early days our sturdy pioneers were bitterly opposed to going into debt, either individually or collectively, municipally or otherwise, and it was no easy task to get authority for our first bond issue of $100,000.[12]

West then went on to say that it was the intent of the council that the debt would be promptly paid, and said of Eccles' financial acuity that "Utah never produced a more careful or success-

---

[10] Edward W. Tullidge, *History of Northern Utah and Southern Idaho* (Salt Lake City, 1889), pp. 171-72.
[11] Milton R. Hunter, *Beneath Ben Lomond's Peak: A History of Weber County, Utah, 1824-1900* (Salt Lake City, 1966), p. 561.
[12] *Ogden Standard Examiner,* September 13, 1925.

ful financier." One of the projects planned under the bond issue was the construction of a $50,000 city hall. When bids were called for the plumbing work, Eccles felt that the bids were all too high. He then called his friend, Bishop David James, for whom Eccles had logged in the early days in the White Pine area, and who now had a plumbing business in Salt Lake City. He asked James to go to Ogden, and go over the building plans, submit a "realistic" and "good wage" bid on the plumbing work. Eccles told James he wanted one of the Ogden firms to do the work but felt their bids were excessive, and would not award the contract to James if one of the Ogden bidders would meet his bid. Bishop James' bid proved to be lower than the lowest bid submitted by W. W. Funge. Eccles then went to Funge and told him what he had done. Funge said he could not do the work for that price, whereupon Eccles replied, "All right, you don't have to do it; Bishop James will do it but I would prefer an Ogden man to get the work." When Funge thought the situation over he accepted the Bishop James' figure. According to Bertha Eccles, Mr. Funge "came out all right" on the deal.[13]

One of Eccles' proudest moments as mayor was the dedication of the completed city hall. Reflecting on the accomplishments of the council during his administration he said on that occasion:

> I bespeak for Ogden a glorious future. We have striven to perform our duties in the past, and whatever party may occupy this place in the future they will find a clean record left by the present administration.[14]

All sources suggest that David Eccles left a "clean record" as mayor. S. A. (for Scipio Africanus) Kenner, a pro-Mormon political commentator, wrote:

---

[13]"Memoirs of Bertha Marie Eccles," pp. 31-32.
[14]*Ogden Standard,* February 9, 1889.

> In 1887 Mr. Eccles was triumphantly elected Mayor of Ogden and gave the city one of the most progressive and pushing administrations it has ever had. It is a great good fortune for any place to have such men in their midst, and the "Junction City" is peculiarly favored in having several such. Any of them is worth a regiment of croakers and inert dreamers, and when Mr. Eccles and his kind are contemplated it is no longer a wonder that Ogden has kept so splendidly to the fore in the presence of much steady and active rivalry.[15]

David Eccles was not a candidate for mayor in the next election held February 11, 1889. Summarizing his administration at an election eve rally, he hinted at the "serious personal sacrifice" that his service had cost, but reflected at the same time his pride in "the confidence which my fellow citizens reposed in me." His summary of his aims and those of his council reflects his characteristic attitude of ecumenism: "We have tried to serve the people well and faithfully — not one class or party, but all the people, rich and poor, high and low."[16]

In the election the following day the trend which was beginning as David Eccles entered Ogden politics found confirmation: Liberal nominee F. J. Kiesel beat People's candidate John A. Boyle for mayor, and in a clean sweep the Liberal candidates replaced People's Party members. Ogden became the first major city in Utah to pass out of Mormon control. (Park City, a Gentile mining town, was already governed by non-Mormons; Salt Lake City would have non-Mormon government a year later.)

Eccles could not let the defeat pass unprotested. He suspected underhanded politics, and said so to an Ogden *Standard* reporter who quoted him:

> I am satisfied that many fraudulent votes have been cast by the Liberal party and many legal votes of the People's party have

---

[15] S. A. Kenner, *Utah As It Is* (Salt Lake City, 1904), p. 538.
[16] *Ogden Standard,* February 10, 1889.

been cast out. . . .

I think an outrage, unworthy of American institutions, has been committed. A number of arrests have been made, but I think we ought to have a good many more.[17]

No official protest was made, however, and the People's Party accepted its defeat.

Two days after the election ex-mayor Eccles gave a dinner in his home in honor of the outgoing city officials. The warmth of the account in the *Standard* almost veils the reality of the situation: the party was in fact a wake darkly celebrating the demise of Church political power in Ogden. David Eccles was the last mayor of an Ogden council composed exclusively of the faithful. The story does truthfully reflect, though, the relief felt most certainly by Eccles, and most probably by his colleagues.

> The occasion was one of enjoyment and genial and thoughtful reminiscence, and the recollection of it will live long in the memory of every participant. The men who had served long and amicably together in the public service were glad to pause for a moment — as they were about to lay down their burden of official care — and renew and intensify the friendliness and mutual trust begotten by their years of experience with each other. As men loyal to their party and its principles, they could not but feel regret for the political defeat which that party had suffered, and this regret they expressed in a manly and straightforward style; but this was not in any personal sense, for individually they were glad to be relieved of burdens which weigh heavily and involve loss of time and neglect of personal business.[18]

Nathan Tanner, Jr., the city attorney, delivered a moving panegyric, a part of which deserves quoting here:

> We need to do [David Eccles] honor, not because he holds the exalted office to which his constituents have elected him, nor

---

[17]*Ogden Standard,* February 12, 1889.
[18]*Ogden Standard,* February 14, 1889.

is it because he is on the eve of retiring therefrom; but, we honor him because with all his goodly qualities of head and heart, in this day of heated political strife and sullied official consciences, he has trod the official wine press a full term and come out without a stain upon his garments so that his bitterest political enemies have naught to say against the honesty or efficiency of his administration.[19]

David Eccles' service in public office, though relatively short, was an interlude in his own life between Utah-based concerns and wider spread interests, and an interlude in Ogden's development, between Mormon and non-Mormon rule — a transition in personal scope in the context of a transition in territorial history.

Within a decade the Liberal and People's parties were dissolved and Utah's citizens aligned themselves with the Democratic and Republican parties. Utah finally attained statehood in 1896, and the bitter struggle between the Mormon and the Gentile moved towards amicable cooperation. The Mormon-Gentile dichotomy was replaced, politically at least, with the two party system still current.

---

[19]"Remarks by City Attorney N. Tanner Jr.," REC.

LDS Church Archives. Logo of Oregon Lumber Company, 1889.

LDS Church Archives. Logging teams, Chenowith, Washington

LDS Church Archives. Early Eccles Sawmill, Baker, Oregon.

LDS Church Archives. Loading logs in Sumpter Valley, Oregon.

LDS Church Archives. Eccles Sawmill at Chenowith, Washington.

LDS Church Archives. Steamer "Pearl" and Lumber Rafts, Viento, Oregon.

9

Lumber and Railroads In Oregon

EIGHTEEN-YEAR-OLD David Eccles saw more than scenery on the long trek to Oregon with his family in 1867. The huge stands of timber, which settlers swore at as they cleared the land they wished to farm, must have appeared to Eccles as representing more gold than dross — certainly once he got involved in lumbering in Utah he would remember the thick forests of Oregon as the raw wealth they were.

Nearly two decades after that first venture into the Northwest, in 1883, Eccles' interest in lumber led him to buy from John Stoddard a small mill for cutting railroad ties at North Powder, his first investment in Oregon's resources. The ease with which the timber could be cut and hauled, and the completion of the Oregon Short Line Railroad, which would connect Ogden with nearby Baker, was an enticement. Besides that, the restrictions of the 1878 Timber and Stone Act which forbade shipping of stone and lumber between territories — from Idaho to Utah, for example — but permitted it from a state — Oregon to Utah — encouraged Eccles to attend more diligently to the possibilities he was discovering in Oregon. In 1887, between his duties on Ogden's civic government, he made a special trip to complete his incorporation, with Thomas F. Hall and O. N. Ramsey, of the parent of the Oregon Lumber Company, then known as Spencer, Ramsey and Hall. Eccles had closed the Beaver Canyon, Idaho mill, and brought H. H. Spencer, who had been managing that enterprise, into the Oregon firm to represent him in the corporation.

Not just one mill, but several grew into the enterprise that year. There was a sawmill near Viento, Oregon and another at Chenowith, Washington, on the north slope of Mt. Hood. Douglas fir and ponderosa (Oregon white) pine were cut, and in a highly efficient operation, floated down a flume and slid into the Viento railroad station, or in the case of the Chenowith mill, floated across the Columbia on barges or rafts to the Viento yard for shipping. Hundreds of cars of railroad ties were thus dispatched from the area, centering some fifty miles east of Portland.[1]

Charles W. Nibley, a Mormon and a business promoter, entered the milling enterprise in that same year, 1887, and participated with Eccles in the events which would lead to the founding in 1889 of the mammoth Oregon Lumber Company. In 1888-1889 the holdings in Oregon and Washington expanded, timber interests in the Hood River region grew, and Eccles shipped one of the mills from the Scofield, Utah plant to Telocaset in Pyle's Canyon. Located about thirty miles west of Baker and nine miles from North Powder, Telocaset was an important railroad shipping point. Although Eccles owned this plant entirely, he operated it under the name of William Eccles and Company, William being either David's father—the source is unclear — or his younger brother, the manager of the mill.

---

[1]Memoirs of H. H. Spencer, REC.

The move of the mill from Scofield to Telocaset is representative of the shift of Eccles' major interest from Utah to Oregon. Government harrassment in the Utah timber lands had become awkward, and relocating seemed a judicious solution. It seems that Utah lumbermen consistently cut the timbers on the government reserves, protecting their efforts by paying off the inspectors one by one as they came. J. E. Inglis, manager of Eccles' operation in Scofield, remembered the situation as follows:

> All the mills that were operated in Utah had never received permits to cut the government timber. They cut it on their own responsibility. Every year a government agent would come to see about the cutting of the timber. We compromised with the government men, each mill paying a certain amount, and the government man kept that for himself. There was a new government man every year and he never gave the money to the government and hence there were complaints made — mostly by the government agent who thought he didn't get enough.[2]

The practice had become so widespread by 1885 that Eccles, in an attempt to facilitate timber cutting within the law, organized a Lumberman's Convention in Logan. His efforts at changing regulations were not really successful, and the misunderstandings between lumbermen and government continued to plague them both.

The "complaints" Inglis speaks of resulted in a full investigation in 1886, as a result of which government officers attached some million feet of lumber which Eccles had in Scofield. Eccles secured its release, but the problem gave no indication of permanent solution. Conditions in Oregon, both natural and governmental, promised to be much more amenable to the logging industry, so Eccles turned his attention increasingly toward his concerns there.

---

[2]Memoirs of John E. Inglis, REC, p. 10.

By spring, 1889, when Eccles had finished his term as mayor of Ogden, Charles Nibley had involved himself in the Oregon project to the extent of selling out his Bear Lake interests and moving to the area. He and Eccles, and Eccles' father-in-law John Stoddard, settled on arrangements to consolidate Eccles' Oregon properties under the title of the Oregon Lumber Company, launching the organization with $75,000 in invested capital. Eccles, of course, held the majority of the stock, with Nibley holding 10 percent and Stoddard a small but unknown percentage.[3]

During these years of growing business interest in Oregon, Eccles also had a personal investment in the country. He moved his second wife Ellen, along with her mother, her brothers Willard and Henry, and her sister Jessie to North Powder, near the mill which Ellen's father John Stoddard had built and which Eccles now owned. The move was a propitious one politically: both Eccles and Stoddard were polygamists, and the chance of the persecutions of the marshals reaching beyond Utah was slim. Even so, Ellen took care to preserve her anonymity, travelling under the name "Mrs. Ellis."

Even in her own family Ellen's marriage to Eccles was unknown, despite the intimacy of the cabin into which the family had moved. With rough-hewn lumber from the mill and a jack plane, the ingenious young wife fashioned not only furniture for the dwelling — table, chairs, and a wash stand — but also built walls dividing one end into two bedrooms, one for her and one for her mother and the children. When David would visit, the couple timed his entrances and exits so carefully that not even Ellen's brothers and sister were suspicious.

Such visits were far too few, at least from Ellen's point of view. Eccles seemed to come long enough to establish busi-

---

[3] "From the Story of Charles W. Nibley," in Kate Carter, ed., *Treasures of Pioneer History* (6 vols., Salt Lake City, 1952-1957), I, pp. 292-93.

nesses and business procedures, and then left good men in charge of dispatching his instructions. In the case of the Oregon ventures, his man was Charles W. Nibley. But Nibley was not one to be content with merely conducting an established business; his spirit was more adventuresome, and his enthusiasm carried Eccles along into new ventures.

During the fall of 1889 Nibley was occupied with the North Powder and Hood River concerns. That November, while investigating some land titles in Baker he learned from the county surveyor of an excellent body of timber in Sumpter Valley. It would be easy to build a railroad up to the Powder River, he suggested, some twenty miles into the valley. Waiting for the train that evening Nibley wrote Eccles a long, enthusiastic letter detailing his conversation with the surveyor and suggesting they investigate. A week or two later Eccles arrived. On saddle horses, with the surveyor's son as their guide, the partners explored the country, following the river into Sumpter Valley timberlands.

Until that time, according to Nibley, Eccles had not "branched out in any expensive way," but rather had limited his operations to narrow tracts and small "cheap" 25-horsepower sawmills. He had involved himself closely in every detail of the business, Nibley said, and thus had little time or inclination to search out new opportunities. Nibley, on the other hand, detested details but "fancied that [he] could tell a good thing and a big one" when he saw it. The two made a good team. Within a few months Nibley, with Eccles' backing, had made an agreement with Charles Francis Adams, president of Union Pacific Railroad, to build a railway into Sumpter Valley.[4]

The system was a frugal one: Union Pacific was replacing some of its narrow gauge trackage for standard gauge, and was willing to exchange the retired equipment — engines, cars,

---

[4] "From the Story of Charles W. Nibley," pp. 292-93.

switches and such — for bonds in the new line. The Union Pacific insured a profit on the new enterprise by contracting for 500,000 ties annually to be bought from Oregon Lumber and shipped on the new line. Baker townspeople supported the railroad with a promise of financial backing, and though their money was never needed, the goodwill of the community must have augured well for the new system.

Stories of the Sumpter Valley Railway are legends now. "Polygamy Central," the line was once called, suggesting that the religious convictions of its founders were not entirely unknown. Or the "Stump Dodger," a nickname it won because of the rough-laid roadbed through the forest terrain. Railroaders told stories of "highballing," speeding the train down the steep inclines; of "joining the birds," jumping out of an imperiled engine before it crashed; of trains stalled on a four percent grade in the midwinter snows before the snowplow came; of the runaway train and the daring leap of a logging engineer who stopped her before she could stage a "cornfield meet" with a passenger train on the same track.

Between August 1, 1891, when the first trainload of logs pulled into Baker, until the summer of 1947, when the last steam locomotive was replaced with a diesel engine, the line built its own legend. Financially, its story was one of success: it eventually extended eighty-four miles from Baker to Prairie City, and operated on a capital of $1,500,000. Commercially, it opened a whole new area for logging-related industry and settlement along its route.

In 1892, soon after the incorporation of the railroad and the Oregon Lumber Company, Eccles constructed a large sawmill at Baker, later incorporated into the parent company. Joseph B. Evans, one of the Scofield men whom Eccles brought to Baker, tells of the planing mill where he directed much of the work. On one occasion, he recounts, young Jim and Merrill, sons of Charles Nibley, were working at the mill under Evans' supervision and that of William Childs. One morning early, Evans recounts, Jim and Merrill went to the mill to "fire-up." Choking the fire box with shavings, the boys accidently set fire to the plant. The only recourse for Childs and Evans was to cut the dam above the millrace and flood the yard. The factory, which had not yet operated one month, was destroyed. Although there was no insurance on the mill, in seven days they were again shipping lumber.[5]

The year 1893 brought another potential disaster to the Oregon Lumber Company and its employees. Severe economic depression dropped prices and curtailed employment. During the panic that followed, Eccles and Nibley called all the employees of the company to Baker, some five hundred of them from the mills around Baker. In straightforward terms they explained the situation to the assembled workers. The future was uncertain. There was enough money for this coming payroll, but they were not sure when they would be able to pay again. They would keep the mill running — there was the commitment for ties to be met — and workers would be furnished with clothing and provisions. It was uncertain when a subsequent payday would come, but when it did, the men would be paid in full. Out of the five hundred employees, only two quit. Said Joseph Evans, "We never knew there was a panic," for on the next payday, the money was forthcoming.

The mammoth Oregon Lumber Company listed principal mills in 1893 at Hood River, Meacham, North Powder, Baker, and Pleasant Valley. Nor did the expansion stop there. Huge tracts were being purchased well into the next century as areas became depleted and new ones must be found. Early in the expansion, when timber land was unlimited, Eccles bought the valuable Middle Fork of the John Day river tract, which pro-

---

[5]Interview, Royal Eccles with Joseph B. Evans, August 16, 1929, REC.

vided timber for more than forty years of continuous operation.[6] It may well have been at the purchase of that tract that the following anecdote of Eccles' business character originated.

Eccles was at The Old Grand Pacific Hotel in Chicago, planning to purchase "that large and wonderful timber tract in Oregon" from a Mr. Jones of Appleton, Wisconsin. During their negotiations, Jones frequently interrupted the conversation with visits to the bar, insisting that Eccles accompany him. Homer C. Hutchinson of New York, a cousin of Eccles, had arranged to meet Eccles that evening and told later of his cousin's growing annoyance with Jones:

> David Eccles suddenly turned to me and said, "This fellow always wants to take a drink, and I don't drink liquor. This fellow is a regular nuisance. He can't talk very long without taking a drink." I told . . . [Eccles] I would go into the bar with Jones and share his hospitality at the bar. This was most agreeable to Jones. When at last he came out, he talked with . . . [Eccles] for such a length of time that the point was reached, where they were to go upstairs to a room, and come to a definite understanding. On the way to the elevator, Jones again wanted to visit the bar. It was then that David Eccles turned around and remarked that they go upstairs at once, or there would be no further going ahead with the matter. As usual, when . . . [he] put his foot down, he meant what he said. The remainder of this conversation regarding the timber land, Jones would have pencil and paper with data before him. In every point that came up he would stop to figure . . . . [Eccles] needed no pencil or paper to figure with at any time. When a point came up as to amount of timber of what it would scale, . . . [Eccles] put his hand to his forehead and would say, "Well, what do you get?" Jones would figure. Sometimes he was right and again as often he was not . . . [Eccles] would quickly remark, "You are mistaken, that is not correct. Jones would say, "Here it is in black and white. I have figured it out . . . ." [Eccles] would say, "I don't

---

[6]James Canse, "History of the Oregon Lumber Company," December 2, 1943, REC.

care what you figure, you are wrong, and I will show you where you are wrong." And he did so in a very short time.⁷

In retelling the incident Homer would not likely have known of the early embarrassment in his cousin's life, of the job of tally clerk which he lost because he could not reckon with figures. But perhaps the memory in Eccles' own mind put a sharp edge on his own pride in his mathematical ability; certainly he had justification.

With the addition of timber tracts and construction of sawmills throughout the state, the Oregon Lumber Company continued to grow. In 1902 Eccles opened a mill at Inglis, Oregon, thirty miles west of Portland, which was operated by his cousin John Inglis. From the mill, located in a fine body of fir timber, workers cut and shipped lumber successfully for many years. The mill was later absorbed by the Oregon Lumber Company.⁸ At the same time he began negotiations with Leslie and Truman Butler for purchase of the Lost Lake Lumber Company, with operations at Hood River. In 1903 the transaction was completed, and two years later the Lost Lake Lumber Company was merged with the Oregon Lumber Company.⁹

Operations at Hood River were facilitated by the construction in 1905 of the Hood River Railroad, which extended from the town of Hood River sixteen miles to the heavy fir timber and later a full twenty-five miles to Parkdale. At the time all kinds of engines were used on logging railroads: second-hand rod engines, discarded after many years of use on regular railroads; new locomotives; steam "dummy types," driven from

---

⁷Interview, Royal Eccles with Homer C. Hutchinson, December 31, 1930, REC.

⁸Memoirs of H. H. Spencer. In 1903 Eccles purchased timber and started the mill operation at Inglis as part of the Lost Lake Lumber Company. See Canse, "History of the Oregon Lumber Company."

⁹Truman Butler to Royal Eccles, n.d., REC; Canse, "History of the Oregon Lumber Company."

street and suburban railways by electricity; and Forney types, that once served the elevated lines of eastern metropolises. Art Sayre, an employee on the Hood River Railroad, recalled that the construction engine he fired was

> a small 2-4-2 steam dummy that was formerly used on street railways in Ogden, Utah. This kettle had no water glass, and the firemen had to try the gauge cocks frequently to avoid blowing her to Kingdom Come. Like many of her sister engines in logging road service, she burned slab wood, a by-product of sawmilling that offered cheap fuel.[10]

The mill and railroad were merged the following year into the Oregon Lumber Company.[11]

In 1906 the Oregon Lumber Company discontinued operations at Hood River and Chenowith-Viento and built a mill at Dee, Oregon, on the line of the Mt. Hood Railroad, for the production of ties and timber. The company had large holdings of Douglas fir around the base of Mount Hood, originally selected with this type of business in mind. After a fire in 1913 destroyed the mill, a modern mill for the production of all types of lumber was built in its place. That same year the pine sawmill at Austin was erected on the line of the Sumpter Valley Railway.[12]

One of the knottiest problems with which the lumber companies were faced through these developmental years was

---

[10]George B. Abdill, *Pacific Slope Railroads: From 1854 to 1900* (New York, 1954), p. 169. This source, p. 176, carries a photograph of a 2-truck wood-burning shay of the Mount Hood Railway Company, with William H. Eccles, Ham Brightson, and S. M. Osborn aboard. The photograph carries the following caption: "Numbered *1,* she was named the 'Bud' in honor of 'Bud' Eccles, a teen-aged son of one of the owners of the Oregon Lumber Company [William H. Eccles, brother of David], who controlled the Mount Hood Road. Young Eccles met an awful death when he became entangled in the cable and drum of a donkey engine used for pulling lumber cars up an incline at Viento, Oregon, about 1900."

[11]Memoirs of H. H. Spencer.

[12]"Dates and Data Concerning the Life of David Eccles," REC, p. 22.

the acquisition of new timber lands. In the case of the Oregon Lumber Company the problem was multiplied by the very size of the company, the number and capacity of its mills, and the demands of its contracts. Constantly there was the need to secure additional forests as the existing ones were stripped of their mature growth in those years before enforced reforestation.

Federal regulations governing the use of public timber lands were unreasonable and shortsighted. Designed as they were to administer fair use of frontier lands where small trees could be cut for individual use, they in no way allowed for use of the massive forests of the Northwest, whose trees could be removed only in large quantities by big and expensive equipment, experienced lumberjacks, skid rows, railroads and barges, and huge sawmills. Both the Timber and Stone Act and the Timber Cutting Act of 1878 permitted the settler to clear his 160 acres, chop down a few trees, saw them up, and then use them for his house and farm. They did not recognize the economic realities of logging.

In the face of such ill-designed legislation, lumber interests found ways to circumvent the law. A frequent foil was for lumber companies to encourage their employees, settlers, or anyone else to file on 160 acre tracts. Agents would scout out good timber lands and advertise openly their desire to purchase the lands from anyone who might enter them under the Timber and Stone Act. Companies drew up applications, took affidavits as notaries public, provided and paid witnesses, in other words, looked after the mechanics involved, requiring the "entrymen" to provide merely their names. Entrymen were usually paid $50 to $150 for their services. Proving fraud in such cases required the government to provide evidence that there had been an agreement prior to the application, difficult evidence to produce.

When in the early 1900s the government began to crack

down on such practices, Eccles and the Oregon Lumber Company were indicted for past offenses just three days before the statute of limitations ran out; litigations dragged on, and it was not until after Eccles' death that the case against the Oregon Lumber Company was settled, in the Supreme Court in 1922. The suit was dismissed on a technicality: the government had waited too long to prosecute.

Eccles' interests in Oregon were far from solely lumber-related. In the 1890s, for example, he and Charles Nibley took over the Baker City Electric Light Company. In 1898 Eccles, after an unhappy split with Nibley, oversaw the construction of the LaGrande Sugar Company to process sugar from beets grown in the Grande Ronde Valley,[13] some on lands owned by the company. Eccles held stock in banks and mercantile institutions in the state, and title to extensive lands in the eastern part of Oregon.

Nor were Eccles' enterprises beneficial solely to Oregonians or the happenstance settlers who drifted by. Friends whom he invited, or who, hearing of his lumbering operations, invited themselves, left their by now overcrowded towns and villages in Utah and migrated into the areas of Oregon where Eccles' concerns were located. There they found work, lumbering in the Sumpter Valley, working the sawmills at Baker, Meacham, Hood River and the like, or, later, running the beet sugar factory at LaGrande. Some of these persons, one can be sure, homesteaded forest lands and then conveyed them to Eccles. So widespread was the migration from Weber Valley and Cache Valley in the 1890s that Latter-day Saint Sunday Schools sprang up, first in Baker, and later in the other towns. In 1898 the newly organized Northwestern States Mission set up its headquarters in Baker, and by 1901 Union Stake, consisting

---

[13] *Baker Morning Democrat,* 1891, as quoted in "David Eccles, Empire Builder," *Ogden Standard.*

of several wards in the area, was created with its center in LaGrande.

There is no way to assess just how much immigration into Oregon can be credited to employment opportunities created by Eccles enterprises, any more than it is possible to assess with any accuracy the total amount of his Oregon interests for any one year. Suffice it here to generalize that without Eccles' involvement, the economic development of the state would have been much different.

LDS Church Archives. Oregon Lumber Company Plant at Dee, Oregon.

LDS Church Archives. Oregon Lumber Company Plant at Baker, Oregon.

LDS Church Archives. Sketch of Plant of
Grande Ronde Lumber Company.

Nora Eccles Harrison Collection. Eccles employees at first mill at
Baker, Oregon in 1891. David Eccles is wearing
the derby on the far right.

Royal Eccles Collection. Oregon Lumber Plant and related enterprises at Baker, Oregon, about 1898.

LDS Church Archives. David Eccles and Charles W. Nibley, about 1890.

10

David Eccles and the Development of Utah: The 1890s

DURING THE 1890s, while David Eccles' interests in Oregon were mushrooming, his concerns both public and private in his adopted home state, Utah, were increasing. At home in Ogden, Bertha's family had grown to six by 1890 with the birth in 1889 of Joseph Merrill, and would increase again in 1891 when Lila was born. Ellen, David's second wife, had returned to Utah, staying with her family in Logan, long enough to give birth to her first child, Marriner, in 1890.

Eccles was wise in keeping his two families separated by distance. The best protection against federal prosecution was to maintain each wife in a different state; once Ellen came back, caution was doubly important. Ellen, visiting with her family back in Logan, did not disclose her marriage even to them until six years after the fact. Pregnant during the trying times just prior to the issuing of the Manifesto, the 1890 document which announced to the world Mormonism's discontinuance of plural marriage, Ellen would keep to her room, careful not to reveal her secret. When, for instance, her Grandmother Eckersley came to visit, Ellen stayed out of sight the entire time, coming from her room only when the older woman had gone out visiting. The child once born was harder to keep hidden, but Ellen carefully hung drying diapers under sheets on the clothesline in order not to broadcast the fact of her marriage to whispering neighbors and federal marshals.[1]

In the meantime Eccles kept his "legal" residence in Ogden and conducted his businesses in both Utah and Oregon. The concerns in Utah were quite different from those in Oregon; somehow they seemed to begin with altruistic motives on Eccles' part, assisting the Church, rescuing a financially distressed company, or purchasing and improving a run-down business. His desire to help individuals and the community, however, never led him into unsound business practices, and where he ventured he usually made sure he could dictate success.

One enterprise which Eccles regarded with grave skepticism was the processing of sugar from locally grown sugarbeets. That industry later became one of the foundations of his fortune. That he would be doubtful initially was natural. Attempts at sugar refining in Utah had had disastrous results since 1852 when Brigham Young's costly imported beet sugar manufacturing equipment was forced to lie unproductive in the old Sugar House in southeast Salt Lake City, having produced some three year's worth of syrup, but never any sugar. Others had tried to build a beet sugar industry with the same eventual failure, up to 1887 when Arthur Stayner, a Mormon horticulturist, persuaded LDS Church and business leaders to

---

[1]Recorded interview, Nora Eccles Treadwell with Ellen Stoddard Eccles, typescript in possession of the writer.

finance further investigations into the production of sugar.[2]

In 1889, with the financial support of the Church, the Utah Sugar Company was incorporated, with sufficient capital stock subscribed and paid that plans were made to build a sugarbeet factory at Lehi. Unfortunately, little more than a year later, many of the original subscribers were either unwilling or unable to fill their commitments, and the Church found itself lacking $35,000 of the first $50,000 down payment on the construction contract due that December. Determined to assure the establishment of an industry which would give employment to its people, the Church borrowed money so that construction of the factory could begin. Next, the First Presidency issued a formal call to the prominent financial men in the wards and stakes of the Church to subscribe for stock, and thus raise money to meet the company's notes and construction costs as they came due. Among those called upon was David Eccles. Heber J. Grant, one of the members of the Council of Twelve Apostles, representatives of the First Presidency who were visiting Church conferences and priesthood meetings to elicit support, later wrote of his discussion with Eccles:

> I took individual letters to different men asking them to subscribe. I delivered a letter to the late David Eccles, than whom I never met a clearer-headed business man in my life, and I have met men who draw their hundred thousand dollars and more every year in salary. He had a comprehensive grasp of business affairs which to me was superior to that of any man I ever met. David smiled when the letter was presented him, signed by President [Wilford] Woodruff and his counselors, asking him to invest five thousand dollars, or seven thousand five hundred dollars.
>
> He said, "Well, I would like to get off at the lowest figure.

---

[2] For fuller exposition of the materials in this chapter see my *Beet Sugar in the West: A History of the Utah-Idaho Sugar Company, 1871-1966* (Seattle, 1966), and *Great Basin Kingdom: An Economic History of the Latter-day Saints, 1830-1900* (Cambridge, Mass., 1958).

You can put me down for five thousand dollars." Then he added: "I hope they will buy lumber from me, so I may make a profit on a part of the five thousand dollars; and after I get my stock, if you can find someone who would like to buy it for twenty-five hundred dollars, I will be much obliged to you if you will come and get the stock."[3]

It was characteristic of Eccles to exercise caution in making investments. Grant, a good friend of the entrepreneur, credited him with

> a wonderful capacity to look into every detail and analyze every proposition from beginning to end. You could never hurry him into anything, he was never afraid of losing a bargain. He wanted to wait and weigh every proposition and examine it, as the saying goes, from A to Z, before he invested his money.[4]

Nevertheless, with no faith in the business itself, Eccles was willing to respond to a request from the leaders of his church. A year later, in 1891, he was elected a director of the Utah Sugar Company.

Eccles' cautious approach to the investment is easily understandable. The factory at Lehi was only the third beet sugar factory erected in the United States, the first to be built with American machinery, and the first to attempt to process sugarbeets grown on irrigated lands. Adding to these causes for concern was the memory of Brigham Young's earlier sugar failure. Nevertheless, the leaders of the Church became convinced that the beet sugar industry was the answer to the industrial needs of the Intermountain West and proceeded in their efforts to finance it.

The Churchwide response to the First Presidency's request for aid to the sugar industry was typically niggardly. More and

---

[3] Remarks of Heber J. Grant, *Ninetieth Annual Conference of the Church* (Salt Lake City, 1919), pp. 9-10.
[4] Response of Heber J. Grant to questionnaire of Royal Eccles, REC.

more, Mormon capitalists were becoming independent of the operations and suggestions of the Church. Many wealthy men whom Grant approached declined to help, responding that "they did not believe the Church had any business to put money in a sugar factory, that it was not within the province of the Church to do such things."⁵ Finally in January 1891 the Church saw no other alternative than to assume itself the responsibility for manufacture of sugar, and appropriated $50,000 in tithing funds to make the first payment on the factory. Eventually added to this was additional money borrowed from Salt Lake banks and subscriptions from Mormon stockholders.

This was 1891, and the Panic had tightened purse strings all over the country. With only $100,000 lacking to complete construction of the Lehi plant, negotiations were begun with the Wells Fargo Bank of San Francisco for that sum. As Church financial agent, Heber J. Grant proposed that if the banker, cashier, and manager of Wells Fargo would write the names of twenty-five of the strongest financial men in Salt Lake City, he would guarantee payment of the $100,000. The Wells Fargo banker had once employed Grant as an office boy in Salt Lake City, and Grant pleaded with him "that as he believed in me as a boy, to believe in me now as a man and as one of the leaders of the Mormon Church." Laughing, the reluctant banker replied, "Why, Heber, that is an impossibility, no set of men on the face of the earth would guarantee four Church notes for $25,000 each." After Grant persisted, he was given the names of thirty strong financiers and proceeded to obtain their signatures.

Seventeen men had endorsed the notes when Grant called at the Deseret National Bank in Salt Lake City for two more

---

⁵Remarks of Heber J. Grant, *Seventy-Fourth Semi-Annual Conference of the Church* (Salt Lake City, 1903), pp. 9-10.

signatures. As Grant approached the two men and explained the situation,

> one of the brethren [said] that the Church had no right to borrow money to aid a private corporation — that it was bad financial morals — that it was no part of the thing a Church could properly do etc. etc. . . . I said all you need to say is yes or no to my request for your signature on these notes and he said "No." The other brother also declined to endorse and approved the position of the one who had been talking. Brother Eccles was sitting at a table writing; he looked up and said, "Heber I have heard your story. Is my name one of the thirty men." I said no, that I had not thought it necessary to suggest to Mr. Dooly to go out of Salt Lake City for the endorsers. He answered "Let me see the notes."

To Grant's astonishment, Eccles

> . . . did not look at the notes; he turned them wrong side up and wrote his name on the back of them, and said, "My name won't hurt them." Then he said, "You tell President Wilford Woodruff that David Eccles always keeps two or three hundred thousand dollars in Bank Certificates where he can put his hand on the cash by giving thirty days' notice, and that, as these notes fall due, if he will give me thirty days' notice, I will take them up, and he can pay me in one year or five years or ten years, or whenever convenient." He remarked that when the Church's note for $100,000 or two or three times that amount was not good, this country would be too hot for a Mormon to live in; that it would be all the same as Nauvoo, Illinois at the time our people were driven away from that city by a mob.

Concluding his reminiscence, Grant said he didn't know "when I ever wanted to hug a man any more than I did [Eccles] when he signed those notes."[6] Eccles followed his signing of the first notes with the offer to Grant of the hospitality of his Ogden home for "supper, bed and breakfast," and the guaran-

---

[6]Recollections of Heber J. Grant, October 28, 1929, REC.

tee of a further $100,000 should the Church need it. Both offers were later accepted.

The struggles of the Lehi plant were multiplied by the deepening economic depression, and the lack of knowledge on the part of the beet producers about growing conditions. But the farmers learned by their experiments, and backers from the East, impressed with Mormon industry and cooperation, invested heavily to keep the plant operating. Their trust proved well placed when, by 1898, the company was not only solvent, but producing dividends. In fact, it proved by then able to assist the Church in its need.

That turn-about convinced Eccles that sugar manufacturing could indeed be made profitable. Armed with that confidence, and the knowledge he had gained of the workings of the beet sugar industry, Eccles returned to Oregon to establish the Oregon Sugar Company with a mill at LaGrande. Typically, he came back to Utah the same year, determined to build a sugar factory at Ogden.

Eccles wanted the Ogden plant to be a community enterprise, and so called a meeting at the opera house in order to give the public an opportunity to subscribe for stock. In his usual eagerness that business cooperation should cross denominational lines, he appointed as chairman of the meeting a Catholic priest, Father Cushnahan. The plans laid before the people, the chairman turned to Eccles for his comment. One of the audience later recalled his terse reply: "Money talks," Eccles had responded. Citizens, confident that any enterprise controlled by Eccles would deal fairly with them, subscribed liberally. A few who later attempted to speculate on their shares found how fair Eccles would indeed be when, on learning of their scheme, he inserted in the local newspaper a statement that any person who desired to be released from his contract for any reason would have his money gladly returned. The speculation ceased.[7] The Ogden factory was followed shortly by the establishment of a similar plant in Logan. Both operated successfully under the control of local businessmen.

The factory at LaGrande, Oregon, was another story. From the first it was troubled, but the owners were optimistic that the factory would eventually become as efficient as those in Ogden and Logan. They were wrong. In the first place, the plant managers were as inexperienced as the factory workers and the farmers. Whereas in Utah there were apparently many young men needing work, in less settled Oregon too few hands could be found to work the sugarbeet fields. It was thought initially that Chinese workers brought from California could fill the need, but the ones who actually came proved to be unsuited for the work.

The result was that the beet crops were simply not large enough to supply the factory on a profit-making basis. Even though the factory managers would contract with the farmers at the beginning of the growing season for a set acreage to be planted to beets, the amounts promised in the spring and the amounts delivered in the fall were two different things. The LaGrande factory never did approach the efficiency of the Ogden and Logan plants.

During the 1890s while Eccles was building his sugar and timber fortune, he solidified his reputation as a financier. He had been a stockholder and, in 1883, director, of the First

---

[7] Recollections of James Canse, September 25, 1943, REC. Another version of the incorporation of the Ogden Sugar Company was related by John Watson, who said that Eccles called a meeting of representative citizens, presented his reasons, and outlined the benefits which he said would accrue to the community through the building of the sugar mill. According to Watson, "he stated that he wished to build such a mill, but he wanted all the people of the community, as well as the farmers, to become interested with him, and that if the community would get back of it he would undertake to build a mill. At that, the people agreed and were enthusiastic and anxious about the new undertaking," Interview of Royal Eccles with John Watson, 1929. REC.

National Bank of Ogden; by 1892 he was vice president of that bank, and in 1894 was named its president. In 1898 he was elected director of the Deseret Savings and Deseret National banks in Salt Lake City.

It was at that time that he was asked again by the Church to serve its interests. Suffering an enormous deficit and under constant harrassment by creditors, the Church had decided to fund the debt by issuing bonds. Lorenzo Snow, who became Church president after the death of Wilford Woodruff in September 1898, desired as trustees two of the strongest financial men in the state. David Eccles and Lewis S. Hills, an officer of the Deseret National Bank of Salt Lake City, were approached. Both responded. As well as undertaking the sale of the bonds, Eccles himself subscribed to the first $100,000 and agreed to purchase the last $100,000 in the event it became necessary. Heber J. Grant recalled that not all of the bonds were subscribed, and Eccles did indeed purchase the remainder.[8]

Not all of Eccles' ventures in Utah commerce, of course, were for altruistic motives. His first railroad venture in Utah, for example, was the organization, with A. W. McCune of Salt Lake City, of the Utah and Pacific Railroad Company. In 1899 and 1900 the new company built a standard gauge line 125 miles from Milford, Utah to Uvada, a point on the Utah-Nevada state line.[9] While additional trackage was being constructed, the railroad was sold to the San Pedro, Los Angeles, and Salt Lake Railroad, later part of the Union Pacific Railroad.

The railroading venture which involved Eccles most extensively and for a longer time, however, began with another of

[8] Recollections of Heber J. Grant, REC.
[9] The distance is given as eighty miles in "David Eccles," Noble Warrum, *Utah Since Statehood* (4 vols., Chicago, 1919), II, p. 54.

his "rescue" ventures, and grew into a mammoth enterprise which seems almost to dwarf the Oregon organization. Corey Brothers Construction Company of Uinta, Utah, had struggled to survive over-diversification and the economic instability of the depression of the early 1890s; it floundered a couple of times, seemed to recover, but finally appeared to be sinking for the last time. Eccles, the banker, was faced with the logical, if expensive, course of letting the company liquidate and redeeming what he could of the amount owing the bank. Or Eccles, the entrepreneur, could risk the backing and invest some of his own financial and organizational genius and reorganize the firm. He chose the latter course.

In 1900 the firm was reorganized into the Utah Construction Company, with Eccles himself holding one-third of the stock. Another third was carried by William H. and Edmund O. Wattis, brothers who had been with the original firm, and one-sixth each by two of Eccles' business associates, Thomas D. Dee and Jim Pingree. Dee was made president, but the major responsibility fell to W. H. Wattis, a man whom Eccles held in esteem, as general manager. The Corey brothers, founders of the firm, were removed from the top controlling positions in the reorganization.

Eccles had not shown much relish for the construction side of railroading, but with his usual adaptability, accepted the new challenge. When in 1905 tenders were let for bid by Western Pacific Railroad on the stretch of track from Salt Lake City to Oroville, California, Eccles not only approved the bid, but actively sought it by using his influence to insure that the Utah Construction bid would be well received by Western Pacific. An associate through the sugar factory transactions, Henry O. Havemeyer, was known among eastern financiers; it was to him that Eccles turned for introduction to decision makers of the Western Pacific. Havemeyer's recommendation to the railroad executives was concise: "If you get Mr. Eccles' signature on your contract, you will get your railroad."[10] The contract for the 700 miles stretch, said to be the largest railroad contract ever let west of Chicago, was awarded to Eccles' Utah Construction Company.

The task was immense. The route passed through a narrow defile so precipitous that, where there was insufficient room for the roadbed, masonry walls had to be built up from solid foundations beneath. The finished railroad would have forty-three tunnels and over forty steel bridges, with a combined length of over 55,000 feet. Despite the terrain, however, there was not one grade on the entire trackage over one percent, one of the greatest engineering feats of its time.

One of the financial feats was the fact that the company remained solvent throughout the construction. By now it was 1907, and another panic was distressing the country. Firms such as Utah Construction were folding, caught in the bind of enforced cutbacks in labor force on one hand and uncompleted contracts on the other. The railroad could not pay the contractor for half-finished contracts, so the contractor could not pay its workers in order to lay them off. Eccles negotiated a compromise with the railroad and maintained the company. By the completion of the railroad, Utah Construction was able to liquidate all its incurred debts.

Now well into heavy construction, Eccles and his sons watched Utah Construction continue its lead as it branched out into other interests and other places, into ocean shipping in South America and real estate in the United States, into mining in Australia and Peru, and dam construction in Thailand and

---

[10]Royal Eccles, "Life of David Eccles, Pertaining to Utah & Pacific Railroad, Western Pacific Railroad," REC.

Pakistan. Charles Nibley's early accusation, that Eccles' wider vision was narrowed by his concern for detail, certainly no longer applied, if indeed it ever had.

Still, with all his growing interest in wider horizons — Eccles took his wife Bertha on a 1893 tour to Europe, and thereafter went several times abroad — he was most concerned with situations close to home: the street cars which passed along the Ogden streets near his office, for example. By 1900 the Ogden Electric Street Railway Lines, owned by the Omaha firm of Jarvis and Conklin, were badly crippled for want of better equipment. Eccles purchased the lines and incorporated the Ogden Rapid Transit Company of which he became president. He acquired new cars, extended the lines in the city, improved service, and otherwise directed reorganization until in 1902 it had become "a street-car system of which a much larger city might well be proud."[11] During the same two years, while he was involved with the Ogden lines, Eccles and his associates purchased and improved the Ogden and Hot Springs Railroad, developing there a health resort whose reputation spread favorably.

Again concerned with metropolitan Ogden, Eccles recognized, with others, the woeful inadequacy of the city's water system when a fire on the top floor of the Utah Loan and Trust Building could not be controlled because of insufficient water pressure. The appointment of Eccles to an advisory committee led, through negotiations which will be outlined in a later chapter, to his purchase of the waterworks, which he then improved, turning the facility into not only a satisfactory public utility, but also into a successful financial venture.[12]

During these years of frenetic activity, Eccles' families were growing, and growing up. By 1900 David C., Eccles' eldest

---
[11]"David Eccles," in Warrum, II, 54.
[12]Interview, Royal Eccles with John Watson, September 29, 1929, REC.

offspring, was twenty-three; Bertha had presented her husband with twin girls, Flora and Laura, in 1894, and just fifteen months later, with another son, William Jack. Anna Vivian was born in 1897, and in 1901 Homer Gordon would arrive, the last of the children of David and Bertha Eccles. After the birth of her first three children in Logan, Ellen had moved back to Oregon, and by 1900 had given birth there to Jessie in 1896, and to Emma in 1898. As the century turned, George was born, as the others, in Baker.

But all was not increase and growth, even in Eccles' family life. On December 3, 1903, the year after the birth of Nora in Baker, David Eccles stood by his father's bedside in Ogden as the old Scotsman succumbed to pneumonia. As William Eccles was eulogized in services at the little Mound Fort meetinghouse, it became evident that part of the success of David Eccles, entrepreneur, was a quality inherited from his father:

> Although possessed of means to enable him to live a life of ease he [William Eccles] has, during the closing years of his life, insisted on busying himself at his farm near the city limits, preferring a life of activity to home ease with all the luxuries that money could buy.[13]

[13]"William Eccles, Sr., Dead," *Deseret News,* December 5, 1903.

Eccles Utah's First 'Tycoon'

Ogden Standard, *March 21, 1945.* David Eccles had widespread mining, railroad, banking, cattle, and beet sugar interests. When he died in 1912 he was rated the wealthiest man in Utah.

LDS Church Archives. One of Nevada Ranches of the Utah Construction Company.

LDS Church Archives. Deseret National Bank Building, Salt Lake City, Utah. David Eccles was an active officer of Deseret National; his family financial firm, First Security Corporation, owns this building and corner in Salt Lake City.

LDS Church Archives. Ogden First National Bank Building, Ogden. Ogden First National was a key enterprise in the Eccles empire.

11

Frontier Capitalist

DURING THE EARLY 1900s Eccles emerged as a financier, a capitalist. During the last decade of his life he became identified with countless enterprises, continually financing new plans and ideas. Interests which he had established earlier, he now developed into multiple businesses, or, in the case of separate enterprises, combined into large organizations. The expansion of his beet sugar interests is an example.

In 1902 Eccles entered into an agreement with H. O. Havemeyer, president of the American Sugar Refining Company, to sell one-half the corporate shares of the Ogden, Oregon, and Logan sugar companies. After negotiating the transfer in New York, Eccles told the western stockholders that he had personally agreed to deliver a full one-half of the outstanding shares of the three companies and that he would perform the commitment, even if it took all the shares he owned. He extended to each, however, the privilege to join with him for one-half their respective shares at the same price he would receive. The stockholders of the three companies were so pleased with the price per share which he had negotiated that several joined in sponsoring a banquet in his honor at the Weber Club at which he was presented with a large chime hall clock with their names inscribed on a silver plate. Immediately thereafter the Amalgamated Sugar Company was incorporated from the Ogden Sugar Company, the Oregon Sugar Company, and the Logan Sugar Company. Eccles, who had been president of the foregoing companies, was elected chief officer of the new corporation.

The western factories had been profitable and thus merged into the new company at greatly increased values. Stock in the Ogden factory was worth three dollars for one dollar, or $300 per share. Amalgamated Sugar later erected additional factories in California, Montana, and Smithfield, Utah and participated in the immense growth and prosperity of the beet sugar industry in northern Utah and Idaho, Montana, Oregon, and Wyoming. Almost all its factories increased in size and more than doubled their original capacities.

Not all Eccles' sugar interests were part of Amalgamated. In 1901 he had joined Jesse Knight of Provo and E. P. Ellison of Layton in building a beet sugar factory at Raymond, Alberta Canada.[1] In 1905 he completed construction of a sugar mill at Lewiston, Utah, which became known as the Lewiston Sugar Company. Eccles was its president throughout his lifetime. Eccles continued as well with his direction of Amalgamated and supervised the 1912 move of the LaGrande, Oregon, factory to Burley, Idaho. He owned the factory site, which he at that time deeded to Amalgamated as a gift outright, along with the right to the lower Snake River Valley for the expansion of the company.

---

[1] E. P. Ellison to Royal Eccles, December 5, 1929, REC; also J. Orvin Hicken, ed., *Raymond 1901-1967* (Lethbridge, Alberta, 1967), pp. 38-40.

Nor was Eccles' curiosity about sugar restricted to the beet-produced type. Though he never developed his interests beyond the intermountain country, in 1906 he did look to the possibilities of cane sugar in the Caribbean. As so often happened, the look was accidental: Eccles had gone to Cuba, taking with him his wife Bertha and daughter Lila, with the thought of examining some timber and investigating the feasibility of building a mill there. He was not impressed with the lumbering possibilities, but did consider investing in the cane sugar industry. With his usual thoroughness he visited cane fields and factories, noting in the industry real competition for the sugarbeet developments in the United States because of the economy of the cane sugar production in Cuba. The possibilities must have seemed little more promising than the lumbering potential, however, for he never followed through with either.[2]

The incident illustrates a characteristic of Eccles as a man of affairs: he could not travel as a simple tourist with an offhand interest in what he was seeing. After his first return to Europe in 1893 he made other visits; by 1911 he had made his fourth crossing, once again visiting in native Scotland. One can imagine that on these visits Eccles saw more than merely tourist scenery; his inquisitiveness and the breadth of his interests would make the business and industry of the old world as intriguing to him as his involvements in the new frontier.

Hardly an industry could be found which did not at one time or another interest David Eccles. His investments reached into practically every type of commerce or production. In 1904 Eccles and his associates purchased the Wyoming Coal Company of Rock Springs, of which he became president. Five years later he acquired a section of land in Carbon County, Utah, and opened a coal mine there, incorporated under the title Black Hawk Company. Some years later this property was

---

[2]Memoirs of Bertha Marie Eccles, REC, pp. 30-31.

purchased by the U.S. Fuel Company. In 1910 Eccles procured another section of coal land near Rock Springs, Wyoming, and organized the Lion Coal Company, which developed and operated the property. That company developed a reputation for dependability by providing coal during shortages when other companies could not. In 1919 Lion Coal merged with the Carbon County mine, retaining the name of the Lion Coal Company.

Another undertaking was Eccles' investment in a large cattle ranch in Nevada, the Vineyard Land and Livestock Company. The original owners of the company, ex-Governor Sparks and his partner Herrold had died, and relations among their successors were strained. Adam Patterson, who operated an extensive sheep business in Nevada and Wyoming, was familiar with the ranch and wanted to interest some associates in acquiring it jointly. Thus he brought the property to the attention of Eccles, the ranch was purchased in 1907, and Patterson become general manager with Eccles as president of the resulting company.[3] The Vineyard Land and Livestock Company controlled almost one million acres. Mile after mile along the water courses the company owned in fee every other quarter section of land, some 300,000 acres in all. As the land in-between was owned by the government, the company controlled this for its own grazing stock.

Several times in those years the intervention of Eccles alleviated problems for banks and financial institutions, particularly in Ogden. To facilitate construction of the Utah Loan and Trust Building near 24th Street and Washington Avenue, he loaned $75,000 to the Ogden Investment Company. Then, through a combination of unfortunate factors, the Utah Loan and Trust Company became insolvent. Although Eccles offered to release the mortgage if the stockholders could pay

---

[3]Royal Eccles to C. J. Doon, November 8, 1962, REC.

$70,000 of the original amount, neither the bank nor the stockholders were in a position to accept the offer. A decision was made to give the building to Eccles. He cancelled the mortgage and after the doors of the Utah Loan and Trust Company closed, he took possession of the building.[4] The 1892 structure, built at a cost of $340,000, was damaged twice by fire. The first, only a year after its completion, was serious enough; the second, in 1911, caused its total destruction. By that time, because of the improvements he had made in the building, Eccles' loss was more than $250,000.

In the year of his death he initiated construction of an eight-story fireproof building there, but an injunction suit pertaining to the removal of the south wall of the building stopped work for two years. When the controversy finally was settled, the original plans were enlarged to include additional frontage and a larger building. The structure became known as the David Eccles Building.

Ogden's failing water system had initially been purchased by John R. Bothwell, an eastern financier, to help the citizens procure an adequate water supply. Through foreclosure of a deed of trust given for $1,500,000 to the Jarvis Conklin Mortgage Trust Company, which later went into the hands of a receiver, Bothwell lost the property. It was at this time, knowing the city could not borrow the money to meet the requirements of the situation, that Eccles offered to buy it himself. After purchasing the waterworks from the Omaha firm in 1900, he offered it to the city at the exact price he had paid but was refused. Under his direction in the following eight years, the system was significantly improved, provided an abundance of water, and became a splendid revenue producer. Suddenly strong agitation developed that the city should own its water system, and a resolution was introduced in the city council to

---

[4] Interview, Royal Eccles with John Watson, September 20, 1929, REC.

obtain the waterworks through a process of law. Although Eccles had repeatedly petitioned the city to purchase the works from him without success, he patiently sent a representative to inform the council that the city could buy the water system, and invited one of their members to see him and make arrangements. In 1909 Eccles sold the waterworks to Ogden City for $450,000, a figure much lower than he could have received, had he insisted on a fair value.[5]

Cache Valley was another outlet for Eccles' municipal interests. D. C. Budge of Logan, a close associate whom Eccles retained as physician for the employees of the Logan and Lewiston sugar factories, worked with Eccles in developing community services. Dr. Budge and some colleagues felt strongly that an interurban railroad in Cache Valley would be a good investment and sought the cooperation of Eccles from time to time, but the businessman produced figures and arguments proving the plan a folly. The idea was a joke all over Cache Valley, in fact, because of the number of proposals which had already been suggested and defeated. One transit company had run two short and inadequate lines since before 1902, but the community had grown, and the need was evident to provide wider service.

Occasionally afterward Eccles would ask Budge what he thought of the railroad proposition, and Budge always replied that he thought it feasible. Finally Eccles asked Budge how much he would invest in the scheme, persuaded him to raise the figure, and then told a committee of leading citizens that if they agreed to raise fifty percent of the needed funds, he would contribute the balance. After the citizens of Logan and Cache County raised about $70,000 Eccles furnished an equal

---

[5]Joseph A. West, letter to editor of *Ogden Standard Examiner*, September 20, 1925; Interview, Royal Eccles with John Watson, September 20, 1929.

amount.⁶ He was made a director of the resulting railroad company.

Thus in 1910 Eccles built the city traction lines at Logan and incorporated the Logan Transit Company, of which he became president. His projected plans included construction of an extensive rapid transit system for northern Utah, based on the Ogden and Logan organizations. After his death this scheme was carried out by his estate under the direction of his sons.

Some time before construction of the Logan Rapid Transit system, D. C. Budge had acquired a water power right in Blacksmith Fork Canyon, southeast of Logan, at an approximate cost of $750. As plans were made for construction of the transit lines, Budge told Eccles of his holdings and suggested that they should own their own power to operate the railroad. Eccles was impressed and promised to work out the details. The next time they met, Eccles declared, "we will build that power house and pipeline and furnish our own power for our railroad and sugar factories." The year 1910 saw the organization of the Blacksmith Fork Light and Power Company, which was constructed on the Blacksmith Fork east of Hyrum, Utah — a hydroelectric plant capable of generating 4,000 horsepower. The power house was built by Eccles at a cost of about $250,000, but he gave Budge an interest in the plant, compensating him for his right and title to the water and making him a director in the power and light company.⁷

Simultaneously Eccles was expanding his lumber interests in Oregon, constructing mills at Inglis, Dee, and Austin and financing the Mount Hood Railway Company as the impressive

⁶D. C. Budge, "David Eccles As I Knew Him," typescript, REC, pp 5-6; "David Eccles," *Utah Since Statehood* (4 vols., Chicago, 1919), II, p. 54.

⁷Budge, "David Eccles As I Knew Him," p. 6; and *Ogden Evening Standard,* June 18, 1912, p. 7.

growth of the Oregon Lumber Company continued. In the province of Alberta, Canada, he joined with E. P. Ellison in building flour mills and elevators, and held a substantial interest in the Knight Sugar Land and Livestock Company there.

The list of Eccles' involvements is overwhelming: he was president of such varied enterprises as the Promontory-Curlew Land Company of Box Elder County; the Ogden Furniture and Carpet Company; the Grant Opera House Company of Ogden; and the Grass Creek Coal Company of Utah.[8] In many more companies Eccles was a director: Utah Condensed Milk Company of Richmond; Thatcher Brothers Banking Company of Logan; State Bank of Brigham City; Consolidated Wagon and Machine Company, Utah Implement Company, and Utah Lumber Company, with headquarters in Ogden or Salt Lake City; and the Utah-Idaho Sugar Company. He was also a director in the $500,000 Austin Brothers Association, dealers in sheep and cattle, which he also financed.

Not all of Eccles' interests demanded his service on executive boards: he had interest in such firms as the Anderson Lumber Company, the Nevada Douglas Mine and Railroad Company, and Nibley-Mimnaugh Lumber Company, the Shupe-Williams Candy Company, the Utah Canning Company, and the W. H. Eccles Company. In total, at his death Eccles was director in thirty-five industrial corporations operating in Utah, Idaho, Nevada, Oregon, and Wyoming, while acting as president of seventeen of those. Further, he was a director in thirteen banking institutions in Utah and Idaho, and president in seven of the thirteen. His estate in 1913, "when a dollar measured a gold dollar," was appraised at almost $7 million.

A peculiar trait which set him apart from most wealthy men was that Eccles never took a salary from a partnership or

---

[8]Paul C. Bates, "David Eccles, Captain of Industry," typescript, pp. 3-4, REC.

from any corporation in which he was interested. A single exception was forced upon him, four or five years before his death, as a result of an antitrust suit brought by the federal government against the American Sugar Refining Company of New York City, which owned fifty-one percent stock interest in the Amalgamated Sugar Company. Since its organization Eccles had been president and general manager of Amalgamated and obviously was managing a subsidiary of the American Sugar Refining Company. Only at the insistence of the New York attorneys, who affirmed that Eccles must place himself on the payroll as a proper matter in the defense which they were preparing for the antitrust proceeding, did Eccles accede and take a modest salary as president and general manager of the Amalgamated Sugar Company. Whenever the subject of working without a salary was brought up, he would invariably demand, "why should I want a salary? I don't need it. I get my salary from my dividends."[9]

Before entering any new enterprise, he always made a careful investigation, often calling in one expert after another, with the view of having his own convictions tested. When the new undertaking was decided upon, he offered his associates the opportunity to invest with him. At the time of his death, he held no majority stock control in any business with which he was identified. A large number of stockholders was more important to him than were personal majority holdings.

Perhaps more amazing than his manifold interests and the fortune he accumulated was Eccles' ability to absorb and recall all the details of each particular industry. The relevant figures and financial reports of each were stamped on his memory. Anyone meeting him at one of his sawmills would be greatly impressed with his grasp of the entire situation, from the cost of production to the possibilities of the market. At any

---

[9]"Dates and Data Concerning the Life of David Eccles," REC, p. 25.

sugarbeet factory his knowledge of the operation would equal or exceed that of the local general manager, including costs of manufacturing, condition of the market, and yield per acre. At the National Conference of American Bankers he appeared to be one who had devoted his life to the banking business, and in the railroad world he could discuss the subject from both construction and operating standpoints.[10]

The kind of mind which copes as readily with minutia of production as with the complexities of high finance must be exceptional. David Eccles the man was as unique among men as David Eccles the capitalist was among businessmen.

[10]Bates, "David Eccles," p. 4.

12

The Man David Eccles

THERE IS MUCH complexity, even paradox, in the man David Eccles. He was "close" with his money, but he might buy his twin girls new hats or pay off a destitute couple's mortgage. He disdained social status, but he was proud of the profits he had earned. He was not particularly active in his church nor meticulous in heeding all its precepts — a glass of forbidden champagne seemed not to bother his conscience — but he paid a full tithe and volunteered on several occasions to help the church in a business way. He loved his wives and children, but his life revolved around his business enterprises more than his homes. He was honest and straightforward in all his business dealings, yet most of his fortune was made by taking advantage of situations arising out of legislative and administrative loopholes in the use of forest lands. How does one explain David Eccles?

The three keys to an understanding of David Eccles are his upbringing in a condition of acute poverty, his Scottish heritage, and his Mormonness.

The family in which Eccles was reared was on the verge of starvation until he was twenty-one. During this period it was literally a matter of life or death how the family's resources were used. Eccles' hatred of waste, his habits of thrift and frugality, and his preoccupation with keeping costs down were all developed during this period and remained with him throughout his life. The adhesiveness of his childhood and boyhood immersion in poverty is suggested by his frequent admonitions to his wives and children to be frugal, long after there was any need for him to be concerned about their spending. Although he allowed Bertha and Ellen to have their own checkbooks, David still went over their accounts, raised questions about what they spent their money for, and admonished them to be thrifty. He is said to have been particularly pleased with Ellen, who kept a cow, raised chickens, and in other ways "saved" money. This tradition was passed on by Ellen to her children, some more than others of course, and some of the family have continued to follow the "penny saved-penny earned" advice of Benjamin Franklin.

Every year the Union Pacific Railroad Company sent Eccles, as one of its important customers, a two-inch by three-inch record book. In these little books, still possessed by the family, David often recorded his personal expenditures — purchases of newspapers, candy, theater tickets, railroad fare, an occasional suit of clothes, and other outlays of cash. He was methodical in making expenditures, whether for consumption or for business, and he encouraged his family and friends to be likewise.

To a poorly educated person from a family with no savings or social status, the only way out of poverty was hard work and careful use of time and resources. Eccles therefore concentrated his efforts toward the goal of accumulation. He did not expend his energies in "church activities," nor in striving for social recognition, nor in unproductive political debate, nor in the pursuit of pleasure. Every moment, every ounce of energy, every expenditure had to count toward the goal of accumulation and profit. This was not a driving preoccupation but a pattern of life he knew was right. He was neither tense nor humorless; he enjoyed his work and his endeavors to turn a profit. He worked with gusto, relished the attempt to make business succeed, found pleasure in investing in new enterprises. But he was careful, prudent, and shrewd. This was habitual with him and not just a "show" to induce a spirit of economy among his employees.

A revealing story about David Eccles is told by Eric Ryberg, an important figure in the beet sugar industry of the West. When still in his teens, Ryberg was employed by Eccles in the construction of the Logan Sugar Factory. One of Ryberg's first assignments was to be the stock boy; that is, he received nails, pipe fittings, small tools, and other supplies and equipment as they came in and placed them in appropriate drawers and bins. As the sugar plant neared completion, Ryberg observed that there was loose material around the plant and he began to gather up such items as bolts, nuts, screws, machine parts, buckets, brooms, shovels, and picks. He went around the plant with a wheelbarrow, collecting all the large material, and dumped it in the corner. Then he gathered the small loose material with two buckets, dumped that on the floor in another corner, and began to sort it out for storage purposes. While building these shelves, necessarily crude because they were made out of used materials, Ryberg was suddenly accosted by David Eccles, who had come to Logan on an inspection trip. "What are you doing?" asked Eccles:

> I explained to him what I was about, and he said, "Fine, fine." I completed the shelves and bins and then began segregating the materials and placing them in the bins. Several days later Mr.

> Eccles said, "Give me a couple of buckets; I will find some more material." Within an hour or so he returned with two buckets full of nails, spikes, nuts, and bolts. He said, "We have to save these. Gather a couple more buckets and we will both go out and pick the material up." He led me down to the pulp silo and there we filled the buckets with nails, some that had never been used, and others that were crooked and spoiled and had been pulled out of lumber. We cleaned the place up as clean as a hound's tooth. He spent an entire afternoon with me. The following day he spent an hour or so with me around the plant. I remember he had me crawl up in the rafters to take down a plumb line, which he said would come in handy. I received a liberal education in thrift from David Eccles in those few hours.

Ryberg then goes on:

> I had no further contact with Mr. Eccles until several years later. I had left the Sugar Factory and was engaged in the contracting business with my brother, Bill. Through Mr. H. E. Hatch, President of Thatcher Brother's Bank, we were contacted by Mr. Eccles to go to Oregon and look over his lumber railroad, called the Sumpter Valley Railroad, to do some underpinning and foundation work on bridges and trestles on the railroad. We had arranged to go and look the work over and submit to him a proposition. Just about the time we were to go he met me in the old Thatcher Bank and advised me that he could furnish a pass from Logan to Baker City, Oregon and that if we were successful and were awarded the job the transportation would not cost us anything. But if we did not give a low enough bid we would have to reimburse him for the transportation. I was somewhat taken back, but did not answer him at the time. Later I went to Mr. Hatch and told him that when he saw Mr. Eccles he could tell him we were not interested in the job — that if Mr. Eccles was that small he could "go to hell and take the railroad with him."[1]

Cutting costs applied not only to picking up nails and disinclination to pay more than going wages. It applied as

---

[1] Eric Ryberg, "Autobiography," typescript, HDC, pp. 47-50.

well to business management. As we have seen, Eccles himself never collected a salary from any of his businesses, preferring to make his income from dividends. A perusal of the minutes of the Anderson Lumber Company show only one instance in which David Eccles was voted down in board meeting. He had opposed a motion to increase the directors' remuneration from $5 to $10 per meeting!

"Small" he might be; unfeeling toward his employees he was not. While presiding over one of the several banks he supervised, Eccles received word that a certain employee was embezzling bank funds. Calling "Smith" into his office, Eccles asked him to make a list of his shortages and the length of time he had been stealing. When the bank president asked Smith what he thought should be done with him, the unhappy worker broke down, genuinely penitent, and explained that he had taken the money only to meet home expenses. A careful examination of Smith's expenditures revealed a lack of economy to be the reason for his shortage. As he had done on the rare occasions when such a situation had occurred, Eccles told the employee that he wanted neither to punish nor discharge him, as the results would be a bad reputation for him and disgrace for his family. For the sake of the family, Eccles concluded that the company would accept Smith's note in the amount of his defalcation and at the same time raise his pay sufficiently so that he could meet the payments on the note over the same period of time. When the note was satisfactorily paid and if Smith had behaved himself honestly, his salary would continue at the same increase, with nothing said about the entire matter.[2]

One other product of Eccles' lowly upbringing was his unassuming nature. Democratic and unpretentious, he enjoyed being with "ordinary" people; he felt inadequate in "society" and did not enjoy "small talk." Neither assertive nor com-

---

[2]Source not disclosed.

manding in nature, he was not the type who enjoyed power and the perquisites of wealth and position. He was energetic in pursuing an opportunity but he did not "order people around." According to Heber J. Grant, his business associate who later became president of the Mormon Church, Eccles was eminently approachable, and was equally comfortable with the white-shirted executive and the sunburned farmer. He discussed the business problems with manual workers as well as with office workers. Said Grant:

> I have seen him as cheerful and happy at a dance in the little meeting house at the mill near Baker City as anyone of the employees with whom he was mingling. He was the same man with the day laborer as with the millionaire. There was nothing put on about him . . . . In nothing did he show his greatness more, in my estimation, than in the fact that he was at home and made his companions feel at home when they were poor men, and than that he was equally at home when in the society of the men of millions.[3]

A second key to David Eccles' character was his Scottishness. Born a Scot, raised to the age of fourteen in Scotland, Eccles remained a Scot throughout his life. His closest friends were fellow Scots, converts, and immigrants. He was proud of his Scottish heritage, went out of his way to meet a fellow Scot in the business world, enjoyed "Bobby" Burns and Harry Lauder, used Scottish expressions and told Scottish jokes, took pleasure in rolling his r's and maintaining his "little Scotch accent," and to the end of his days called his girls "gettles." Eccles expressed the opinion that "Men of Scotch descent becoming citizens of the United States were doubly fellow countrymen."[4] One daughter admits her father was discriminatory: "If two men wanted a job and one of them was a Scot, the Scot got the job."

---

[3]Heber J. Grant to David C. Eccles, December 18, 1912, REC.
[4]D. C. Budge, "David Eccles As I Knew Him," REC, p. 1.

Although his boyhood life in Scotland was hard, David was rather grateful for it; it taught him valuable lessons. His wife Bertha later told her children:

> When we were in Scotland, the children on the streets — bootblacks, newsboys, and street urchins — were anxious to earn some money and would often do some stunt or say a piece. They always interested your father — I suppose it brought him back to his childhood days and reminded him of himself when he was earning a living on the streets and sleeping in parks and hallways. When I began to lament the condition of these boys, David said, "That is what makes men of them — when they have to get out for themselves." He liked to talk with them and learn what they were doing. He told me, "There is nothing to worry about; these lads will get along alright."[5]

Thus, a principal part of his Scot heritage, Eccles believed, was the spirit of enterprise. Proud of his own use of that heritage, he attributed much of his enterprise to his Scottish beginnings. His oft-expressed motto was "never let a dollar lie idle." His active business mind was ever searching for ways to develop the natural resources of a locality he visited. One associate remembered:

> One time I accompanied David Eccles on a trip to Bear Lake. While there he collected data as to the amount of land under irrigation and cultivation. His investigation comprised many things that would assist him in making a decision as to how he could organize some industry there to assist the people in taking advantage of their possibilities. Had his life been prolonged he no doubt would have established some industry there that would have been of lasting benefit to the people.[6]

Eccles is reported to have said that "people need enterprise, not money, to achieve success."[7] Eccles' partner C. W. Nibley observed of him that "he could analyze a business proposition,

---

[5]Memoirs of Bertha Marie Eccles, REC, p. 1.
[6]Budge, "David Eccles As I Knew Him," p. 7.

and dissect it, turn it inside out and upside down, and look at it from more points of view than any other man I ever knew; and it was nearly always with unerring accuracy."[8]

David Eccles also placed great emphasis on living up to one's word, "as a Scotsman should." He was a man of his word in business, and he expected others to be the same. Two incidents illustrate this facet of his character, which on occasion revealed itself in almost grotesque forms. A woman who was poor needed support and asked for work. He said he had no opening in his business, but he could use her around the house if she would care to work out her room and board. She agreed to do so. After several weeks she found other employment, and came to him for her pay. He reminded her of the agreement they had made about her working for room and board alone, and said that since that was their agreement it was not proper that he should pay her more.

On another occasion, he took his family East to meet his son Marriner, who was due to return from his Mormon mission in Scotland. Accompanied by Ellen and their daughter Jessie, then sixteen, David stopped off to see Niagara Falls. David made arrangements with the driver of a horse-drawn taxi, for a certain fee, to take the group to see the Falls from both the American and Canadian sides. After they had visited the American side, they headed for Canada, and soon reached a point where a $1 toll had to be paid. The driver asked David to pay it. He refused, reminding the driver that he had contracted to take them to both sides at no further expense. "You must carry out your terms of the bargain." The driver was adamant; his "package deal" did not include paying the toll, he said. David was angry at the driver's failure to live up to his agreement. David's daughter Jessie, equally angry at

---

[8]*Deseret Evening News,* December 6, 1912.
[7]Budge, "David Eccles As I Knew Him," p. 5.

her father's obstinacy, said that she herself would pay the driver, and "let's get going." David would not let her. Both the driver and David being equally stubborn, there was an impasse. The driver finally turned round, and the family went back to their rooms without going over to the Canadian side. To the daughter, mere pigheadedness had marred the pleasure of the visit; to David, it was simply a matter of a correct business principle — one was bound to one's agreement.[9]

Business associates of Eccles, of course, had great respect for that principle. Horace Havemeyer wrote that his father "would have taken David Eccles' word on anything without a question and . . . would have advanced him any sum of money within his power on his word alone." Regarded with respect and confidence, Eccles enjoyed a reputation for being "scrupulously . . . just and fair with his associates and with everyone."[10]

Associates say that around the mills he operated, if things failed to go right, Eccles "gave the dickens" to whomever was responsible. One of his children remembers an occasion when he lost his temper upon visiting the Logan Sugar Factory. He visited the bookkeeper to check over the accounts. The accountant was unable to strike a balance, being off a few cents in some account which he couldn't quickly find. He observed to Eccles, "It's only a few cents; it isn't important enough to waste time hunting it down right now." That remark was a mistake. It set off David and he gave a snappy lecture on the importance of "a few cents" — told the bookkeeper he must watch every cent — that in a large business a cent here and a cent there would eventually amount to a great deal — the difference between profit and loss.[11]

David Eccles' confidence in his own analytical ability,

---

[9]Interview with Mrs. Joseph Quinney, January 27, 1973.
[10]G. L. Becker to Royal Eccles, November 7, 1929, REC.
[11]Interview with Mrs. Joseph Quinney, January 27, 1973.

bolstered as it was by uncanny success, may have been responsible for his disparagement of higher education. Quick to acknowledge his own indebtedness to Professor Moench for the development of his reading and calculating abilities, he still observed that many well-educated people failed to exercise good judgment. The son of one of his business associates went to an eastern school and came back a typical fop — excessively concerned about his appearance and manners, and not at all useful as a worker. "The educated fool" was David's name for him. David determined that that would not happen to his sons, and for many years resisted the desire of their mothers to send them to college. It is therefore of interest to note that approximately three years before his death, Eccles was asked by David O. McKay and John Watson to become a member of the Weber Academy (now Weber State College) Board of Trustees. Eccles immediately took as much interest in the school as he did in any of his business enterprises and began to encourage manual training for boys. The minutes show that David did not hesitate to give suggestions on matters which came before the board. He remained a trustee until he died.[12]

A third predominating influence on the character of David Eccles was his birth as a Mormon. While no adequate studies have established the parameters of "the Mormon mind" in the nineteenth and early twentieth centuries there is general agreement that Mormon group life was distinctive and carried with it a certain mentality. The Mormons had a well-developed respect for group activity, found satisfaction in working together, and got enjoyment out of mutual association with fellow Mormons. Eccles' closest business partners were almost invariably fellow Mormons. He consulted Mormon leaders on the wisdom of business deals, reared his families within the context of the Mormon community, regarded himself at all times

---

[12]Homer Hutchinson to Royal Eccles, December 31, 1930, REC.

as a member of that community, and took some pride in the fact that he had contributed mightily toward "the building of the Kingdom."

Mormonism touched his life at all the key points. As a young man, he advanced in rank in the "priesthood" — the lay leadership role in the Church from "teacher" to "priest" to "elder" to "seventy." He was married to Bertha in the Endowment House in Salt Lake City "for time and all eternity." That church authorities permitted him to marry a second wife, also for "time and eternity," suggests that they regarded him as orthodox, obedient, and reasonably faithful in carrying out his religious obligations. David never regarded himself as the preaching type and resisted invitations to speak in church, and although throughout his life he rarely attended church meetings, he nevertheless regarded himself as a loyal member. He recruited Latter-day Saints in Ogden, Weber, and Cache valleys to work for him in Oregon; he helped them to build a chapel and organize a congregation there; he helped support his brothers on their preaching missions; he encouraged his own sons to go on missions; he occasionally held family prayers in his home; and he insisted that the food be blessed before meals, even in lumber camps. (According to Bertha he blessed it himself when he was there.) He depreciated profanity, expected his employees to honor the Sabbath, and always spoke respectfully of Mormon officials. He gave no consideration to leaving the Mormon community, but rather expended his money in establishing beet sugar and other enterprises which would contribute to the community's welfare.

Eccles was always grateful to the Church for assisting his father's family to migrate to Utah; thought the Church a worthy organization; and made important contributions to many of the programs of the Church, in addition to paying a full tithe of his income. Papers left by Eccles demonstrate that he paid tithing as early as 1871. In that year he turned over to his bishop 40,000 board feet of lumber, which would suggest that he had produced 400,000 board feet of lumber during his work that season. To give another example, he contributed two yoke of oxen in 1875; these were apparently sent to Southern Utah to help in the construction of the St. George Temple. Indicative of his income, he paid tithing valued at $77 in 1876, $181 in 1877, and $125 each in 1878 and 1879. During the last years of his life, his tithing usually exceeded $10,000 per year, and in several years, he was the leading tithepayer in the Church. Eccles was particularly pleased with the request that he serve as one of the trustees of the Church's bond issue.

At one point in Eccles' married life church authorities suggested that Eccles' go on a mission to help preach the gospel. His answer was that he felt he was worth more to the Church as an employer of many Latter-day Saints who would otherwise have to look elsewhere for jobs and would possibly have great difficulty in finding them. Apparently, the church leaders agreed with his reasoning. The call was withdrawn.[13]

Heber J. Grant, after becoming a member of the Quorum of Twelve Apostles, was called by the First Presidency of the Church to secure the necessary money to keep the *Ogden Daily Herald,* organ of the all-Mormon People's Party, from failing. The *Herald* not only could not pay its running expenses but owed $51,000. The decision was made to incorporate a new company and give the property of the old to the parties paying its obligations. According to Grant, "Many refused to take stock knowing it could not be sold for half what it cost, but Brother Eccles took all that I appealed to him to take, and he did it cheerfully."[14]

---

[13]George Reynolds, secretary of the Church Missionary Committee, to David Eccles, November 9, 1892, REC.

[14]Heber J. Grant to David C. Eccles, December 18, 1912; and Heber J. Grant Recollections, October 28, 1929, REC.

When John Watson became bishop of the Ogden LDS Fifth Ward in 1900, the ward was owing about $7,000. After steady but small payments had reduced the debt to $4,000, Watson approached his friend Eccles for help. Eccles promised to ask Church President, Lorenzo Snow, if he could turn $3,000 of his own tithing toward the ward debt and visited the office of the First Presidency with that purpose. His request was granted, and the load of Ogden Fifth Ward was lightened. It is said that this action initiated a policy on the part of the general church to "participate" in the financing of local meetinghouses and tabernacles by advancing half the cost.[15] The Fifth Ward later honored Eccles by presenting him with a gold-headed cane, in gratitude for his contributions to their budget.

After he had the financial wherewithal and the social incentive to do so, Eccles made no attempt to move his families out of the social circle of the Mormon wards in which they resided. The story of a nephew may illustrate David's respect for the Mormon Church. When his brother Stewart was foreman of the William H. Eccles mill in Austin, Oregon, in 1912, David paid an overnight visit to his home. After dinner, he sat in a comfortable armchair and took a nephew on each knee. Holding a handful of coins and selecting a dime, he counseled young Stewart and his four-year-old brother: "If you boys will save one dime out of every dollar that comes into your hands, you'll one day be rich men." Taking another dime, he continued, "And if you'll pay one dime out of every dollar that comes into your hand to the Mormon Church, you'll be good men."[16]

His Mormonness probably played a role in Eccles' practice of "cutting in" friends and associates on every important venture. Seeing his friends succeed seemed as important as making gains himself. One associate observed that "at one time when

---

[15]From a brochure published by Ogden Fifth Ward in 1902.
[16]Interview with Stewart B. Eccles, April 29, 1971.

he handed me a stock dividend from the Lewiston Sugar Factory he seemed happier to be able to hand it to me than I was to receive it."[17] He enjoyed performing little services for others, "running here or there, . . . seeing to this matter or that for some friend or relative or even for a person with whom he was not well acquainted."[18]

One associate wrote:

> As I knew David Eccles . . . his love for his fellowmen was evidenced in the splendid manner in which he came to the rescue of his friends whenever he learned of their financial distress.
>
> It was never his intention to do injury to any man. He would never advise an investment that he was not willing to enter himself.[19]

Nevertheless, Eccles' generosity was not extended to those who were unwilling to help themselves. David was a firm believer in the freedom of the individual to control his life. When queried about his unfortunate fellows living in slums or other poverty areas, his remembered response was, "well, there is always new territory to which the ambitious can move and where they can improve their lot through hard work."[20] This attitude may have been a product of his continued association with Mormonism, a religion which has taken a certain pride in the independence and self-reliance of its members; more significantly, it may be the essential link which binds an upbringing in poverty, a Scottish hardiness, and a deep sense of Mormonness into the man David Eccles.

---

[17]Budge, "David Eccles As I Knew Him," p. 6.
[18]*Deseret Evening News,* December 6, 1912.
[19]Budge, "David Eccles As I Knew Him," p. 7.
[20]Marriner S. Eccles, *Beckoning Frontiers: Public and Personal Recollections* (New York, 1951), p. 5.

LDS Church Archives. President Joseph F. Smith of the Mormon Church, a close associate of David Eccles.

LDS Church Archives. President Heber J. Grant of the Mormon Church, a long-time financial associate of David Eccles.

Royal Eccles Collection. David Eccles in 1900, after he had become a millionaire.

13

The Ogden Family

DAVID ECCLES FATHERED two large families, twelve children in one and nine in the other.¹ By the time he took his second wife, under Church-condoned but state-condemned polygamy, the time had passed for merging both wives and all the children into one communal family. Eccles kept his two families apart, the first in Ogden, the second in Baker and later in Logan. Despite distances, both families knew their father well —he was that expansive that his concern could include them all. But because of distances, and the independence of having to make

---

¹That David Eccles may have had a second plural wife is suggested by a suit brought in 1915. Margaret Geddes, widow of William S. Geddes, claimed to have been married in 1898 to David Eccles and asserted that her son Albert Eccles, born in 1899, was a son and heir of David Eccles. The jury found for Mrs. Geddes and Albert. I have not included Mrs. Geddes and Albert in this account of families because, for whatever reasons, they were not publicly recognized or acknowledged to be David Eccles' wife and child while he was alive. Mrs. Geddes died in Salt Lake City in 1954 at the age of 90. A prominent Salt Lake City businessman and long-time active member of the LDS Church, Albert Eccles has been active in theatrical and musical circles in the Salt Lake Valley. A review of Albert Eccles' suit is given in Cleo G. Geddes, "The Eccles Case," Plan B Paper in History, Utah State University, 1969.

decisions they gained the maturity of having to take responsibility. Their mothers taught them what their father would have them learn.

Bertha Eccles, first wife, mother of twelve, matron of Ogden society, began her marriage with David in the small adobe house on Lincoln Avenue, adjacent to the Ogden lumber yard Eccles and his partner owned.[2] She ended her life in the mansion on Jefferson Avenue now known as the Bertha Eccles Community Art Center. The present use of the mansion as a center for the cultural arts links it to the simple life of the first, for Bertha's first purchase from the $1,000 dowry with which her father blessed the marriage was a small organ which she played, and which she encouraged each child as it grew to play.

The first move from the adobe house was to a larger home across the street, and it was from that house that the family, by then consisting of parents and ten children, moved in 1896 to the three-level, sixteen-room house which had been built three years earlier by James C. Armstrong.[3]

The house was architecturally significant, one of the eastern style which dominated small residence architecture in Utah until well into the present century.[4] The Eccleses made some changes in the home, laying all new hardwood floors, removing partitions and replacing hardwood. Bertha's sense of the importance of beauty of surroundings coupled with their mutual warmth of hospitality guided the decorating, and from its ten-foot-wide wainscoted front hall, to the library with its leather furniture, to the ornately carved oak dining room, the mansion reflected luxury and friendliness. On the main floor was a 15

---

[2]"Bertha Marie Jensen Eccles: The Wife of David Eccles Relates Her Story," prepared by Cleone R. Eccles, p. 1, REC. The early experiences of Bertha Jensen Eccles are based primarily on this source.

[3]Alice Pardoe West, "Bertha Eccles Hall Echoes with Joys and Romance; Recalls Fabulous Ogden Era," *Ogden Standard Examiner*, May 10, 1953.

[4]Federal Writers Project, Works Progress Administration, *Utah: A Guide to the State* (New York, 1941), p. 186.

by 32 foot living room with comfortable furniture, a grand piano, and statues. There was a sunny conservatory filled with ferns and plants; a breakfast room and kitchen; and the Rose Room, or drawing room, with mirrored French doors, German rose satin wallpaper ornamented with hand-painted cherubs, and an arched mirror over the mantle. It was here that Bertha kept most of her *objets d'art* mementoes of various trips to Europe: paintings, sculptures, woodcarvings. Bertha's concern for the arts probably explains David's interest in the Ogden Opera House and the Salt Lake Theatre.

Not all the art works were European; on the second floor of the house was a large conservatory hall whose walls were lined with pictures of all the family. The conservatory led to a horseshoe-shaped veranda. On both the second and third floors were bedrooms with maple, cherry, oak, and bamboo furniture. The master bedroom, on the second floor, had "Circassian walnut" (gumwood) furniture and an ornate fireplace. The room opened onto an alcove veranda.

"The house had a lot of living," her mother's namesake, Bertha Eccles Thomstorff, said later. "I don't believe there ever was a time when that house didn't have someone in it besides members of the family. It seemed Mother was always helping or training someone. We used to laugh and call them her prodigies."

And there were always parties. Another daughter, Lila Eccles Brimhall, recalled:

> Whenever the Salt Lake City guests would miss the late Bamberger, we had them sleeping in their tuxes and formals on the couches, on the floor, and every place. Mother didn't mind the confusion and "mess" they caused and always made them welcome — no matter how many. But I noticed she always kept her eye on us to see that everything was going on just as it should.[5]

---

[5] West, "Bertha Eccles Hall."

A dozen children didn't prevent Mrs. Eccles from engaging in social, civic, club, and church work, and her home was the scene of activities of the Child Culture Club, the former Martha Society, Daughters of the Utah Pioneers, Children's Aid Society, and the MIA and Relief Society of the LDS Church. There the Ogden Drama Club and the Ogden Girl Scouts had their inception.

One of the major events which took place in the mansion was the 1903 celebration of the sixtieth wedding anniversary of David's parents, William and Sarah Eccles. People from all parts of the state, including many Scotsmen, attended a special program and banquet. That evening David Eccles and his brothers and sisters presented their parents with a group of family pictures in a frame surrounded with lovely cut glass. In later years that picture hung in the "art gallery" conservatory hall on the second floor of the Eccles' residence.[6]

The opulence of their home and the ease of her life with David Eccles did not significantly change Bertha Eccles. "Mother came from the good old pioneer stock," commented the younger Bertha, "and she was not afraid of work." Efficiently she reared the children and managed the home. Each child was given a job to do. Saturday mornings Royal and one of the girls helped with the washing, Royal pushing the handle on the washing machine back and forth, his sister moving the clothes into and out of the sudsy water.

Regardless of the number of maids or hired girls employed in the household — and they often had Scandinavian immigrant girls after David was well-to-do — Mrs. Eccles would never let them wait upon the older children. She was ever hospitable and generous. If a visitor happened to like a piece of furniture or some decorative object, she would readily give

---

[6]"Eccles Diamond Wedding," *Ogden News,* May 6, 1903; also West, "Bertha Eccles Hall."

it to him. Lila recalled, "One time she gave a leather couch to one of our relatives, just because he admired it. And I practically furnished my sorority house with our furniture."[7]

The twelve sons and daughters raised under her care were David Christen, LeRoy R., Vida, Royal, Bertha Olivia, Joseph Merrill, Lila, Laura, Flora, William Jack, Anna Vivian, and Homer Gordon Eccles.

David became president of the David Eccles Company and administered the bulk of his father's estate for several years; LeRoy was president and manager of the Amalgated Sugar Company; Vida married Ray T. Savage, who was active in mining enterprises; Royal was a lawyer in Ogden and president of the Oregon Lumber Company; Bertha married Arthur Wright, a long-time Mormon missionary, and in her own right was a drama coach and reader; Joseph was president of the Wyoming Sugar Company and operated other properties in western locations; Lila married Dean R. Brimhall, a psychologist and administrator of New Deal agencies in Utah and elsewhere, while Lila herself followed an independent career in theatre arts and speech at the University of Utah. Laura, one of the twins, married Alonzo Romney, a high school football coach and manager of the David Eccles Building; while Flora, the other twin, married Orson Douglas, a sugar broker in Chicago. Jack was associated with the Oregon lumber industry; Vivian married Joseph Scowcroft, an Ogden merchant, who died at an early age, after which she married Addison Richards, a character actor in Hollywood. Homer was an officer of the Oregon Lumber Company and of other enterprises on the Pacific Coast.

David Eccles didn't live to see all of his children established in adult lives; Homer, the youngest of this family, was only eleven when his father died. But as long as he lived he

---

[7] West, "Bertha Eccles Hall."

enjoyed his children, taught them, played with them. To play one of their favorite games, he and an older son would sit on the floor with their feet together, both grasping a broomstick to see who could pull the other up. Eccles was usually victorious. As countless and weighty as his business concerns were, he managed to leave them elsewhere when he came home in the evening. Of prime concern then was the whereabouts of each of the children. Hearing voices from the living room, he would ask who was there. "Oh, just friends of Bertha and Royal," his wife would answer. Then, if the clock showed a later hour than he thought proper, he would gently pull open the big doors, greeting the group with a kindly "good evening." Then, pulling out his watch, he would say, "my father, like all godly men, stickett his doors at half past ten. It is now nearly eleven o'clock, and I think it is about time that all of you young folks should be in bed getting your rest. Good night."[8]

His family felt the strength of their father's attitudes about work and education. Royal, for instance, wanted to go to college, but his father felt that experience in the commercial world would be better training. He seemed to think that college made a man unfit for useful work. Still, he did consent that Royal study engineering at the University of Michigan. When after the first term the young man wanted to study law instead, he was afraid to tell his father of his change and of the extra courses he would have to take that summer. School began, the money didn't come, and mornings Royal sat in the pool hall near campus. Mr. Genereau, the proprietor, learning of the situation, handed Royal some bills, and the young man proceeded to "work like the deuce" to make up the week he had lost. The money did come from his father eventually, and Royal lost no time in repaying Genereau. When Royal graduated from law school, his father evidenced his characteristic

---

[8]Homer C. Hutchinson to Royal Eccles, December 31, 1930, REC.

humorous pride: He would introduce his son as "the liar — oh! I mean the lawyer."

Twelve children grew to adulthood in the Ogden home of David and Bertha Eccles. Despite their father's absences from home for business, for travel, and for his second family, they knew him, were taught by him, felt the warmth of his wry humor and the strength of his firm discipline.

Royal Eccles Collection. David Eccles and Bertha Eccles.

Royal Eccles Collection. David Eccles about the time of his marriage to Bertha Jensen in 1873.

The six eldest children in the Ogden family of David Eccles. From left to right, from top to bottom: David Christen Eccles, LeRoy R. Eccles, Vida Eccles Savage, Royal Eccles, Bertha Olivia Eccles Wright, and Joseph Merrill Eccles.

The six youngest children in the Ogden family of David Eccles. From left to right, from top to bottom, they are: Lila Eccles Brimhall, Laura Eccles Romney, Flora Eccles Douglas, William Jack Eccles, Anna Vivian Eccles Snowcroft Richards, and Homer Gordon Eccles.

Royal Eccles Collection. David Eccles at the time of the establishment of the Eccles Lumber Company in 1878.

14

The Logan Family

WHILE DAVID ECCLES' one family was establishing itself firmly in the social life of Ogden, his other children were being born under a veil of necessary secrecy. Apprehension and imprisonment for polygamy was still a threat in 1890 when Ellen gave birth to Marriner and in 1892 when Marie was born. In fact, those few years which Ellen spent in Utah early in their marriage were fraught with fears and tensions. She recounted later that once when Marie was a baby, she and the two children hid out in the fields of Erastus Cole's property west of Logan until Eccles could come for them. He did, and took them across the state line to Franklin, Idaho where they remained until spring.[1]

There was some safety in Idaho, but, as Ellen later recounted, little comfort for most of the women, plural wives whose husbands had brought them there to avoid discovery. She gives a picture of their plight in her description of her

---

[1] Recorded Interview, Nora Eccles Treadwell with Ellen Stoddard Eccles, typescript in possession of the writer. Most of the details of the early marriage of Ellen Stoddard and David Eccles are from this source.

neighbors — among the six families on her block, only one had a man living there. Ellen felt favored among the women: her husband came often to visit, and provided well for her during his absences. Other women, Ellen explained, would be weeks without visit or sustenance from their husbands.

The Eccleses were never raided by the federal deputies, probably because of the precautions Ellen took. But the fear was always there. In Logan, she recounted,

> "I never went to bed at night that I didn't look where I put all my clothes in case I had to run before morning."

That David Eccles was a polygamist was, in fact, known to very few. He, as well as Ellen, found it trying, and on one occasion told his wife in Logan that Dr. Ormsby, a leading psysician in Cache Valley, "could fix it with a deputy that we could be a little free." A price, of course, would have to be paid the deputy. Ellen, with characteristic caution and foresight, replied, ". . . we're not going to start being bled. I've lived this long the way I've lived, and I'll continue to live the same way."

Eventually, however, in 1893, David was summoned to the Fourth District Court to answer charges, but under the amnesty for those whose marriages were contracted before 1890, charges against him were dropped.

In late 1894, after the birth of Spencer, Ellen moved with the three children back to Oregon. She would not be entirely alone there: her husband's lumbering and sugar business brought him often, and her father, associated with Eccles in a sawmill enterprise, had made his home there. There was a branch of the Mormon church in the community, and Ellen became an active leader in the Primary Association, a church auxiliary for children, and in the women's Relief Society.[2] The

---

[2] Noble Warrum, *Utah Since Statehood* (4 vols., Chicago, 1904), IV, p. 350.

three children born in Logan soon found themselves in a large family: Jessie, Emma, George, Nora, and her mother's namesake, Ellen, all were born in Oregon; only Willard was born after the return to Logan.

Eccles necessarily divided what time he had for domestic matters between his two families, so the responsibility for rearing their nine children necessarily fell to their mother Ellen. The oldest son of this family, Marriner, recalled, "she reared us all to share her own view of David as a man who was to be respected and loved, and not to be annoyed by noise and tumults on the occasions when he was home with us."[3] And his sister Nora concurred, adding that, even though Eccles kept unorthodox hours — in his later years he often came home as late as ten o'clock in the evening — her mother would attempt to have a full dinner for him, and a family of happy, if tired, children to greet him.

The children loved to wait for his arrival. He would play games with them, such as dropping nickles and dimes on the sofa for them to find. When they would bring the lost coins to him, he would reply in his Scottish burr, "Losers weepers, finders keepers!" and laugh heartily.

Once back in Logan, Ellen and the children fit into a pattern of weekend visits from David. Some of the children recall that Ellen had on her shelf a bottle of champagne out of which she poured a glass for David upon his arrival every Friday evening. David was not a drinking man in the proper sense of that word, but he did enjoy champagne. After he had spent a weekend in Logan, Ellen would prepare a sandwich for him to eat on the train as he headed out for Oregon. On more than one occasion Ellen found the same sandwich in his pocket days later — he had forgotten to eat it and could not

---

[3]Marriner S. Eccles, *Beckoning Frontiers: Public and Personal Recollections* (New York, 1951), p. 22.

bring himself to throw it away.

Ellen accompanied David on one of his trips to Europe, as had Bertha before her. Two of the girls, Bertha's Lila and Ellen's Marie, went with them — apparently to visit missionary friends there. Ellen also accompanied David to Mexico. On one occasion David took Ellen with him on a business trip to New York City to meet Henry Havemeyer and other important persons in the sugar trust. Not accustomed to meeting persons of great wealth and high station like this, Ellen was nervous about this trip.

Ellen and David Eccles shared a belief in the virtue of labor, and their children were taught from their earliest years the importance of real work. Marriner, for instance, earned five cents an hour for ten hours' work daily the summer he was eight years old. He carried his own weight in boxes in the box factory of the Oregon Lumber Company in Baker. And George, at the age of eleven or twelve, was a water boy on the interurban railway then under construction between Logan and Preston. David Eccles saw that all his children worked. "He wanted none of us to grow up in idleness or acquire a taste for easy living," recalled Marriner.

David Eccles' stern philosophy was effective. At his death his son Marriner, then only twenty-two, was capable of taking full charge of the family's estate, organizing and expanding the Eccles Investment Company to further increase the family's interests.

David Eccles was no advocate of university education, for his children any more than for his employees. Of the latter group it is said that he hired only two college educated persons in his life: a motorman and a conductor in his Ogden transit line. Of the children, Spencer is an example: though he went beyond the usual high school level, attending Utah State Agricultural College and Columbia University, he left before earning a degree at either university. Not that Eccles was adamant, his children could persuade him to let them continue their education into universities, and several did. It was more that he valued a course which led to development, as in Spencer's case, of practical skills and business acumen.

From David Eccles' Logan family came Marriner Stoddard Eccles, chairman of the Board of Governors of the Federal Reserve System, 1934-1951, and chairman of many corporations including First Security Corporation and Utah International Inc.; Marie Stoddard Eccles Caine (Mrs. George E.), whose husband was for many years head of the Department of Animal Husbandry at Utah State University; Spencer Stoddard Eccles, who was an officer of First Security Banking Company through most of his adult life and managed the Mountain States Implement Company; Jessie Stoddard Eccles Quinney (Mrs. Joseph), whose husband has been in a well-known Salt Lake City law firm and conducts legal work for many of the Eccles enterprises; Emma Stoddard Eccles Jones (Mrs. LeGrand Jones), who has made a career as an elementary school teacher; George Stoddard Eccles, president of First Security Corporation, and active in national and international financial organizations; Nora Stoddard Eccles Treadwell Harrison (Mrs. Richard), whose imaginative ceramics have appeared in many American and European shows; Ellen Stoddard Eccles Merrill Harrison (Mrs. Hugh), and Willard L. Eccles, vice president and secretary of First Security Banking Corporation.

The mother of the Logan family, Ellen Eccles, sometimes called by her nickname "Bammy," was a warm and affectionate person, practical and frugal (when David wanted to buy her diamond earrings she said, "they would cost too much"). She was an excellent housekeeper, good cook, prudent manager, and demanding mother. As Bertha had done before her, Ellen served a term as cook for David's sawmill crews and was noted for her succulent hot bread. She was ambitious, self-reliant, independent, and determined. With flashing dark eyes and fair skin, she was a beauty whom David enjoyed "showing off." Although only forty-five when her husband died, Ellen at no time considered marrying another. "Nobody else could have stepped into his shoes," she told her children.

In her Logan Mansion, built in 1907, and finished with the finest lumber produced by David's mills in Oregon, Ellen was the grande dame of Logan society, and was often noted driving her electrical automobile around Cache Valley and its lovely adjoining canyons.

Nora Eccles Harrison Collection. David Eccles' Logan family taken at Logan in 1909. Left to right: George, Emma, Jessie, David Sr., Marriner, Ellen, Ellen Stoddard Eccles, Marie, Willard, Spencer, and Nora.

Royal Eccles Collection. David Eccles, prosperous businessman.

Ellen Stoddard Eccles *Royal Eccles Collection. David Eccles at the time of his venture at Beaver Canyon, Idaho, in 1883.*

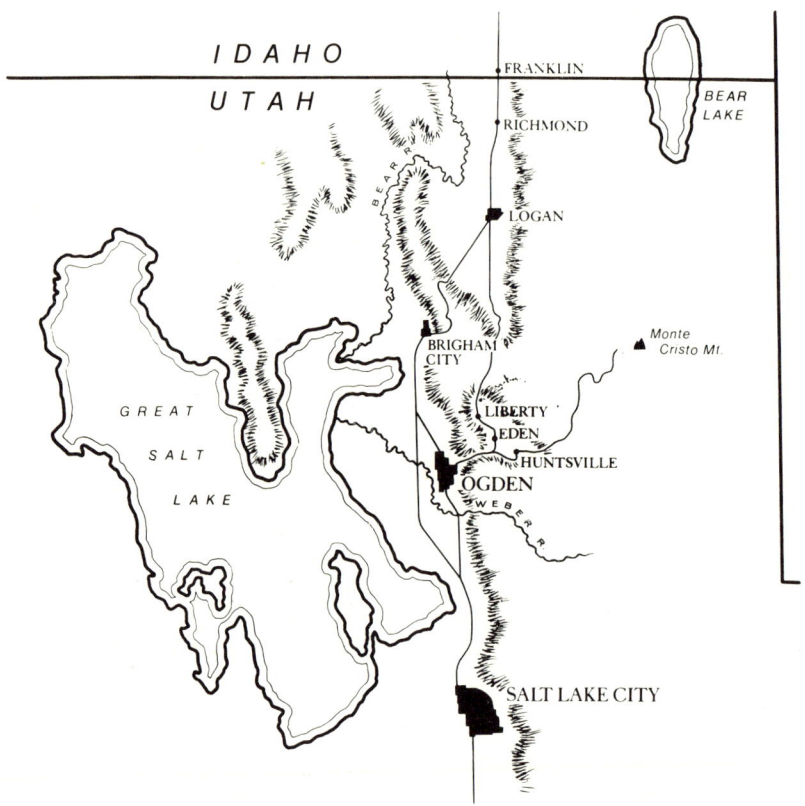

The Salt Lake Valley, Ogden Valley, and Cache Valley region where the William Eccles and David Eccles families lived

15

David Eccles, Paterfamilias

HOW DID DAVID ECCLES manage his two wives and their families? For one thing, he always kept Bertha and Ellen at arms-length from each other. During nearly all of their married life, Bertha maintained her home in Ogden. After their marriage Ellen was in Baker for three years, then Logan and vicinity for another three years, then back in Baker for another twelve years, then in Logan all the years after 1906. During the "Oregon years," David went to Baker for a week or two or three, then back to Ogden for a week or two or three. Later, because most of his work was in Ogden, David spent most of the week there with Bertha, and rode on the Oregon Short Line ("Cache Valley Limited") to Logan, usually on Fri-

---

This chapter is based partly on interviews in 1971, 1972, 1973 with Mrs. Nora Eccles Treadwell Harrison, Oakland, California; Mrs. S. J. Quinney, Salt Lake City, Utah; Mrs. Marie Caine, Logan, Utah; Mrs. Lila Eccles Brimhall, Salt Lake City, Utah; Mrs. Cleone Rich Eccles, Ogden, Utah; N. B. Salisbury, Logan, Utah; Reed Bullen, Logan, Utah; Wendell Budge, M.D., Logan, Utah; and S. J. Quinney, Salt Lake City, Utah.

The chapter also uses material in the interviews conducted by Royal Eccles, and statements in letters to the Eccles family written after the death of David Eccles.

day night, stayed with Ellen, and returned to Ogden on Monday.

Eccles did not portion out allowances to each wife, but permitted each to draw from accounts he set up for them. If either wife tended to get out of line by spending too much on clothing or food or some other item, he would call it to her attention. The sons in both his families began working for one of his enterprises as soon as they were capable of working. The youngest would be waterboys for work crews; as they became older they piled lumber, made boxes, kept books, and performed other tasks. Eccles tried to integrate the daughters in the two families to some extent by taking one of Bertha's girls with him when he went to stay with Ellen, and vice versa. Thus, the girls in the two families developed a friendship that has continued throughout their adult lives.

The older Eccles children, particularly, the girls, also became friendly with "the Salt Lake crowd" by going to Salt Lake City occasionally for matinees and theatrical performances, and to attend dances and parties. In Salt Lake City they usually stayed at the Beehive House (former Brigham Young home) as guests of Julina Smith, wife of Joseph F. Smith, the president of the Mormon Church. "Aunt Julina," as they called her, usually had convert girls from England or Scotland to help with housework and enjoyed having "out of town" company. David and Bertha or Ellen, when in Salt Lake City, usually stayed at the home of Hyrum S. Young, son of Brigham. Hyrum had been cashier of Ogden First National before going with Deseret National in Salt Lake City.

In his later years Eccles tried to combine his trips to Europe with visits to his sons who were on preaching missions there. He would take first one wife and then the other, and occasionally with Bertha he would take an older daughter of

Ellen, or with Ellen an older daughter of Bertha. In general, these relationships and associations were harmonious. There were occasional outbursts of little jealousies, but these seemed never to have developed into tense or strained relationships. Nevertheless, the two families were distinct units and tended to think of themselves as independent and separate.

Eccles' typical working day began late; he often rose at eight or nine or later in the morning. He would read the paper, eat a modest breakfast consisting of milk toast or a bowl of warm cereal and two or three cups of hot cocoa, and on special occasions maybe a can of kippered herring. During the morning hours he would go to the barber shop for a shave; he rarely shaved himself. He was always clean shaven, except for a small mustache, though during the early years of his marriage when he worked at sawmills in the mountains, he wore a full beard. Careful in his dress, he always wore his business suit, with celluloid collar on his shirt, and a bow-tie which was tied by Ellen or Bertha, or perhaps pinned on. Mid-morning or later, then, Eccles would walk to work, if he was in Ogden, or in Logan, to the depot.

He returned to his home around eight o'clock in the evening, or later. By that time his children had already eaten, and he ate alone. Again, his meal was simple. Hot biscuits, a little meat and vegetables, and lots of buttermilk — he once joked that if he could find a cow that gave buttermilk, he would pay any price for her! He was not a heavy meat eater, did not go in for rich desserts, but enjoyed fruit. He also enjoyed toasted cheese sandwiches. Coming home from a trip or from an exciting business deal, he would often go into the kitchen and do a little Scottish dance while humming or whistling a Scotch ditty as his supper was being prepared. Or if the day had not gone so well, he would complain of being tired with "a bit of a headache," in which case his wife might bring him a cup of hot cocoa or tea. After dinner he might play with his small children for a while, then go to his desk and work on business papers until midnight. He put in a long day at his work.

Frequently on Sunday afternoons the family all had dinner together. On these more formal occasions the food was placed in dishes at his end of the table and he would serve the family. He served small helpings, explaining: "you may have an additional serving when you finish this, if you like, but we musn't waste by giving you food you won't eat." Bertha specialized in Scandinavian cooking; Ellen in Western America preparations. On a cold evening, when he brought one of his Scottish friends with him, they might gather together and share a "toddy"—not necessarily hot — of Scotch whiskey, or a glass of champagne. David was not a drinker, but occasionally indulged in a drink with his friends. His wives were both teetotalers, but most of his father's family enjoyed an occasional drink as did most of his business associates.

Although Eccles was a strong family man, there were times when business must take precedence. He did not encourage his children to run down to the depot to walk back with him because he often brought along one of the Brownings or Scowcrofts—someone to talk business with, and perhaps put up for the night. He did not engage in long conversations with his wives or family. His interest was in business transactions, not ideas or "gossip." When his children were little he might play "horsey" with them on the floor, and he enjoyed doing tricks. His children always called him "Papa," and on more formal occasions, "Father." He was not a great reader, but was informal and his family felt at ease around him. He enjoyed bringing small gifts to his children and his wife. He might bring home a necklace or other piece of jewelry, and he often carried some hardtack candy or peppermints to give to children.

He was informal and democratic around his employees. Though he dressed well, he never wore a tuxedo and never "put on airs." One daughter remembers an occasion when her father was negotiating for the purchase of saw blades to be placed in one of his mills. Not finding his little notebook in his pocket she recalled that he wrote down the prices on his shirt cuffs and refused to allow his wife to wash off the writing until he had concluded the bargain several days later.

David felt ill at ease at social gatherings of "high society," and preferred associations with his Scottish cronies and with his employees. On a Sunday or holiday, at one of his milltowns, he might sponsor a footrace, and then run in it himself. His employees might let him win — and he was good enough to win occasionally without their letting him, and then have another race for the rest.

Eccles, as most Mormons, was not profane in his speech. He might occasionally say "Dammit!" when considerably irritated, but did not habitually use profanity or indulge in "cussing." Bertha and Ellen never felt out of place cooking for his lumber crews because "there was never a word off-color." Occasionally, Eccles might become angry and upset, and at such times he would call his wife "Bertha" or "Ellen," whereas under normal circumstances he would simply call her "Mamma."

Eccles was "close" with his money, but he was not stingy. The family have been told by business associates of Eccles that he never foreclosed on anyone. He enjoyed cutting friends in on his business deals so they could make money along with him. In a number of cases, people were allowed to buy stock on credit and pay for it later with the dividends they earned. Eccles' sons and daughters recalled some instances in which older persons came to them after their father's funeral and told them that David had "given them their home," by paying off their threatened mortgage, or giving them other kinds of help.

Eccles' recreation was business and family. He did not fish, hunt, or engage in sports. He enjoyed traveling and found relaxation in occasional trips to Europe.

His first trip for pleasure was taken to Scotland in the summer of 1893. It was at the time of the World's Columbian Exposition in Chicago, sometimes called the Chicago World's Fair, and David and Bertha spent five days there before proceeding on to New York from where they sailed on a German steamer, the *Augusta Victoria,* and landed in Hamburg. They went from Hamburg to Lübeck, then sailed over to Copenhagen where they spent a week. In nearby Aarhus they visited Bertha's relatives. Next, in London, they met a Logan friend, Erastus Cole; they then moved to Glasgow. David and Bertha remained about two weeks in Scotland, the only place, according to Bertha, where David was an enthusiastic sightseer. They spent time with his Eccles and Hutchinson relatives, visited the scenes of his childhood, and traveled about in Edinburgh. They enjoyed a few days in the Northern Highlands, visited Loch Katrine (just east of Loch Lomond) and the wooded Trossachs, immortalized by Sir Walter Scott in *Lady of the Lake* and *Rob Roy.* They also visited the home of Robert Burns, Sterling Castle, and the monument to the Scottish patriot, William Wallace, "the hammer and scourge of England," who drove the English out of Perth, Stirling, and Lanark when he was still in his twenties. Sailing from Glasgow, they spent a few additional days in Chicago before returning to Ogden, having been gone more than three months.

David and Bertha and their daughter Vida returned to

Europe in 1900 to see the World's Fair in Paris and once more visited England and Scotland, as well as Belgium and Holland. In Scotland, they again spent time in Paisley, Glasgow and Edinburgh, and also Aberdeen and Inverness, sailed through the Caledonia Canal to Oban, and from Oban went up through the Northern Highlands again.

In subsequent years, there was a trip nearly every year to the East, to Cuba, to Mexico, or to Europe. Eccles enjoyed these weeks of respite from his gruelling business responsibilities.

His trips also provided opportunities for Eccles to be generous with his wives and children. He usually brought back nice gifts to his children — bracelets, necklaces, and scarfs for the girls, toys, knives, and cufflinks for the boys.

A man as involved in affairs of business as David Eccles was had little enough time for family life; when that time had to be divided between two families, it became even less. Yet he did well by his two wives and their twenty-one children. Each group constituted a strong family unit, and the children were high achievers. Taught from an early age to help and support their family, the children developed qualities of industry, frugality, and leadership, mainly because their parents demanded it of them. Eccles and his wives encouraged their children to be self-reliant and creative; they insisted upon high standards of performance. Above all they demonstrated warmth and respect for their sons and daughters, providing them stability and security, and the kind of encouragement which breeds self-confidence.

The two families of David Eccles were stable, well conducted, respected households, both of which had felt their father's guiding hand. In 1912 the oldest child of the Ogden family, David Jr., was thirty-five years old, the youngest, Homer Gordon, was eleven; the oldest child of the Logan family, Marriner, was twenty-two, the youngest, Willard, was three. In all, Eccles had twenty-one living children (some said twenty-two), and two living wives (some said three). Estimates of his wealth varied from six or seven million to twenty-five million, but most of the estimators at whatever the figure called him the richest man in Utah. That was what he left behind him when he boarded the train on December 5, 1912, for a series of business conferences in Salt Lake City.

16

Death and Burial

THE DAY IN Salt Lake City followed Eccles' normal pattern of formal and informal business and social conferences. He attended a meeting of the directors of the Deseret Savings Bank, and he called at the offices of the Utah-Idaho Sugar Company, where he talked for an hour with George Austin. Around four in the afternoon he dropped in at the *Deseret News* office, as he frequently did when he was in the city, to chat with H. G. Whitney about sugar and banking business. There he met Emma Lucy Gates, operatic prima donna, and talked about her professional prospects with her. To the people in the office he seemed "careworn," but in good spirits as he picked up a paper to read on the train that evening and left the office.

At the Deseret National Bank the financier talked with former Utah Governor John C. Cutler and with bank colleague W. W. Riter. From shortly after five o'clock until eight, his whereabouts were unknown, although he had mentioned several engagements.[1]

---

[1] "David Eccles Stricken with Heart Failure," *Deseret Evening News*, December 6, 1912.

With some time to spare before the 9:00 P.M. train to Ogden with possible connections to Logan, Eccles stopped at the box office of the Empress Theater around eight to discuss with manager D. F. McCoy the proposed building of a theater in Logan. They were absorbed in discussion when Eccles mentioned his plan to catch the train. McCoy reminded him that train time was only seven minutes away, and Eccles left, hurrying toward the depot.

Frank A. Hyde, of 228 Brown's Court, saw Eccles walking at a rapid pace near 132 West South Temple Street, and later reported:

> I did not know Mr. Eccles, but was standing in front of Chep's tavern and saw him coming west toward me on South Temple street. I noticed that he was absolutely undisturbed until he was within a few yards of where I stood. He then began to stagger and groped blindly for a few steps and would have fallen had I not caught him. He did not seem hurried or excited in any way and until he started to stagger appeared all right.[2]

Soon Hyde was assisted by patrolmen H. C. Schrans and Ernest Leaser, who carried the unconscious man into Chep's Cafe and notified authorities. A flashing red beacon and wailing siren announced the arrival of a police ambulance, which quickly took Eccles to the emergency hospital at police headquarters. As Eccles was placed on the operating table, his faint heartbeat stopped. Until the attending physician, H. B. Sprague, pronounced the well-dressed, distinguished-looking man dead and authorized a search of his clothing, none of the rescue team knew that they were trying to save the life of the wealthiest man in Utah. Then a bank book and personal papers made his identity clear.[3]

---

[2]*Ogden Evening Standard,* December 6, 1912.
[3]*Deseret Evening News,* December 6, 1912.

While David C. Eccles, the oldest son, who was attending a theatrical performance in Ogden, was being notified by Chief B. F. Grant, and while arrangements were being made for him to reach Salt Lake City, word of Eccles' death spread rapidly. At first his friends found the news incredible; many of them had talked with him, in apparent good health, that very day. Four close associates, C. W. Nibley, Presiding Bishop of the Mormon Church; W. W. Riter, president of Deseret Savings Bank; H. G. Whitney, secretary of the Utah-Idaho Sugar Company and director of Deseret National Bank; and D. S. Spencer, assistant general passenger agent of the Oregon Short Line Railway, were among the first to visit the emergency hospital, notify family members, and take temporary charge of the body.[4]

A private railroad car took David C. Eccles and his brothers LeRoy and Joseph to Salt Lake City, while their two sisters who lived there, Vida (Mrs. George W. Davis, wife of a Salt Lake attorney) and Lila, a student at the University of Utah, were notified. All the other children of Eccles' "first family" resided in Ogden, except for twins Laura and Flora, who were attending the Cumnock School of Expression in Los Angeles. Although each was informed of the death, the news was withheld from their mother, Mrs. Bertha Eccles. Seriously ill and under the care of the family physician, she was not told for several hours. That evening the family gathered at the undertaking parlors of Joseph William Taylor, 25 South West Temple, and at noon on the following day the Bamberger line returned the body of David Eccles to Ogden.

Nearly three weeks earlier Ellen had gone with David to Oregon for two weeks. They had returned to Logan the preceding weekend with Christmas presents for the children

---

[4] *Deseret Evening News,* December 6, 1912.

that they had bought in Portland. Wednesday night David had telephoned Ellen from Ogden to say, "I'll see you tomorrow night."

Early in the afternoon of Thursday, anticipating their father's visit that night, Nora and George, ages ten and twelve, had gone to a neighborhood creamery to get a gallon of the buttermilk he loved. Their route took them along the large irrigation ditch that ran by the home of an uncle and aunt. On their return they were told the chilling news of his passing.

Marriner, the oldest of Ellen's family, had returned from his preaching mission to Scotland in May of 1912 and had been assigned by his father to keep the books and handle the payroll of the hydroelectric power plant being built far back in Blacksmith Fork Canyon, southeast of Logan. Late at night, sleeping in the camp at the project, Marriner was informed by a messenger of his father's death. He returned immediately to be with the family.

The next day Ellen and the children took the Union Pacific train to Ogden. They were escorted by Heber J. Grant, apostle of the Church and man of finance, who had come from Salt Lake City to be with the family of the man he had been associated with, in a business way, for almost twenty years. Little Nora would never forget that she sat on Brother Grant's knee the entire trip.

The suddenness of Eccles' death was puzzling. His sons David C. and LeRoy knew of no similar previous attack and observed that their father had seemed in good health when he left them that morning, although a little pale, probably from overwork, they assumed at the time. They could only attribute the attack to overexertion and resulting heart failure when he tried to catch the train. William Moyes, A. R. Heywood, and other long-time friends were likewise at a loss to account for his death. However, the family physician, Dr. Ezra Rich, after talking with the widow, Bertha, felt that the probable cause was apoplexy. Bertha had mentioned that her husband had been suffering from frequent headaches; this led the doctor to believe that high blood pressure could have been the cause.[5] D. C. Budge of Logan, who had been the millionaire's personal physician since 1901, offered a similar explanation:

> Only a few weeks prior to his death I informed him that he had developed hardening of the arteries. I advised him to put his business affairs in shape and to prepare his final will, fearing that something unforeseen may happen.[6]

While doctors were determining the cause of his death, David Eccles' associates were assessing the importance of his life. From Ogden, from Logan, from Oregon and elsewhere came tributes to his character and acumen. Several statements were printed in the *Deseret News*. Joseph F. Smith, president of the Mormon Church, called Eccles' death "a state-wide misfortune and calamity" and credited Eccles as having provided employment for thousands of people in Utah, Idaho, and Oregon. In Logan, H. E. Hatch, president of Thatcher Brothers Banking Company, said:

> The passing of Mr. Eccles is a personal loss to everyone in this valley; not alone to those closely associated with him, but also to those who had no direct connection with his interests .... no one is left who can just fit into his place.

A close associate of Eccles' for thirty years, Bishop C. W. Nibley wrote:

> He was a man of strong and dominating powers, and yet he was most easily approached by anybody and everybody .... His judgment in business affairs was better than that of any other man whom I ever knew. He could analyze a business proposition,

---

[5]*Salt Lake Tribune,* December 6, 1912.
[6]D. C. Budge, "David Eccles As I Knew Him," REC, p. 7.

and dissect it, turn it inside out and upside down, and look at it from more points of view than any other man . . . and it was nearly always with unerring accuracy. To his family and his relatives he was most patient, and in many ways even extreme in his patience and helpfulness. He is gone now and his place will never be filled. There is no other like him . . . . No financial loss that could come to his state or his people in the way of development and building up the country can equal the loss that the state and his people suffer through his passing away.

A stunned W. W. Riter, who had chatted with Eccles that afternoon and then found himself at the emergency hospital five hours later taking temporary charge until the sons arrived, expressed his feelings:

> In the death of David Eccles the country had lost one of its most useful citizens . . . . His force and resoluteness of purpose have had but few equals and no superiors in my acquaintance. His capacity for business was almost unlimited. He had a faculty and discrimination for business affairs that were unapproachable. . . .

Finally, John Pingree, cashier of the First National Bank of Ogden, said:

> Because of Mr. Eccles' quiet nature, no one but those intimately connected with him in business affairs can realize what a truly great man he was. The business affairs with which he was connected are so complete and so well organized under his direction that his death will have no effect upon the institutions established by him. He was a master in organization, perfecting his works and then choosing the employees to carry on the work.[7]

The leading commercial establishments of the West passed resolutions of respect for Eccles' work in building up the region.

While the press was honoring Eccles, his family and friends were solemnly preparing for his burial. The day fol-

---

[7]All of the preceding statements from *Deseret Evening News,* December 6, 1912.

lowing his death several of his sons and business associates accompanied the body to Ogden on the train. Scores of friends gathered at the station to await the party. These willing hands helped place the casket in the hearse and then accompanied the family to their home. Because of the necessity of waiting until all the members of the family and close associates could return to Ogden, the funeral was delayed until the following Tuesday.[8]

Larkin & Sons, the undertaking establishment, telegraphed east for a large Springfield bronze casket, the exact duplicate of the one in which President William McKinley had been laid to rest. The Weber Club sent postal cards with black bordered edges to their members, urging them to attend the funeral as a group. The city draped herself in black mourning and a certain quietness bothered her citizens. On Saturday the body was taken to the home where it lay in state until the funeral.

On Tuesday of the funeral, shortly after 12 o'clock, friends and relatives gathered at the Eccles' home to accompany the family and hearse to the Ogden Tabernacle where the service was to be held. The cortege, several blocks in length, was led by the members of the Weber Academy School Board, followed by the faculty and four hundred students. Next in the procession were the members of the Weber Club, numbering some two hundred. These two groups walking four abreast led the cortege down Twenty-sixth Street and then along Washington toward the Tabernacle. Several carriages followed carrying the President of the Mormon Church, Joseph F. Smith, and other speakers at the funeral. The honorary and active pallbearers came next, accompanying the hearse. The first carriage behind the hearse was occupied by Mrs. Bertha Eccles and several of her children, followed in another carriage by Mrs. Ellen Eccles and her young children. Then came the other friends

---

[8] *Ogden Evening Standard,* December 7, 1912.

and relatives in carriages, or, since the supply of carriages in Ogden was not sufficient, on foot to the Tabernacle. The long cortege moved slowly down the mourning-draped streets of Ogden.

> Business was temporarily suspended in all business houses along Washington avenue while the procession passed. No one thought of making a purchase and clerks and proprietors stood before their stores. Many uncovered and bowed their heads.[9]

The Tabernacle seating had been divided and allotted among the different groups. A certain section was reserved for the family and for different groups as the Weber Club and employees of the Ogden Sugar Factory. By the time the cortege arrived it was plainly evident that only a very small portion of the crowd could gain admittance.

> So many people gathered around the entrances that it was with difficulty that the members of the family could enter and the crowd had to be requested time and time again to stand away from the door. As each carriage was emptied, the gathering believed it to be the last and a general rush was made for the door. It was 2 o'clock before the last carriage had drawn up and the members of the Weber Club had entered in a body. What few remaining seats were vacant were soon filled and every nook and corner held those willing to sacrifice comfort to hear the services. Many lingered about the doors and windows in the hope that they might hear the music or catch a few words that were spoken.[10]

The bronze casket was placed directly below the flower-draped pulpit. Lilies of the valley, supposedly Eccles' favorite flowers, were profuse. L. W. Shurtliff, president of the Weber Stake of the LDS Church, presided over the service which was conducted by Bishop Henry C. Jacobs of the Eccles' own Fifth

---

[9] *Ogden Evening Standard,* December 10, 1912.
[10] *Ogden Evening Standard,* December 10, 1912.

Ward. The speakers at the funeral included many of Eccles' closest associates. Charles W. Nibley spoke first, followed by John Watson and then George Romney, all of them not only prominent businessmen but important officers in the Mormon Church. After a musical interlude, Apostle David O. McKay expressed eloquently some of the community's feelings about David Eccles. He observed:

> That simple act of hurrying to the train on foot instead of hiring a taxicab, illustrates one of the dominant traits in Brothers Eccles' life. Plain living and high thinking were ever characteristic of him. The lessons of industry, economy, and frugality that he learned in the days of his poverty, remained with him to the last, and David Eccles, the multimillionaire, was the same modest unassuming David Eccles that worked and plodded in the mountains to earn his first fifty dollars .... A man who can produce a million dollars and at the same time contribute a million dollars to the wealth of the community is a public benefactor. Such a man was David Eccles.[11]

Joseph F. Smith was the concluding speaker at the funeral. As President of the Mormon Church he offered official as well as personal condolences to the family and mourners. During his talk he spoke almost entirely of religious matters, using Eccles' life as text and example for his sermon:

> I will say to you, friends, here today, if you can improve upon his religious life, do it. You cannot, I believe improve upon his financial life and capabilities, but you can follow his example. There is one thing in this connection I wish to impress upon you: when you run, stop before you become weary; when you walk, rest before you faint. When you have done your duty, give nature a chance to recuperate. Do not deceive yourselves into believing that you can run and not tire .... I told David that he was going too fast, that he ought to stop and enjoy the fruits of

---

[11]*Ogden Evening Standard,* December 10, 1912.

this life, but he said that he did not know the meaning of fatigue and enjoyed his manner of living.[12]

At the conclusion of the funeral the pallbearers removed the heavy casket to the hearse and the solemn cortege reformed. It moved slowly down Twenty-Second Street and Jefferson Avenue to the city cemetery. Once there, David Eccles' two large families and close friends formed a somber half-circle around the flower-lined grave. In the brief graveside service, Bishop Jacobs dedicated the site. David Eccles' body was lowered into the waiting grave.

---

[12]*Salt Lake Tribune,* December 11, 1912.

17

Settlement of the David Eccles Estate

WHEN DAVID ECCLES died on the streets of Salt Lake City in the early winter of 1912 he left behind myriad legal and financial problems for his family and associates to solve. He left no will and few accurate written records of his financial operations. His family and associates spent the next year-and-a-half trying to piece together his involvements and interests, to effect a settlement among the various heirs. (Federal income taxes and the regulation and demand which they made for accurate records had not yet been imposed.) Added to these difficulties was the necessity of dividing the estate among two households. The legal questions involving the inheritance of a plural wife and her children were at this time not entirely resolved. Because of these problems and the sheer size of the estate the proceedings attracted great public interest.

At the time of Eccles' death the various papers estimated his wealth to be near $10 million, with some estimates as high as $25 million.[1] Most writers overestimated his estate by mis-

---

[1] *Salt Lake Tribune,* December 6, 1912; *Deseret News,* December 6, 1912.

takenly assuming that he owned a majority interest in all of the twenty-three companies of which he was president. Although he controlled many of these companies he did this not so much by personal stock control as by having a large block of stock, which, added to the stock of his close associates, gave him operational control. For example, the Amalgamated Sugar Company, of which he was president, was worth several millions, yet he owned only $633,000 worth of stock in the company. Eccles' vast influence over the company resulted from the fact that he was the organizer and founder, the acknowledged leader of the Ogden interests, and the go-between for the American Sugar Refining Company and local stockholders. This was typical of many of the industries in which Eccles participated; his control and influence could not be measured by the monetary value of his stock.

When Eccles' estate was appraised, many were surprised to learn that it was as small as it was. The following excerpt from the *Salt Lake Tribune* a few days after his death indicates the nature of the speculations:

> If the late David Eccles left an estate of $10,000,000 as has been estimated by some, the state of Utah would thereby be enriched to the extent of $500,000, according to the inheritance tax law. The law requires a tax of 5 per cent on all estates, with a $10,000 exemption. At any rate, the estate promises to bring a large sum of money into the state coffers. . . . Attorney General A. R. Barnes is of the opinion that it will probably be unnecessary for the state to issue bonds for the construction of the capitol building, if the next legislature will set aside the tax from the Eccles estate to be used for the building of the structure.[2]

The newspapers not only wishfully predicted the size of the estate, but suggested the logical use of the money before it was calculated and paid. The Eccles settlement followed closely

---

[2]*Salt Lake Tribune,* December 10, 1912.

upon the windup of the estate of Henry Harriman, the railway magnate, which had just been settled, with the state of Utah receiving inheritance taxes to the amount of $1.4 million. (Harriman was not a Utahn, but the Union Pacific Railroad was incorporated in Utah and his estate paid large inheritance taxes in Utah.)

Shortly after Eccles' death a controversy arose concerning a possible heir and marital relation. In his lumber operations in Oregon, David Eccles had employed William Geddes as a manager. When Geddes died, Eccles helped to support two of his widows with small amounts of money. One of the widows, Margaret Geddes, instituted suit to establish her son Albert, born in 1899, as the legitimate offspring of David Eccles, following a plural marriage which she stated took place in 1898 in Richmond, Utah. The Ogden and Logan families of David Eccles responded negatively to the suit. A lengthy trial involving many witnesses eventually resulted in a jury decision in favor of Mrs. Geddes' claim which caused an award of $250,000 to be made to Albert Eccles.[3]

The first step in the final settlement of the estate of David Eccles was the naming of an administrator. By law the legal widow was entitled to that position, but in this case Bertha Eccles declined in favor of her eldest son, David C. Eccles. On February 4, in Ogden, Royal Eccles, as attorney, began the estate proceedings listing twenty-two heirs, including Bertha Eccles and her twelve children as well as the nine children of Ellen Eccles, but excluding their mother, and representing the total value of the property at not more than $4,500,000. The publication of the administrative papers was disappointing to those Utahns who looked forward to a large tax:

---

[3] A review of the trial and of the evidence for and against the existence of the marriage is presented in Cleo G. Geddes, "The Eccles Case," Plan B Paper in History, 1969, Utah State University Library, 31 pp.

> Reduced from an estimated value of from $10,000,000 to $25,000,000, the estate as now represented with a valuation of less than $5,000,000 will mean a revenue to the state through the Utah inheritance tax of less than $200,000, as nearly as can be ascertained from the represented value of the Utah properties and securities.[4]

The federal estate tax was not enacted until 1916, so the only meaningful tax was the 5 percent levy by the state of Utah on all property above $10,000. The district court which had responsibility for the estate settlement appointed appraisers to review the figures presented by the administrators.

> While the heirs to the large estate declare that they have exercised every possible means to ascertain the true value of the property owned by the late David Eccles and have represented that valuation to be not more than $4,500,000, it is admitted by Attorney Royal Eccles, who is the legal representative of the estate at present, that the court appraisers may alter those figures. The estimate of the property . . . was largely for the guidance of the court in fixing the bond of the administrator.[5]

The process of appointing appraisers, combined with the waiting period of ten months to allow creditors to present claims against the estate, promised to delay the settlement. Attorney Royal Eccles announced that he expected a minimum wait of eighteen months.

On May 20, 1913, the appraisers appointed by the court, Thomas Whalen, A. McFarland, and C. F. Middleton, began their arduous task.

The unraveling of the estate, originally envisioned as requiring a week, eventually required a year. Eccles owned property in seven states and Canada. He was the president of sixteen industrial corporations and seven banks. He was a director in some twenty-four other banks and industries, mak-

---
[4] *Salt Lake Tribune,* February 6, 1913.
[5] *Salt Lake Tribune,* February 5, 1913.

ing a total of some forty-seven corporations in which he was an officer. He owned stock in seventy-six industrial corporations and banks, many of which were intertwined in financial ways which no one but Eccles himself understood. The Eccles family assisted the appraisers, but even they were not certain of the different financial involvements, and David Eccles had not left an accurate, overall account of his businesses. The administrator furnished the appraisers with some twenty-five pages of typewritten material concerning the involvements, but he did not attempt to give a valuation to the personal property or real estate.

Several interesting aspects of the estate provide an insight into the manner in which David Eccles conducted his financial operations. There were large deposits of cash at several banks: Eccles had approximately $400,000 in bank certificates of deposit at the time of his death, in addition to some $67,000 in his personal checking account.[6] He also had substantial amounts in negotiable securities which could easily be converted to cash. Eccles regarded the paying of interest as wasteful, and so maintained this financial condition in order to avoid the necessity of borrowing money. His large liquid holdings enabled him to start businesses, expand them, and even pay advances on the sugarbeet crop out of his own funds. His son characterized the financial operations of the Amalgamated Sugar Company as being similar to those of a bank: when the farmers brought their beets to the factory they were paid immediately from a large cash reserve. Later, when the refined sugar was marketed to the various retailers, the cash reserve was replenished.

On May 11, 1914, the state appraisers finally announced

---

[6]The large sums in bank certificates and personal checking account do not square with "Never let a dollar lie idle." Perhaps Eccles was accumulating funds to make a purchase.

the actual value of the estate to David C. Eccles, the process of valuation having taken almost a year to complete. The total value placed on the estate was $6,034,554. Personal property amounted to $5,404,824, and real estate holdings were valued at $629,730. The most important Eccles holdings were Amalgamated and Lewiston Sugar companies, Utah Construction Company, the Ogden Rapid Transit Company, the First National Bank of Ogden, and the Eccles Lumber corporations.[7]

The final step in settlement of the estate was the division among the heirs of the amount remaining after the inheritance tax was paid. In a series of interesting and unique decisions the Utah Supreme Court and the United States Supreme Court had derived a system for distributing estates among plural households. These decisions betray an unambiguous distaste for what Mormons called "the Principle." The estate of David Eccles was not a landmark decision, but was one of the earliest examples in which a large estate was divided under precedents already developed.

One of the first acts passed by the Utah legislature provided that illegitimate children and their mothers might inherit from the father in the same manner as legitimate children.[8] This was passed long before the Mormon Church had publicly relinquished the practice of plural marriage and may have been designed to protect the rights of plural wives and their children until the legality of the marriages was clearly established. Later, the non-Mormon courts of Utah and the United States ruled that polygamous marriages were illegal and that the issue of such were illegitimate. The Statute of 1852 then, of course, became applicable — a right not clearly established under common law. With the growing national

---

[7] *Deseret Evening News,* May 11, 1914.

[8] Territorial Act of March 3, 1852. I am grateful for the assistance of George Daines, student at the Yale University Law School, in following these cases.

disapproval of polygamy, attention focused on the territorial law as one which helped and fostered Mormon marriage practices. In 1862 Congress passed the Anti-Polygamy Law, which provided that all acts or statutes passed by the Utah Legislature "which establish, support, maintain, shield, or countenance polygamy" were annulled. On the basis of this act, the Utah Supreme Court (Mormons were ineligible to serve) later ruled that children born through polygamous marriages were not legal heirs.[9] But when this decision was cited in a later appeal to the United States Supreme Court, the latter ruled that the Anti-Polygamy Law of 1862 did not annul the previous statute passed by the Territorial Legislature of 1852.

> The distribution of and the right of succession to the estates of deceased persons are matters exclusively of state cognizance, and are such as were within the competence of the Territorial Legislature to deal with as it saw fit, in the absence of an inhibition by Congress.[10]

To prohibit the children of plural households from sharing in the estate of the father, the court observed, was to visit a punishment on the child who was not culpable for the relationship of his parents. The court also pointed out that the statute was not passed with the intention of protecting only those children born through plural households, but all children whether they be illegitimate, polygamous, or legal issue. "Our conclusion," said the court "is that the appellant George A. Cope is entitled to share his father's estate, and the decree of the Supreme Court of the Territory must therefore be reversed."[11] This decision for the time stopped the controversy and the pattern became part of the standard legal procedure in the territory and later in the state.

---

[9] In Re the Estate of George Handley, *Utah Reports,* Vol. 7, 1890, p. 49.
[10] *Cope v. Cope,* January 19, 1891, 137 *US Supreme Court Reporter.* p. 833.
[11] *Cope v. Cope.*

Although the issue of children receiving from the estate was resolved, there was still the question of the legal rights of the widows of polygamous husbands. The decision *Raleigh v. Wells* clearly illustrates the attitude of American law toward the plural wife. When the plural wife in this circumstance sought to retain the house in which she had lived and served as a polygamous spouse, the court ruled against her, stating that it could grant her no dower right since under the law she did not have the status of lawful wife.[12] As suggested in this precedent, Ellen Stoddard Eccles, the second wife of David Eccles, had no right to any inheritance from her husband. As the legal guardian of her minor children, however, she might exercise some control on their use of the money they inherited.

The accounts left by the various sources usually referred to the estate as having been divided between the first and second families. Each family tended to view its property as belonging to *the family*, rather than to individuals. The actual division of the estate of David Eccles among his heirs which would include his first wife and twenty-one children was accomplished on the basis of Section 2826 and 2828 of the Compiled Laws of the State of Utah, 1870.[13] Bertha Eccles, as the first and legal wife, received one-third of the estate, with the remainder to be divided equally among the twenty-one children. Under this formula each child received two sixty-thirds (2/63). This partitioning left the first family with five sevenths of the estate and the second family with two-sevenths. Bertha Eccles received approximately $1,962,322, and each child received $188,793.[14] The estate paid a total of $297,348 in inheritance taxes to the

---

[12]*Raleigh v. Wells,* July 11, 1905, Vol. 29, *Utah Reports,* p. 221.
[13]In Re Bullen's Estate, 47 Utah 98, decided April 22, 1915.
[14]There seems to be some conflicting data on the value of the total estate. The newspapers of May 11, 1914 indicated it was $6,034,554, and this seems an accurate statistic.

state of Utah.¹⁵ This was pronounced to be "the largest ever received by the state from a single estate, with the exception of the Harriman tax."¹⁶

An interesting incident of the estate settlement was the effort to extort money from the Eccles family. This was probably triggered by all the newspaper speculation on the wealth of the family. Evidently the Eccles family of Ogden had received some letters demanding that a certain sum be turned over in exchange for their lives, or for not dynamiting the house. The *Salt Lake Tribune* presented a melodramatic account of this incident:

> The Eccles home in this city was once more turned into a "House of Mystery" last night, at least so far as the neighbors were concerned. The actions of members of the household and the comings and goings of "mysterious strangers", presumed to be private detectives, revived rumors of black-hand death threats.
> It will be recalled that some time ago menacing letters were sent to the Eccles family in an evident endeavor to extort from them some portion, large or small, of the millions left by the late financial Napoleon, David Eccles. Up to date the cool nerve and shrewdness of the Eccles boys have held the black-handers at bay.¹⁷

The so-called Eccles boys reportedly spent the night patrolling the house with shotguns and automatic pistols. On one occasion two newspapermen who came to investigate were almost mistaken for the phantom "black-handers". The next day the

---

[15] David C. Eccles to Jesse D. Jewkes, State Treasurer, June 1, 1914, REC. It is interesting that Jewkes, after having carefully gone over the figures of the estate, located a descrepancy of 11¢. This tiny sum triggered a series of letters and explanations between the family and the Treasurer's Office. Whether the Eccles family ever paid the 11¢ is academic, but it is a commentary on the parties involved that this very careful treasurer and this very Scottish family bothered with the tiny sum.

[16] *Salt Lake Tribune,* November 12, 1913.

[17] *Salt Lake Tribune,* September 25, 1913.

police and sheriff became involved in efforts to apprehend the criminals. It does not appear that the black-handers were ever foolhardy enough to risk an encounter with "the cool nerve and shrewdness of the Eccles boys."

After the estate settlement many forces encouraged the two families to remain united in the various industrial and banking enterprises. The second family had children who were considerably younger than the first — in fact, six of the nine were still minors. Despite his youth and seeming inexperience, however, Marriner Eccles and his family decided that it would be advantageous to separate the interests of the two families. As a result of this split, two companies were formed to represent their interests: The David Eccles Company held the interest of the first family or five-sevenths of the estate; the Eccles Investment Company held the remaining two-sevenths for the second family. Ellen Eccles, as second wife, turned over to the Eccles Investment Company all of her stock, which was valued at some $250,000 and which David Eccles had given her during his lifetime. Marriner Eccles became the president of this concern, which in 1972 was still in existence. Slowly, over a period of years, the various businesses in which the two families held stock were partitioned, went out of business, or were sold. Some ten years after separation the two companies were not operating together in any concerns. The Eccles Investment Company, originally the smaller of the two, grew into a major force in regional and national business, while the David Eccles Company declined into relative obscurity. In 1972 Eccles Investment was absorbed into Utah International, Inc.

Arnold D. Quantrell, associate of David Eccles in Lost River Mines in Idaho.

Matthew Sandefur Browning   Judge Thomas D. Dee

18

Epilogue: Reasons for Eccles' Success

How does one explain David Eccles — a poor immigrant boy who in the Mormon setting in Ogden Valley had few opportunities, few incentives, and no models? The studies of entrepreneurial historians have taught us not to look for business leadership in such a setting.[1] One explanation, of course, would emphasize the manner in which he took advantage of opportunities, beginning with his early start in riding the construction boom in Ogden after the completion of the Pacific railroads in 1869. He supplied lumber for the construction of railroad branch lines, for business establishments, and for homes, and profited from doing so. When a similar boom struck eastern Utah with the completion of the Denver & Rio Grande Western Railroad and the opening of the coal mines in Carbon and Emery Counties, David was there to share in the profits to be made from supplying a similar demand. David took advantage of the stampede of miners to the Wood River

---

[1] William Miller, ed., *Men in Business* (New York and Evanston, 1962).

district of Idaho, and as this began to play out he profited from the construction of a railroad through eastern Idaho up to Montana. In following an identical procedure in eastern Oregon, he added to this the attraction of hundreds of Utah families who signed up for forest land, made remission to him, worked for him, and he was thus able to sell millions of dollars worth of prime lumber which had cost him very little to acquire. He must have been sufficiently careful in all of this that he was never fined or jailed, although at least two suits were brought against him.

This may explain the acquisition of his wealth, but it does not explain the phenomenon of David Eccles. On what basis may we have predicted that an unschooled, poverty-stricken immigrant boy would have seized these opportunities and have had the leadership to make them pay? A second explanation suggests the milieu of his early operations in Ogden. After the completion of the transcontinental railroad, Ogden became a community with two antagonistic systems: the agriculturally-oriented cooperative economy of the Mormons, and the trading-oriented, individualistic economy of incoming non-Mormons, the Gentiles. This clash of cultures created a fluid social system in which a person, although operating from a restricted Mormon background, might find opportunities and stimulus not characteristically found in most Mormon communities. That this explanation has some merit is suggested by the considerable number of creative persons who came out of Ogden: John Browning, who attained international fame for his inventions of firearms; Bernard DeVoto, the distinguished historian and literary critic; and the Coreys, Wattises and others who, with the Eccles', built the Utah Construction Company (now Utah International, Inc.) into the world's largest mining and construction company.

There is still a further possible explanation of the emergence of David Eccles; namely, that his achievement was one of the by-products of Mormon family life.[2] Professor Marian Winterbottom and David McClelland, using the techniques of the behavioral sciences, have attempted to isolate the significant factors which explain the emergence of superior peoples.[3] They have found these things in common among superior cultures: strong family ties, strong religious incentives, and strong intergroup feeling. In particular, they have emphasized the significant role of the mother in implanting high desire for achievement in her children. Strangely, the great deterrent of high achievement, they found, is the ever-present authoritarian father. Indeed, they found high achievement among the seafaring nations where the fathers, as sailors, were absent for extended periods — the Greeks, early Etruscans, British, Japanese, Scandinavians, and Genoese.

That David Eccles demonstrated such high achievement in his adult life, may be explained in the fact that his father, because of his blindness, did not dominate his family and his mother placed heavy responsibilities on David, giving him nec-

---

[2] A number of studies have suggested high achievement among Utahns without pinpointing the cause. For example, Dr. E. L. Thorndike of Columbia University, found Utah a top state in the proportion of former residents who became superior men. E. L. Thorndike, "The Origin of Superior Men," *The Scientific Monthly*, 56 (May 1943), 424-433. Recent studies of *American Men of Science* suggest the same thing. Education studies show Utah with high achievements in education; and a recent study of business leaders shows Utah and Mormon culture ranking high as a producer of executives of large corporations. Most of these studies conclude by saying that "Mormon culture" and its values account for the high proportion of superior people, without trying to assess what it is in Mormon culture that accounts for it. See: Mark W. Cannon, "Mormons in the Executive Suite," *Dialogue: A Journal of Mormon Thought*, III (Autumn, 1968), 97-108; R. H. Knapp and H. B. Goodrich, *Origins of American Scientists* (Chicago, 1952).

[3] Marian R. Winterbottom, "The Relation of Childhood Training in Independence to Achievement Motivation" (Doctoral dissertation, University of Michigan, 1953); David McClelland, *The Achieving Society* (New York, 1961).

essary independence and leadership. He was respected by the mother for assuming a certain amount of responsibility because he was the oldest son at home and "held the priesthood"—an ecclesiastical position of leadership among the Mormons. Taught from an early age to help support the family — to master the principles of selling, operating an enterprise, and assisting the family with its financial and personal problems — he developed qualities of self-reliance, industry, and leadership. The early established personal qualities of David Eccles, then, may explain his emergence as a leading entrepreneur at the turn of the century in Utah, Idaho, and eastern Oregon.

Thoughtful review of his convictions and business pattern suggests that Eccles did not become wealthy through "speculation" in the narrow sense. Because he did not believe in paying interest to others, he did not finance his enterprises with funds from the money markets. He believed that a business, like an individual, could remain free only if it kept out of debt. Like Brigham Young, Eccles spurned speculative enterprises and instead "followed constructive methods which resulted in the upbuilding of the district in which his labors were put forth."[4] Indeed, he avoided any appearance of speculation. At one time a number of the directors of the First National Bank of Ogden became most enthusiastic about a Mexican rubber business in which B. F. Grant was selling stock. At a meeting of the board of directors someone greeted Eccles with, "I see you have gone into the rubber business in Mexico." When Eccles denied any connection and then was told that his name appeared on the company's stationery, he became greatly disturbed:

[4]"David Eccles," in Noble Warrum, *Utah Since Statehood* (4 vols., Chicago, 1919); Wain Sutton, ed., *Utah: A Centennial History* (3 vols., New York, 1951), p. 28; Marriner S. Eccles, *Beckoning Frontiers: Public and Personal Recollections* (New York, 1951), p. 20.

I am not interested and am not going to be interested, and if such be the case that my name is in the letterhead, someone did it who had no authority and I'll have it taken off because no one is going to be led into these wildcat speculations through me.[5]

He avoided the customary money-making devices of borrowing and speculating, yet few individual men have been credited with as much development and improvement of Utah and the West.

From grassroots, then — by capturing opportunities, and by paying careful attention to the minutest details of his interests — Eccles amassed his magnificent fortune. He was an indefatigable worker. From the time when as a youth he walked the long miles around Glasgow to peddle his father's wares, his determination to succeed moved him forward when his empty stomach could not. Although he never knew a year-by-year schoolroom education, he learned through resolution and industry.

David Eccles developed his physical powers throughout his life and was of the opinion that hard work was good for a person. Bertha Jensen Eccles wrote that he was proud of his physical skills and of his good health.[6] Even though he was rather small in stature until he reached maturity (he finally reached 5'11"), he was able to succeed in many kinds of physical competition that took place among the men he worked with. One of his favorite sports was competing to see who could raise a load of lumber in a wagon the highest by lying under the back axle and raising one end of the wagon with the legs. Bertha wrote that David usually won the contest by either raising the load highest or quite often by being the only person to raise the load at all.

---

[5]Interview, Royal Eccles with John Watson, September 20, 1929, REC.
[6]"Memoirs of Bertha Marie Eccles," REC, p. 16.

Working hard, and then seeing the fruits of his efforts was Eccles' greatest pleasure. More than once he would admonish his older sons:

> Never work for money, my boy, because this is the wrong attitude and it can never bring you the most good — on the contrary — you should always work for the success of the business, and if you will keep your mind and attention on the business, you'll never go wrong and the money will come. Now the business is the most important thing and the money is only the yardstick of its success. The trouble with people is that they too often work only for money. Some work so hard to get it they become rascals, and the penitentiaries are filled with them.[7]

As the profits came, the money was utilized. A ruling principle of Eccles' life was to spend his money made in one enterprise in the same one or in another — to use the earnings from sugar, for example, in building a new sugar factory or by investing in a power plant, railroad line, or some other industry needed by the community and likely to make a profit. From others he expected the same ambition and diligence that he expended. His son Marriner observed: "As a Scot, my father did not believe in praising people for doing good work. He seemed to feel it was sinful if they did less than their best."[8]

In addition to his industry, Eccles' sharp intellect was a factor in his success. Heber J. Grant said of his mental powers:

> He had one of the most remarkable minds of any man I have ever met. His wonderful capacity for details and to grasp and comprehend any proposition placed before him gave him an influence among men wherever he mingled with them. He commanded the attention and respect of men great and small.

Known for his foresight and sagacity, he astonished the workers of each of the industries he routinely visited with his exhaustive

---

[7]"Dates and Data Concerning the Life of David Eccles," REC.
[8]Eccles, *Beckoning Frontiers,* pp. 35-36.

knowledge of all facets of the business. He visited the different industries on a somewhat regular basis, traveling many miles throughout the western United States in his efforts to keep each business running efficiently and smoothly. His traveling also included trips to New York, Chicago, and many other large cities where he associated with influential businessmen and took care of any problems that could not be handled in Utah or Oregon. As an example of his extensive travels, Eccles recorded in 1904 that he had traveled 44,211 miles in various business capacities.

Not only among his partners and employees was Eccles' technical and organizational acumen recognized. From long years of association H. G. Whitney, editor of the *Deseret News,* declared:

> No one who knew Mr. Eccles could doubt that he was one of the most remarkable men in the West, especially as a financier. While he had no technical knowledge of bookkeeping, his ability to analyze a ponderous and intricate financial statement, detecting its strong and weak points and reducing it to a plain a-b-c proposition, was marvelous. His business associates, many of whom were the keenest and brainiest men in the community, always respected his ideas and deferred to his judgment.[9]

David Eccles had an awareness of the responsibility of wealth, and managed money with care and thrift. Whether the amount in question was for a few cents or thousands of dollars, none slipped through his fingers. Breakfasting one morning on a dining car, George Romney, the prominent Salt Lake builder, sat opposite the millionaire. Eccles, after eating all he could, offered the remaining egg on his plate to his friend so that it would not be wasted.[10] At one time Eccles arranged

---

[9]*Deseret Evening News,* December 6, 1912.
[10]Response of George Romney to questionnaire sent by Royal Eccles, REC.

for D. C. Budge to take his wife Ellen to the Mayo Clinic for a goiter operation. Subsequently, a bill for one thousand dollars arrived. After the outraged Eccles asked Budge to complain and arrange for an adjustment, the reply from the clinic came that Eccles had not read the bill carefully. On their judgment of his ability to pay, the clinic was charging him *ten* thousand dollars. As a result of heated correspondence and his assertion that even a millionaire was not to be taken advantage of, Eccles finally paid one thousand dollars.

Thrift was not easily learned by all of his sons, many of whom had grown up in ease and plenty. Often he tried to make them see that money had to be carefully earned and handled:

> If I could only teach you the value of a dollar, and the effort behind it. The importance of taking care of it, and why you should always be careful to get a dollar's worth for the business. If I were lax in not getting a full dollar's worth, the salesman would think me an "easy mark" and he, in turn, would tell others, and very soon these business men would not respect me. Now I can't afford to be looked upon as an "easy mark", and the only way I can get the respect of the people and hold it, is to see that I get my full dollar's worth. I owe this to the stockholders of the business, and I owe it to myself. This is true regardless of how much money you have, and if you don't handle it properly, you will soon be thought a fool. I am unable to spend any more money than I can properly use, and if I should try to overdo it, just for the sake of spending, I would become wasteful and then surely people would know I was a fool and I would lose their respect, so you see, . . . there is a great responsibility in having money, and I must see to it that it is put to work, and then to keep it working always. I am no more than a trustee of the money I have, and I must build and make investments for it to accomplish the most good, and I don't see where I can quit, but I can be helped a great deal if my boys grow up to be good and honest men to relieve me of so much work.[11]

---

[11]"Dates and Data," pp. 25-26.

In keeping with his policy of thriftiness, then, Eccles maintained the conviction that the respect of other businessmen was important in becoming a truly successful businessman. He was known to be a man who could not easily be intimidated in business transactions. In fact, his powers in bargaining were reputed to be more than adequate. In his first transaction with Henry Havemeyer, the wealthy and powerful sugar magnate, Eccles informed him that the Amalgamated Sugar Company did not owe anyone any money, and that therefore the bargain would be made on Eccles' terms or not at all. When Havemeyer tried to pressure Eccles to bargain with him he apparently had no success at all. As Havemeyer learned more about the character and business abilities of Eccles his respect for him increased. Eventually, the two became good friends and spent several pleasurable years in business dealings with each other.[12]

Finally, the law of returns brought prosperity to David Eccles in dealing with his colleagues. Although he was ambitious and continually seeking new avenues of expansion, his path was never strewn with the wrecks of other men's fortunes. As technological advancements increased specialization of work, only the selection of responsible associates could have assured him success in so many diversified enterprises. His associations were mutually profitable, for the justice and uprightness which were an integral part of his life were reciprocated by others.

> While he prospered, those who worked with him and for him prospered too. His loyalty to them was unlimited and he was delighted in seeing them share the benefits of his various enterprises. To this end he encouraged and helped them to become his business associates. No man can say that David Eccles was enriched at the expense of those who were identified with him.[13]

Heber J. Grant affirmed that whenever Eccles invited his

---

[12] "Memoirs of Bertha Eccles," pp. 23-24.
[13] "David Eccles," Warrum, *Utah Since Statehood*, II, p. 55.

friends to affiliate with him in any enterprise they felt that a favor was being granted them. Because of his reputation for being a man who was concerned about his friends and generous when others were in need, David Eccles was often appealed to by people who found themselves in financial difficulties. Scattered throughout his personal correspondence are letters from relatives, employees, and friends asking for financial assistance during a certain particular time of need. These letters always contained a promise of the return of the money as soon as possible. There is no way of ascertaining if *all* these requests were met; certainly many were, and many more of which no record survives.

Diligence, an analytical mind, frugality, and fairness were personal qualities which, together with favorable business opportunities, combined to enable the son of a blind, indigent woodturner to amass a fortune of six million dollars and become one of the West's great magnates in business and industry.

Appendices

APPENDIX 1

CHRONOLOGICAL LIST OF COMPANIES FOUNDED BY DAVID ECCLES AND ASSOCIATES

1873 Eccles, Gibson and VanNoy
　　　Gibson and Eccles
1881 David Eccles and Company
　　　Eccles and Quantrell
1883 Sawmill in North Powder, Oregon
　　　The United Order Manufacturing and Building Co.
1886 Home Fire Insurance Company
　　　Hall, Eccles & Company
1887 Spencer, Ramsey & Hall
1888 William Eccles & Company
　　　Ogden Milling & Elevator Company
1889 Eccles Lumber Company
　　　Oregon Lumber Company
1890 The Grand Opera House Company
1891 Lehi Sugar Company
　　　Sumpter Valley Railway Company
1894 Eccles, Spencer & Company
　　　Eccles, Spencer Mercantile Company Ltd.
1897 Ogden Sugar Company
1898 LaGrande Sugar Factory
　　　Oregon Sugar Company
　　　Utah & Pacific Railroad
1900 The Stoddard Lumber Company
　　　Utah Construction Company

	Vineyard Land & Livestock Company
	The Bear River Irrigation & Ogden Water Works Co.
	Ogden Rapid Transit Company
	Ogden Railway Company
	Ogden City Street Car Line
	Thatcher Brothers Banking Company
1901	Ogden Furniture & Carpet Company
	Ogden & Hot Springs Railway and Health Resort Co.
	Ogden-Hot Springs Railroad
	Logan Sugar Company
1902	Amalgamated Sugar Company
	Consolidated Implement Company
1903	Mount Hood Lumber Company
	Lewiston Sugar Company
1904	Knight Sugar, Land, & Investment Company
1907	High Creek Power & Light Company
	Nevada Copper Belt Railroad Company
1908	Promontory-Curlew Land Company
	Richmond State Bank
	Utah Condensed Milk Company
1909	Utah-Idaho Central Railroad
	Grande Ronde Lumber Company
	Logan Rapid Transit Company
	Anderson Lumber Company
1911	W. H. Eccles Lumber Company
	Nibley-Mimnaugh Lumber Company
	Black Hawk Coal Company
	Blacksmith Fork Power and Light Company
	Burley Sugar Company
1912	Austin Brothers Association
	The Esmeralda Mine
	The Lion Coal Company

APPENDIX 2

BRIEF HISTORY OF THE BUSINESS ENTERPRISES WITH WHICH DAVID ECCLES WAS ASSOCIATED

A. **Lumber Companies**
   - Gibson, Eccles & VanNoy 211
   - Gibson & Eccles 212
   - David Eccles and Company 212
   - Eccles, Spencer & Company 213
   - Eccles Lumber Company 215
   - Hall, Eccles & Company 215
   - Oregon Lumber Company 216
   - Mount Hood Lumber Company 221
   - Stoddard Lumber Company 222
   - Grande Ronde Lumber Company 223
   - Nibley-Mimnaugh Lumber Company 224
   - W. H. Eccles Lumber Company 225
   - Anderson Lumber Company 225

B. **Railroads**
   - The Sumpter Valley Railroad Company 228
   - Utah and Pacific Railroad 230
   - Ogden Rapid Transit Company 232
   - Logan Rapid Transit Company 233
   - Mount Hood Railway Company 234
   - Nevada Copper Belt Railroad Company 235
   - Utah Idaho Central Railroad 236

C. Beet Sugar Refineries
   Utah Sugar Company, Lehi 240
   Ogden Sugar Company 241
   Oregon Sugar Company, LaGrande 242
   Logan Sugar Company 243
   Knight Sugar, Land & Investment Company 244
   Lewiston Sugar Company 244
   Burley Sugar Factory 245
   Amalgamated Sugar Company 245

D. Food Processing Establishments
   Utah Condensed Milk Company 247
   Utah Canning Company 248
   Ogden Milling and Elevator Company 248
   Shupe-Williams Candy Company 249

E. Construction
   Utah Construction Company 251
   United Order Manufacturing and Building Company 254
   Eccles Building 255

F. Banks and Insurance Company
   Deseret National Bank 256
   First National and First Savings Banks of Ogden 257
   Thatcher Brothers Banking Company 258
   Burley State Bank 259
   State Bank of Brigham City 260
   State Bank of Richmond 260
   Hyrum State Bank 261
   Home Fire Insurance Company 261

G. Land and Livestock Projects
   Promontory-Curlew Land Company 263
   Bear River Irrigation Company and Ogden
      Waterworks 264

Austin Brothers Association 265
　　　Vineyard Land and Livestock Company 266
H. Other Enterprises
　　　Black Hawk Coal Company 267
　　　Lion Coal Company 268
　　　Consolidated Implement Company 269
　　　Ogden Furniture and Carpet Company 270
　　　Blacksmith Fork Power and Light Company 270
　　　High Creek Power and Light Company 270
　　　Grand Opera House Company 271

A. Lumber Companies

Gibson, Eccles & VanNoy

During the summer of 1872 David Eccles contracted to supply a mill with white pine from the Monte Cristo Mountain. The mill, located about forty-five miles east of Ogden, was being run by Henry E. Gibson and W. T. VanNoy for Ogden lumberman David James. David Eccles was fifteen years younger than the two mill operators but they realized that the twenty-three-year-old Scot was a "hustler." Gibson and VanNoy decided to include Eccles in their plans to purchase their own mill for the following year.

Eccles had made a profit of some $1,500 during the summer of 1872 and planned to use this to purchase his portion of the sawmill. However, his older brother John borrowed the money to finance a furniture business he was starting in Ogden. Lacking the needed capital, David took a contract to haul freight during the winter to Pioche. Upon his return with his share of the money, a sawmill was purchased from George A. Lowe & Company through Warren Childs. Eccles did not have sufficient money to complete his portion and was forced to borrow some money from Childs which he paid back at the end of the season. The partners placed the mill near where they had operated the James mill the previous year. They again cut white pine on the Monte Cristo Mountain near the Bear Lake Divide, and sold their lumber to Barnard White who operated a lumber yard in Ogden.

The first year was profitable and the partners determined that it would be to their advantage to open a retail outlet in lieu of selling their lumber to another concern. They bought a yard on Franklin Street (Lincoln Avenue) about half-way between Third and Fourth Streets. The yard was 132 feet wide and about 198 feet long and contained a planing mill. It appears that David had primary charge of the sawmill while the other two partners operated the retail outlet. In 1877, VanNoy sold his one-third interest to the other two partners; in consideration he also took the portable sawmill.

Gibson & Eccles

David Eccles and Henry Gibson continued their partnership under this new name. A new sawmill was purchased and located in the same area and the business continued. Evidently the two partners did not get along well despite the increasing success that the business was enjoying. Eccles' wife remembered an incident in which Gibson had traded to obtain two yoke of oxen and Eccles became upset because the oxen were old and useless. Gibson kept the retail yard and Eccles took the sawmill. Each had accumulated about $15,000 from the business by the time of its dissolution in 1881.

David Eccles and Company

David Eccles purchased a new lumberyard in Ogden and continued the retail business under the David Eccles and Company title. Probably in 1882 the small portable sawmill was moved from the Monte Cristo area to Scofield, Utah. Stewart Eccles and John Inglis had been operating a small shingle mill previously in this area, which had done business with the Gibson and Eccles partnership. There were several small coal mines in the area and the mills near Scofield probably supplied them and the retail yard in Ogden. Many of the people in Ogden had supposed that Eccles would go out of business when he and the more experienced Gibson divided, but they were soon proved wrong. David Eccles had worked at all the tasks involved in lumbering and was proving to be an astute businessman. His retail business continued to expand each year both in size and volume. In 1881, Eccles also formed a partnership with A. D. Quantrell in a sawmill operation in Gray's Gulch in the Wood River area of Idaho. This partnership supplied lumber to nearby Hailey as well as to the mining camps in that area.

The sawmills were small affairs that could easily be transported from one area to another as the timber ran out. The small, twenty-five horsepower, steam engines were usually placed under a roof with no sides. The mills produced about 20,000 feet daily with a maximum capacity of 36,000 feet. The lumber mills were used to supply mining camps, nearby towns, and the retail yard in Ogden. By 1883 Eccles had expanded his holdings in the Scofield area to three sawmills and had opened a general store in Scofield. Most of the early buildings in Scofield were built with Eccles' lumber. By 1884 he had cleared some $40,000 on his operation in that area. He had also made some $25,000 from the Wood River area operation.

After 1884, Eccles began to move his lumber operations from Scofield into other areas. In Scofield the demand for lumber had decreased sharply with the slump in the mines. The government was also becoming increasingly regulatory in regards to the use of timber lands. On their own responsibility, lumbermen were cutting timber on unsurveyed government lands. In 1886 Eccles was singled out for prosecution in regard to this activity, although (or perhaps because) in 1885 he had made an effort to alleviate the disputes with the government by organizing and presiding over a Lumbermen's Convention in Logan, Utah to work with the government to establish a more reasonable policy. (See discussion of the problem in Chapter 9.) The decrease in local demand and increase in governmental harrassment probably explain Eccles' departure from the Scofield area. After 1884 most of the mills were moved to other areas, although some lumbering continued. In 1894, with Stewart Eccles going on a mission and David more interested in Oregon timber, the store was sold to J. T. Ballantyne for $7,300.

The David Eccles and Company lumberyard in Ogden was successful in competing with other Ogden yards. The Wood River operation was not near a railroad and as the Scofield operation slowed it became necessary to try to locate a good timber source close to transportation. The lumberyard in Ogden demanded large quantities and a ready supply seemed to be available along the route of the Utah and Northern Railroad near the Idaho-Montana border.

Eccles, Spencer & Company

When the Utah & Northern was built from Pocatello, Idaho to Dillon, Montana, some of Eccles' friends were involved in cutting ties in the Beaver Canyon area near the Idaho-Montana border. These friends, the Stoddards and VanNoys, probably recommended this area to him. It was close to the railroad and it would be inexpensive to ship the sawn lumber 275 miles to Ogden. In 1884 Eccles sent his manager, Hiram H. Spencer, to Beaver Canyon with one of the sawmills from the Scofield area. The lumber operation prospered and was successful in supplying the Ogden needs of the David Eccles Lumberyard. While directing the timber cutting operation Spencer also began a large merchandise store. Eccles and Spencer also acquired in that area several thousand acres of land which they stocked with cattle herds.

Despite the profit of the Beaver Canyon enterprise it was decided to move the operation to Oregon just two years after Eccles, Spencer & Company had started. There are probably three reasons why Eccles made this move: (1) The Timber and Stone Act prohibited the shipment of timber from one territory to another. Oregon was a state, so it would be legal to ship the lumber from Oregon to Eccles' yard in Ogden. (2) Oregon timber was superior in quality and almost unlimited in quantity. Having worked in the timber there as a young man, Eccles was well acquainted with the richness of the timber, now that the railroad made transportation feasible. (3) And this is speculative, Eccles may have seen the Oregon operation as an opportunity to escape prosecution as a polygamist. Both Utah and Idaho polygamists and their wives were under constant threat of the law. In Oregon Eccles' second wife, Ellen Stoddard, would probably not be bothered, nor even noticed.

After the lumber operations had ceased in the Beaver Canyon area, Eccles continued with several other enterprises. Large holdings of land at the mouth of the Portneuf River were owned by the Eccles, Spencer Cattle Company of Beaver Canyon and American Falls. The mercantile store in Beaver Canyon became part of a chain of stores known as Eccles, Spencer Mercantile Co. Ltd. They owned and operated general stores at Beaver, Spencer (named for H. H.), and Market Lake (later known as Roberts). These sold everything from chicken feed and underwear to ladies hats and lumber. On June 5, 1900 David Eccles sold his interests in the stores to Spencer Harwood for the sum of $20,000. Eccles cleared a total of $27,000 from this business.

Eccles Lumber Company

In 1884, Gibson sold his lumberyard in Ogden to John Stoddard, who operated it under the firm name John Stoddard & Son until 1887. In that year the Stoddards sold out to David Eccles, who was also running the David Eccles and Company yard. David Eccles operated the two yards separately until 1889. By that year the business had grown so large that Eccles felt it would be wise to consolidate and take a partner. Thomas D. Dee became his partner and the firm was incorporated under the name, Eccles Lumber Company. The new company had a capital stock of $50,000 and included as shareholders N. C. Flygare, D. H. Peery, Joseph Clark, H. H. Spencer, Moroni Brown, Peter Minnoch, H. S. Young, and John Watson. The firm did well, paying 20 percent dividends during the boom times and 10 percent in other years. In 1888, Eccles said he was doing $100,000 in trade every year in Ogden. The lumberyard continued after Eccles' death and on December 31, 1923 was finally sold to Anderson Lumber Company, a firm in which the descendants of Eccles still own a large portion of stock. Anderson Lumber Company continues to run the lumberyard on Twenty-fourth Street.

Hall, Eccles & Company

During their two year stay in Oregon in the 1860s, David Eccles had worked at various locations in the timber industry and was impressed with the superiority of the grand forests of Oregon. In 1882 the Oregon Short Line completed a railroad from Cheyenne, Wyoming, to Huntington, Oregon. Recognizing the opportunity opened up, David Eccles built a small sawmill at North Powder, Oregon in 1883. His father-in-law, John Stoddard, his new wife Ellen, and several other Utah families later moved into the area. With the construction of the Oregon Railway and Navigation Company from Huntington to Portland in 1884, connections were available at Baker, which was near the mills at North Powder. It was now possible to ship lumber to Ogden. While the Timber and Stone Act prohibited the shipment of lumber from Idaho to Utah, it was not illegal to ship from Oregon to Utah. As capital became available Eccles expanded his operations in the Beaver State.

In November of 1886, Eccles bought into a partnership conducting operations near his North Powder sawmill. After reorganization the partnership included Thomas F. Hall, O. N. Ramsey, and David Eccles. The company was known as Hall, Eccles and Co. A letterhead dated September 28, 1887, indicated the following: "Proprietors of Oregon Lumber Company, and North Powder Milling Company (flour). Also dealers in General Merchandise." Eccles owned one-third of the enterprise, which had obtained a lucrative contract to supply ties. Several letters between Eccles and Hall indicate there was some managerial friction between the two men. It became obvious to Eccles that he couldn't adequately supervise his Oregon lumber operations from Ogden. Eccles' Beaver Canyon partner, H. H. Spencer, was then assigned to represent Eccles and on August 27, 1887, the firm was converted from Hall, Eccles & Co. to Spencer, Ramsey, & Hall, with Eccles continuing as a principal partner. The firm continued to operate profitably until later it was purchased by the Oregon Lumber Company.

Oregon Lumber Company

The opportunities in Oregon justified the erection of additional lumber mills. During the winter of 1887-1888 Eccles interested Charles W. Nibley, a fellow Scot from Logan, Utah, who had operated a small lumber mill near Paris, Idaho, in his Oregon enterprise. Nibley was an energetic and far-sighted promoter and together, the smooth-talking Nibley and careful-managing Eccles eventually established the organization which made both of them multimillionaires.

During the same winter of 1887-1888, Eccles acquired timber interests in the Hood River, Oregon, region and purchased the plant of an old firm which had become almost bankrupt. Later in 1888, he shipped one of his sawmills from Scofield, Utah, to Telocasset, Oregon, and operated it under the name of William Eccles & Co. This mill was located about six miles north of Telocasset, the railroad shipping point on the Oregon Railroad & Navigation Company. The mill cut and shipped lumber to Utah and Idaho during the 1888 to 1890 period. In 1887 Eccles established a sawmill near Viento, Oregon. The mill was located about six miles south of the railroad station and the lumber was floated down a flume from the mill to Viento. This sawmill was located on the north slope of Mount Hood about two hundred feet higher than the railroad, and the lumber was floated down and slid into the yard. Eccles also operated a sawmill on the north side of the Columbia River at Chenowith, Washington. From that location lumber was shipped across the river on rafts to the mill at Viento, where it was cut and loaded onto cars for shipping. By 1889 Eccles was operating five mills in Oregon.

On Nibley's recommendation David Eccles incorporated the Oregon Lumber Company in 1889. Eccles was the principal stockholder of the large organization and even advanced money to Nibley to purchase his 10 percent of the stock. The company was originally incorporated at $100,000; later infusions of capital increased it to $1 million. The company took over a fir mill at Haynes Spur and also a pine operation at Pleasant Valley. All Eccles' sawmills were operated by this company in order to streamline the lumber operations. Eccles and his associates replaced the small sawmills which produced rough plank and railroad ties with a centrally located mill capable of producing all sizes and cuts of lumber. This would be made possible when an economical way was devised for getting the timber to the mill from the various cutting locations.

In the fall of 1889, when Nibley, who had now moved to Oregon, was in Baker City to investigate land titles, the county surveyor recommended the excellent timber located up the Sumpter Valley, and said it would be easy to build a railroad up into that area. Eccles and Nibley then rented horses, explored the Sumpter Valley region, and concluded that a railroad would open up a rich stand of timber. It would require an enormous capital, however, not only to construct the railroad but also to build a large lumber mill in Baker to handle the logs brought in by the railroad. A group of men combined with Eccles and Nibley through the Oregon Lumber Company to finance these new acquisitions and building: William H. Eccles, John Stoddard, Hiram H. Spencer, Judge Thomas D. Dee, George Romney, Hyrum S. Young, and the Taylor, Armstrong & Romney Company, lumber merchants. Within a year Eccles and Nibley were ready to begin active construction of the railroad and mill.

Cost of the projected railway was estimated at $250,000, of which $200,000 was advanced by the Oregon Lumber Company and $50,000 by capitalists in Baker. As plans matured, however, Union Pacific Railroad interests furnished some of the equipment so the pledges of Baker capitalists were not needed. The Union Pacific Railroad had purchased the Utah & Northern Railroad and had decided to broad-gauge the track. Narrow gauge cars, engines, and other equipment were supplied in return for bonds. This arrangement apparently was worked out by Nibley and Charles Francis Adams, president of the Union Pacific, with whom Oregon Lumber was promised a contract for 500,000 ties for five years — a contract involving something over one million dollars. Oregon Lumber agreed to furnish the right of way, grade, tie and lay the track, and take the stock of the road for payment, while the railroad received the bonds.

Oregon Lumber Company was amazingly successful — additional mills were established in other locations. The Mormon Church became prominent in the eastern Oregon area because of these lumber operations; the enterprises were often referred to as "Mormon firms," non-Mormons employed by the companies became known as "Mormon Johns." David Eccles was the largest stockholder in the parent Oregon Lumber Company, holding 60 percent of its stock.

The first train of logs was supplied to the Baker sawmill on August 1, 1891. Originally the road extended twenty-five miles to McEwen. Oregon lumber supplied its mill with timber along the line, then it extended spur lines up into the mountains. These spur lines were usually owned and operated by the lumber company rather than the railroad. Constructed primarily to get the timber out, they were hastily built and sometimes had tremendous grades. Once the lines were in operation, the loaded cars would be left on a siding by the main track and when the regular train came down it would stop and pick them up.

The sawmill at Baker was the most modern of its day, possessing 200 horse-power engines. The yard produced about four or five hundred different qualities and sizes of lumber. After drying for a year the lumber was planed and sold or used for boxes. Three hundred men were employed at Baker, earning wages of $7,000 per week. In 1896 the company shipped 2,400 carloads of lumber and ties. Near the sawmill the company operated an electric light plant which supplied the city with electricity. The waste lumber of the mills fueled the light company and the Sumpter Valley Railway. The company also operated a general store for its employees and other townspeople. Besides the large mill at Baker, Oregon Lumber operated and serviced other mills at Hood River, Meacham, North Powder, Baker, Pleasant Valley, Chenowith, Haynes Spur, and Little Salmon River.

With a daily output of 100,000 feet of lumber, the mill at Chenowith was reported to be producing more lumber than any other sawmill on the Coast. Located about 3,000 feet above the level of the Columbia River, the sawmill transported the sawn timber the three-and-one half miles down to the Columbia River by means of an immense flume, one of the largest ever built, which spanned deep gorges, hurtled down steep canyons, and tunneled through mountain caves. After arriving at the river the timber was loaded onto rafts which were pulled across the Columbia River by the steamship *Pearl*. Once across, the lumber was loaded aboard railroad cars. There were many methods of transporting logs used in logging; the Oregon Lumber Company tried most of them. They used horses, oxen, railroads, skid rows, and even steam skidders to bring the logs to the mills.

It had been common courtesy between Eccles and Nibley to involve each other in their business opportunities. In the early 1900s Eccles and Nibley had a dispute which was to lead to dissolution of their commercial relationship. Eccles purchased part of a lumber company, involved in Sumpter Valley logging, which was being run by George Stoddard, son of John. Nibley was not involved. In order to repay Eccles for this slight, Nibley bought the Grande Ronde Valley Lumber Company and purposely excluded Eccles. At the next directors' meeting Eccles removed Nibley from his directorship of Oregon Lumber. He allowed Nibley to continue as a director of the Sumpter Valley Railway but Nibley angrily resigned from this business also. The ex-partners became tight competitors, but later renewed their strong friendship.

The richness of Northwest timber supplies and the spectacular rise in the demand for their product made it feasible for companies to acquire huge tracts and to devise and utilize expensive equipment capable of handling the big trees and hauling them the long distances over rough terrain. Government land policies and timber regulations, as reflected in the Homestead Act of 1862 and the Timber and Stone

Act of 1878, however, were designed to make the land available in small parcels to individual settlers. There was no provision for the type of enterprise which was needed to utilize the vast timber resources of the area, nor was there legislation to prevent its exploitation if its use were made possible. Lumber interests solved this problem by purchasing homesteads from individual settlers who had established a claim. Some companies even went so far as to do the paperwork on the claim itself, paying the "settler" his expenses and an initial stipend while he fulfilled the residence requirement on the land. It is not known that Eccles was guilty of this practice, but certainly many settlers from Cache Valley, Weber Valley, and Ogden Valley in Utah, established claims in Oregon and sold these to Oregon Lumber Company. In the 1900s Eccles was among many lumbermen indicted for procuring homesteaded timber land in this way; but he and the Oregon Lumber Company escaped trial by a technicality: the statute of limitations had run out before the government attorneys could prosecute.

The purchase of smaller lumber interests, and the subsequent diversification of the one organization into segments were other means Eccles employed to take advantage of legal loopholes. In the first instance, Oregon Lumber Company financed the W. H. Eccles Company in 1902 to purchase timber near Inglis, Oregon, and in 1903 bought the Lost Lake Timber Company operations and holdings at Hood River, Oregon. Both of these were incorporated into the larger company. In 1910 the company had a head-on collision with the United States Forest Service over disputed timberlands. The Forest Service charged Oregon Lumber with the formation of several independent but closely related lumber firms which would then continue to obtain timberlands. The main company, however, still continued to push up the Sumpter Valley and construct sawmills along their railroad line.

After Eccles' death his holdings in the Oregon Lumber Company, valued at $650,000, reverted to his two families. The first family, by reason of their greater stock control, ran the company after Eccles' death, with David C. Eccles, oldest son of the first family, as president. In the 1920s the second family, in a transfer of stock, took over control of certain Oregon enterprises, although the Oregon American Lumber Company, a new name for Oregon Lumber Company, remained under the control of the first family. Oregon Lumber acquired the Nibley-Hilgard Lumber Company and later, during the depression of the 1930s, the Cavanaugh Lumber Company. In 1956, the Oregon Lumber Company was sold to a Chicago syndicate.

Mount Hood Lumber Company

The Lost Lake Lumber Company, founded in 1899, operated a sawmill on the Columbia River at the mouth of the Hood River on Mount Hood near Eccles' operation at Viento and Chenowith. Owned by a team of brothers: William F. Davidson, A. J. Davidson, L. M. Davidson, P. S. Davidson, and F. H. Button, the company owned approximately 1600 acres of timberland, and a mill valued at $75,000. It also maintained an office building and boarding house at the millsite, which became known as Hood River, Oregon.

In 1901 the company encountered financial difficulty and borrowed $35,000 from David Eccles. At the same time Eccles acquired an option to purchase half of the company. Eccles then acquired some new timberlands in that area and in 1903 expressed his desire to buy the company's assets. The owners of Lost Lake Lumber Company dickered with Eccles but finally sold their mill, facilities, and other property to Eccles for $130,000. Two weeks later, on April 4, 1903, the Mount Hood Lumber Company was organized to take over the assets of the Lost Lake Company and their mill at Hood River as well as an operation at Inglis, Oregon, which David Eccles had also purchased. The Mount Hood Lumber Company was really an offspring of the Oregon Lumber Company and essentially the same people owned and operated them both; David Eccles served as president, and the stockholders were William Eccles, Charles Early, John Inglis, David Eccles, Thomas Dee, H. H. Spencer, George Romney, W. W. Riter, and Henry Rolapp, all of whom owned shares in the Oregon Lumber Company. The Mount Hood company was originally capitalized at $400,000. Most of the stock in the new company was held by William Eccles, Charles Early, and John Inglis.

The company appears to have been profitable and continued to operate as a separate entity from the Oregon Lumber Company for two years. By 1905 they had exhausted their timber holdings near the mills and it became necessary to build a railroad to tap further timber resources in the area. At this time it was merged with the Oregon Lumber Company; the Mount Hood Railroad Company was incorporated, and a railroad was built to continue serving the mills after the operations were moved to Dee, Oregon. The mill at Dee continued to function until 1913, when it burned down.

Stoddard Lumber Company

David Eccles enjoyed a long series of business associations with John Stoddard in various lumber enterprises, including Oregon Lumber Company. Some of the Stoddard sons spent their early years working for Eccles at his various Oregon enterprises. The eldest son, George Stoddard, opened his own mill at Woolf Creek near North Powder. When the Sumpter Valley Railroad opened the road to McEwen, the Stoddards worked out an agreement with Eccles and the Sumpter Valley Railway under which George and Joseph Stoddard erected a small sawmill on Clear Creek which operated profitably for several years until the nearby timber was exhausted. In 1897, the Sumpter Valley Railway purchased a small engine which was loaned to the Stoddards to assist them in logging farther distances.

The $150,000 mill was burned in 1900. Capital for the rebuilding was furnished by David Eccles in return for one-third of the stock in the company. The new Stoddard Brothers Sawmill was built at South Baker and the Sumpter Valley Railway hauled the logs to the mill from the cutting areas. At the time of his death in 1912 Eccles owned an interest valued at about $50,000.

On January 27, 1914, the Stoddard Brothers Lumber Company changed from a Utah to an Oregon corporation and in the process changed its name to the Stoddard Lumber Company. The principal incorporators were George and Joseph Stoddard and A. S. Shockley. The latter had become involved in the company when the Stoddards had bought the Shockley & McMurran Lumber Company, he having received 758 shares in payment. The company at this time was worth approximately $400,000.

The company prospered, and in January 1929, absorbed the

Grande Ronde Lumber Company. Marriner Eccles became president of the company, replacing George Stoddard, who moved to Salt Lake City and later to Michigan to become a bank executive. The company also joined together with the Oregon Lumber Company creating a common marketing company, the Oregon & Stoddard Sales Company. On April 28, 1948, the Baker mill was closed and the lumber cutting and marketing activities of the firm ended. The company was formally dissolved on June 17, 1953, for lack of timberlands on which to continue its operations.

Grande Ronde Lumber Company

In the late 1890s it become apparent to many timber men operating in the Michigan and Wisconsin area that they would have to shift their operations to the huge virgin stands of the West Coast. Among those who moved to the Northwest to try their luck in those immense forests were five Wisconsin men: J. S. Sherman, George W. Dwinnell, L. C. Stanley, F. S. Stanley, and C. A. Stanley. On February 9, 1889, they organized the Grand Ronde Lumber Company at LaGrande, Oregon. Capital stock was set at $100,000, and L. C. Stanley served as the first president. In 1891 the company moved its operations three miles to Perry where a sawmill, railroad station, post office, and a small settlement were established. In July 1898, David Eccles, who was operating the LaGrande Sugar Factory nearby, purchased some of the cut-over lands from the company.

Although the company was prosperous, paying a dividend of 25 percent in 1902, the original stockholders began to turn their holdings over to the Stoddards and C. W. Nibley. Nibley and the Stoddards eventually bought out the Wisconsin men and assumed control of the company with Nibley as president, and Nibley, George Stoddard, F. S. Murphy, and Alex Nibley, as directors. The minute books indicate a profit of $93,000 in 1903. Capital stock was increased to $500,000, still later to $650,000, and in 1906 P. Mimnaugh was given $150,000 of stock in exchange for 150 million feet of timberlands. Even though David Eccles was not included originally, he bought the Mimnaugh stock and was made a director of the company in 1909. His investment at the time of his death was valued at $45,000. The company paid a dividend of 33 percent in 1917, but suffered in the years that followed, perhaps because Nibley used the company to support some of the other Nibley interests such as the Nibley-Channel Lumber Company and the Nibley-Mimnaugh Lumber Company, which were not financially successful. Having lost heavily on his sugar and other interests during the depression of 1921, Nibley sold his stock to the Stoddards in 1922, and Joseph Stoddard, E. I. Stoddard, G. Earl Stoddard, D. I. Stoddard, and Marriner Eccles became directors. On September 8, 1924, the sawmill burned down, Marriner Eccles resigned his directorship, and the Stoddards found it necessary to borrow heavily.

Nibley-Mimnaugh Lumber Company

C. W. Nibley and P. Mimnaugh were both involved in several lumber companies in the Northwest. Nibley was involved in Oregon Lumber and Grande Ronde, while Mimnaugh was connected with Grande Ronde and several other lumber enterprises there. The Nibley-Mimnaugh company was formed to buy land and cut timber along the Grande Ronde River in Wallowa County, Oregon, not far from LaGrande, Oregon where Nibley had previously helped build a sugar factory.

In need of money in 1911, the company borrowed $10,000 from David Eccles on security of two hundred shares of stock. Sometime later the capital stock of the company was set at $250,000. The most important stockholders were the Grande Ronde Lumber Company (697 shares), T. H. and C. H. Mimnaugh (358 shares), David Eccles (200 shares valued at $20,000), and the Stoddard brothers (222 shares). Nibley by this time had dropped out of the company. Fully 60 percent of the stock of the Nibley-Mimnaugh Lumber Company was owned by the stockholders of the Grande Ronde Lumber Company. Thus, after the Nibley-Mimnaugh Company had depleted its timber holdings in 1923, the stockholders voted to merge with the Stoddard Lumber Company. Subsequently all real property and assets of the Grande Ronde Lumber Company were transferred to the Stoddard Lumber Company in exchange for 3,600 shares in the new company.

W. H. Eccles Lumber Company

In 1910 and 1911 the Oregon Lumber Company came under severe attack by the government for the manner in which it had acquired some of its timber lands. David Eccles and the management of that company were drawn into several lengthy court battles. At this time a large tract of timber in the Blue Mountains was ready to be sold by the government. The Oregon Lumber Company would have bought this timber under normal conditions, it being along the Sumpter Valley line. But because of legal complications, it was unable to do so. W. H. Eccles, a brother of David Eccles, had supervised many of his operations in Oregon, such as the Mount Hood mill and before that the Chenowith and Viento enterprises. The W. H. Eccles Lumber Company, financed primarily by David Eccles, which had been set up to obtain timber lands, was utilized in 1911 to obtain the Blue Mountain tract. Just east of Austin, this turned out to be one of the best timber tracts in the region. The company extended a spur line up the Middle Fork of the John Day River, and bought a Climax locomotive. A mill was purchased from the Wisconsin and Oregon Lumber Company, a lumber firm which operated in Baker. The Company hired H. H. Salisbury to supervise the logging operations; under his direction the W. H. Eccles Lumber Company continued to haul logs out of this section of timber land until 1922, gradually extending the spur lines until they reached almost ten miles up into the Blue Mountain area. Its supply of timber exhausted, logging operations were discontinued in 1926 and the company was terminated. This mill was capable of producing 75,000 board feet daily on the band mill.

Anderson Lumber Company

David Eccles' financial empire was rooted in the lumber industry. Thus it was natural that his counsel and support were sought by others in the same industry. Eccles' involvement with the Anderson Lumber Company, Utah's largest, provides a good illustration of this situation.

Anderson Lumber Company was founded by Anthon Anderson, a Norwegian immigrant who had moved from his carpentry apprenticeship in Richmond, Utah to carpentry and then to contracting in Logan. In 1890 Anderson leased lands, buildings, and later a sawmill from Christian Garff of Logan and began the Anderson Lumber Company. Although at first several other Logan men were involved in the enterprise, Anderson soon decided to retain ownership for himself and his sons, Edward and Robert, thus forming the Anderson and Sons Lumber Company.

After ten years of obtaining their entire supply of lumber from small mills in Logan Canyon, Anderson and Sons terminated their lease with Garff, bought a mill and yard site, and moved to their own property where they continued their millwork and retail lumber business, dealing in products for all aspects of the building trade.

In 1904 the firm was incorporated at an authorized capital of $50,000 — 500 shares of $100 — all of which were held by family members. The next five years were marked by prosperity and rapid growth. Dividends exceeded $35 per share for several of those years.

David Eccles entered into the Logan firm in 1909 and shortly afterwards the articles of incorporation were amended to allow a capitalization of $100,000, divided into 1,000 shares of $100 each. In the same reorganization the Anderson concern acquired the United Order Lumber Company, now owned by Eccles and the George Cole family, by assigning 100 shares to the Cole group. Eccles owned 300 shares under the new scheme. The Coles withdrew from the merger in 1910 and were allowed to repurchase the U. O. Lumber Company.

David Eccles continued to prod the Andersons into expansion and diversification. In his role as prime backer of the Utah-Idaho Central Railroad, for example, Eccles opened up opportunities for favorable contracts. The Eccles investment in Anderson Lumber at the time of his death was valued at $110,000.

In 1916 Anderson Lumber was again refinanced, this time at a capitalization of $500,000. The board of directors was expanded at the same time to include seven members, two of them Eccles' sons, Marriner S. and David C. Although the David Eccles Company, formed by the sons of Bertha Jensen Eccles, held 43 percent of the Anderson stock, Robert Anderson supported Marriner S. Eccles in his move to separate the holdings of David Eccles' two families. By

1921 Marriner Eccles' Investment Company had purchased all of the stock which had formerly belonged to David Eccles. Spencer S. Eccles replaced his half brother David on the board of directors.

Despite the death of its founder, Anthon Anderson, in 1923, the Anderson Lumber Company continued to expand rapidly. The original company acquired many other enterprises in Utah and Idaho, among them Eccles Lumber Company (1923), Bowerman Lumber Company (1923), Cross Lumber Company (1926), Burton Walker Lumber Company (1926), Home Lumber and Coal Company (1928), Mutual Coal and Lumber Company (1941), Livingstone Lumber Company (1947), Tri-State Yards (1948), Boise Payette Yard (1948).

The unstable economy of the 1920s and the depression of the 1930s led to the sale of three Idaho yards and several years of deficits. Salaries, wages, and expenses were cut to a minimum. By 1939, however, the company was in a position to take advantage of opportunities during World War II. During the 1940s and 1950s Anderson repeatedly made ventures into the pre-fabricated home market and met with varied success. Primarily, however, Anderson Lumber Company has remained a supplier to contractors and private builders as it was at its pioneer beginning.

B. Railroads

The Sumpter Valley Railway Company

The Sumpter Valley Railway, sometimes irreverently referred to as "The Polygamy Central," was one of the most picturesque and colorful of the narrow gauge railways. Originally it began as a "logger" to move the timber down to Baker, Oregon and the Oregon Short Line. Later, it took part in the gold rush to Sumpter, and even participated in the cattle industry, hauling cattle out of Prairie City, Oregon.

David Eccles, Charles Nibley, and John Stoddard had been extensively involved in lumbering in eastern Oregon from about 1885. Crucial to the lumbering industry was the need to constantly locate new sources of timber. In 1889, Nibley in the process of checking land titles heard about the tremendous stands of timber in the Sumpter Valley. Later he and David Eccles decided that the only efficient way to tap those forests would be by building a railroad up the valley. They raised money for the railroad from the Baker townspeople, but later the money was returned when a fortunate pact was made with Union Pacific. The latter was in the process of replacing several narrow gauge roads. Nibley talked to its president, Charles Francis Adams, and it was agreed that the narrow gauge equipment would be given to the new railroad in exchange for bonds. Union Pacific also contracted for 500,000 ties annually for five years, insuring business for a new road. In order to acquire the needed capital for construction, each shareholder of the Oregon Lumber Company took as many shares in the Sumpter Valley Railway as he owned in the lumber company, paying 20 percent of the value of the lumber stock to the railway. David Eccles held 60 percent of the lumber company and consequently 60 percent of the railway. The Sumpter Valley Railway was officially organized on August 15, 1891. Eccles was named president and the board of directors consisted of Eccles, Nibley, John Stoddard, William Eccles, and F. M. Shurtliff.

Joseph A. West was in charge of constructing the first portion of the road from Baker to McEwen. Even before it was completed on October 1, 1891, the railroad began to haul logs to the Baker sawmill. F. M. Shurtliff became the superintendent upon its completion to McEwen. Besides the log hauling business the railway was also used for passengers and freight. Because of the winding road and the old equipment — most of it was castoff or reclaimed from other lines — there were always accidents, but because of the ten mile-an-hour speed they were seldom serious. When the timber through to McEwen was exhausted the railroad pushed on to Sumpter, five miles up the valley from McEwen. With the completion of the railroad Sumpter enjoyed a gold mining boom. The road even had to move its lines once when gold was discovered on the tracks. Prospectors and miners arrived, with saloons and supplies to follow. Promoters of the railway became aware of the profit that freight and passenger hauling could bring. By 1908 the boom was over and the gold mining stopped just as abruptly as it had begun. A little later the town of Sumpter burned down.

The main function of the railroad remained the hauling of lumber. Usually the lumber companies would operate spurs from the main line, extending them upward into the pine forests. They would then haul the loaded cars down to the main line where they would be left for the Sumpter Valley train to pick up from each spur as it came down. On the return trip the Sumpter Valley train would leave the empty cars waiting at the spurs to be filled again. As the hills were exhausted the Sumpter would be built even further up into the high country to tap more timberlands. The Sumpter Valley was completed into Whitney in June of 1901. Around Whitney there were immense forests, and some spur lines stretched twenty miles from the main line.

The road made good profits; in 1907 it was even possible to declare a 100 percent dividend. The management of the railroad company became interested in building a connection with the Nevada-California-Oregon Railroad, which was being constructed out of Reno, Nevada. For this reason it was decided to build to Prairie City, some twenty miles southwest. The extension was completed in 1910, but never achieved its aim; the envisioned connection with the Nevada-California-Oregon Railroad never materalized.

There were frequent problems which plagued the Sumpter Valley trainmen. Since the loggers operated year round and the little towns also depended on the railroad it was necessary to run the train through the winter. The high passes were often glutted with snow and many times trains were held up until snow plows and rescue trains could be brought in. When the lumber companies had finally exhausted their timber supply, the railroad's death began. In 1947 the Sumpter Valley Railroad made its last run.

David Eccles had for many years presided over the company and upon his death his ownership, valued at $90,000 in stock and $70,000 in bonds, reverted to his sons. Surprisingly, during the life of David Eccles the railway never received one new engine. Its hand-me-down equipment, however, gave the old narrow gauge railway a certain charm. Sometimes the trainmen were pretty unpopular with the residents, as for example when they tipped a trainload of cattle over and the ranchers had to spend weeks rounding them up again. But they didn't suffer nearly as much as the unfortunate engineer who a few years earlier on the way to a logging camp dumped beer kegs all across the countryside instead of at the camp. One oldtimer published a reminiscence of an occasion when David Eccles was riding in an observation car. Suddenly, the road seemed smooth — no bumps! "Look out," he is said to have exclaimed, "we must be off the track!"

Utah and Pacific Railroad

Operating under the name "Utah and Pacific Railroad," a group of Ogden men began planning in 1895 for a railroad line which would connect Utah with Los Angeles and other cities of Southern California. As a first step, they proposed to build a road from Milford, Utah to Uvada, Nevada, a distance of about seventy-five miles. The Union Pacific terminus had been at Milford since the late 1870s. Surveys were made and construction commenced, but the continuation of the Cleveland depression complicated the financing.

The organizing group included Joseph A. West of Ogden, an engineer for the Oregon Short Line, Abraham H. Cannon, enterprising son of George Q. Cannon, an apostle of the Mormon Church, and others. Cannon's untimely death in 1896 interrupted the company's progress. On February 8, 1897, the vacant place left in Utah and Pacific was filled by David Eccles, who was elected director to replace Cannon; thereafter Eccles was a dominant force in the firm's business.

On August 16, 1898, a contract was entered into between the Oregon Short Line Railroad (owned by Union Pacific interests) and Utah and Pacific whereby Utah and Pacific was given those grading rights south of Milford previously granted to OSL, as well as an option to buy second-hand rails at a favorable price. OSL obtained in return a five-year option for the purchase of the Utah and Pacific line when completed.

Formal articles of incorporation of the Utah and Pacific Railroad were signed on August 19, 1898. These listed A. W. McCune, president; David Eccles, vice-president; William L. Hoge, secretary; and Charles W. Nibley, treasurer. Joseph F. Smith, Richard McIntosh, Thomas D. Dee, and Robert C. Lund were listed as directors. The road was bonded for $1,500,000 — $20,000 per mile — and stock to the amount of $75,000 had already been purchased at the time of incorporation.

Two groups of associates joined together in the enterprise. One group which owned half of the stock consisted of David Eccles, principal owner, plus Charles W. Nibley, Joseph F. Smith, Thomas D. Dee, and Robert C. Lund. The stock and with it the voting power, of all of these men was placed in the hands of David Eccles. The other group consisted of A. W. McCune interests. (McCune was principal owner of Salt Lake City's street railroad system.)

At the time of incorporation the Utah Construction Company was also organized for the purpose of handling the construction of the road. Construction began immediately and the track was completed to Uvada on the Nevada-Utah border by July 1, 1899.

On February 2, 1899, Oregon Short Line interests organized a subsidiary of the company, the Utah, Nevada, and California Railway Company, to continue the line from Uvada to California. Some work was done by this subsidiary company, but the plan was abandoned in early 1901.

During the last part of March 1901, David Eccles and A. W. McCune went to New York to negotiate with the Oregon Short Line Railroad Company for sale of the Utah and Pacific Railroad line.

After ten days of talks, on April 4, 1901, the railroad was sold for $1.5 million. Half of this sum went to Eccles and his friends, the other half to McCune. The decision of Union Pacific interest to complete the line to Los Angeles had made this sale, at a good price, possible. Fair value of the railroad was $1.2 million. The 272-mile line from Milford to Los Angeles, called the Salt Lake, Los Angeles, and San Pedro, was completed in the spring of 1905.

Ogden Rapid Transit Company

The first public transit system in Ogden was begun in 1884 and provided horse-drawn car service to the Ogden residents. The line ran from the old Mound Fort school south to Thirty-Third Street. The Swan Land and Livestock Company purchased the street railway company in 1888 and changed its name to the Ogden Railway Company. Between 1888 and 1890 and lines were extended and small steam "motors" were introduced to pull the company's three small cars. Late in 1890 the Ogden Railway Company went into receivership and was eventually purchased by the Jarvis-Conklin Company of Kansas City. Under Jarvis-Conklin ownership the lines were again extended and preparations were made to electrify the system.

During roughly the same period of time, a series of owners built and improved a railway line running from Ogden to the Hot Springs between Ogden and Brigham City. The Ogden Hot Springs Railway and Health Resort Company capitalized on the supposed curative powers of the hot waters and mudbaths to develop a thriving business. In 1892 the property changed hands for $160,000.

In 1900 David Eccles and Thomas Dee formed the Ogden Rapid Transit Company and purchased the Ogden Railway Company from the Jarvis-Conklin interests. North American Trust, the bondholders, took $80,000 in bonds as partial payment for the system. Early in October of the same year, the Ogden men bought back the bonds and assumed the obligations of the trust company, thus gaining complete control of Ogden's urban railway lines. At that point the new owners pushed ahead with a program of repair and modernization. At least five new cars were put into service on the all-electric line and plans were made to extend into outlying areas.

In 1901 Eccles followed up his purchase of the Ogden Railway

Company by buying the Ogden and Hot Springs Railway and Health Resort Company. He soon separated the railway from the resort and used it as the basis for his new Ogden, Logan, and Idaho Railroad. A trolley car line, forming a branch of the Ogden system, linked the hot springs and the city of Ogden. Eccles' interests in Ogden Rapid Transit at the time of his death was valued at $40,000 in stock and $70,000 in bonds.

Eventually the Rapid Transit Company was combined with the Ogden, Logan and Idaho Central line — Eccles' renovated and expanded Ogden-Hot Springs Railroad. After this consolidation, the new company began construction of a line up Ogden Canyon. Between 1909 and 1911 the line was completed as far as the Hermitage. By 1915 it had been extended to Huntsville.

Economic troubles in the O. L. and I. Central Railroad were felt to result from the unprofitable Ogden and Ogden Canyon part of the system. It was then decided to separate that part from the remainder of the line. In 1919 the Utah Rapid Transit Company was incorporated to control all of Ogden's street railway system, the Ogden Canyon run to Huntsville, and the Logan street trains. In 1933 the company was operating forty-six cars and locomotives over thirty-six miles of track.

When Utah Rapid Transit went into receivership in 1936 because of inroads made in the mass transit industry by private automobiles and incipient urban sprawl, it was purchased for $30,000 by George S. Eccles on behalf of the mortgage bond holder's committee. At that time the company was reorganized as the Ogden Transit Company and began operations with thirty employees and a fleet of eighteen buses. In 1951 the company obtained permission to discontinue operations.

The Logan Rapid Transit Company

In 1902 Cache County, Utah was served by a transit company which owned two short lines in the valley. Although this setup was not unsatisfactory, apparently the people in the area hoped for a more extensive transportation system in the future. In 1905 David Eccles, partly through the urging of his Cache Valley friend, Dr. D. C. Budge, began making plans to establish a railroad line for Logan and Cache Valley.

By the end of 1909 a street railway built by David Eccles was completed and ready for use. The people of Logan, now provided with a street railway which operated within the city, next hoped for an interurban line which would connect Logan to cities such as Ogden. The Golightly Company received a franchise which authorized them to build an interurban railroad. However, construction was delayed so long that the franchise was finally revoked.

Toward the end of 1911 David Eccles went before the city commissioners of Logan and presented a plan for an interurban railroad. He asked to be granted a franchise for fifty years in which he would be allowed one year to commence construction with the stipulation that he have five miles of the road in operation at the end of two years.

To provide for his different railroad lines and other activities which required electricity, Eccles established at an estimated cost of $250,000 the Blacksmith Fork Canyon power plant which generated about 4,000 horsepower. As the Logan lines which were owned by David Eccles and his business friends continued to expand north and south, several other companies also applied for permission to build the line to Ogden. A few franchises were granted, but at the time of Eccles' death in 1912 an interurban line still had not been completed.

Mount Hood Railway Company

David Eccles' lumber operations at Chenowith, Washington, and Viento, Oregon, begun in the 1880s, had easy access to river transportation. The logs could be skidded and dragged to the Columbia River, then floated to sawmills on the river or loaded onto trains for shipment. The same was true of the timber cut in the Mount Hood area for the Lost Lake Lumber Company which was operating a small sawmill on the Columbia at the mouth of the Hood River, down which the logs would be floated from the forests above. In 1901 Eccles loaned $35,000 to the Lost Lake company, and by 1903 had bought it outright, and organized it, together with his other interests in the region, into the Mount Hood Lumber Company, which was owned and operated as a subsidiary of the Oregon Lumber Company.

By 1905 the logging operations had exhausted timber with easy access to river transportation in the area, so under Eccles' direction, and backed by the assets of the Oregon Lumber Company, the Mount Hood Railway Company was incorporated and some twenty-five miles of track were built into the mountain timberland. The railroad originally extended into the Cascades from Hood River, then from Hood River to Dee, where the lumber company built a large sawmill, and then to Parkdale, also in Oregon. The Dee sawmill was the only industry situated on the line, and traffic was wholly dependent on its operation, with the lines from Dee and from Parkdale serving as feeder lines to the Oregon Railway and Navigation Company.

As in the case of the Sumpter Valley Railroad, the Mount Hood company made use of second-hand equipment. The first engine was the old Consolidation, obtained from the Oregon Railway & Navigation Company. Most of the engines were wood-burners.

Before David Eccles' death in December of 1912 it had been announced that a huge dividend was to be paid to the Oregon Lumber Company shareholders. On January 27, 1913, the directors declared this large extra dividend, which consisted of a total distribution of the stock and bonds of the Mount Hood Railway Company. The dividend was valued at $750,000, with 10 percent in cash, 40 percent in bonds of the Hood River Railway Company, 20 percent in stock of the same company and 8 percent in bonds of the Sumpter Valley Railway. From these figures it can be estimated that the Mount Hood Railway company must have been valued at approximately $600,000. This distribution gave the Oregon stockholders control of the railroad whereas previously the Oregon Lumber Company had controlled all the stocks.

The railway continued to be operated by the Eccles interests because the estate was distributed to his surviving families. After the 1920s the lumber companies encountered difficulties and the railway, being completely dependent on the lumber mill at Dee, was shut down.

Nevada Copper Belt Railroad Company

It was reported in 1906 that H. E. Miller, the one-time owner of the Minnie Moore Mine which produced some $8 million, had opened up the Mason Valley and Yerington areas to mining operations. They were supposed to represent one of the best copper districts in Nevada. After preliminary development, Miller sold the Douglas property, as his holdings were referred to, to W. C. Orem, J. D. Wood, and F. J. Hagenbarth of Salt Lake City. A. J. Orem & Co. of Boston also held a large percentage of the company's stock. The Nevada Douglas Copper Company was organized under the laws of Maine; the company was capitalized for one million shares with a par value of $5 each. The officers were J. D. Wood, president; Frank J. Hagenbarth, vice president; Walter C. Orem, secretary and manager; Wendsor V. Rice, treasurer; and directors included the officers and Josiah Barnett, A. J. Orem and Henry R. Bradley. The mines were surveyed and recommended as excellent properties.

In July of 1907, the Ludwig mines, adjoining the Douglas site, were purchased by the Nevada Douglas Company. This brought the company's holdings to 700 acres of land rumored to be the richest mining area in all of Nevada. In 1908, in addition to the continued development of equipment and facilities, the company formulated plans for a spur of the railroad to connect their operations with the Nevada and California railroad. At this point David Eccles, because of his experience through the Utah Construction Company in constructing railroads, became involved. Eccles' contribution to the development of the railroad, so important in the success of the Mason Valley Mining companies, is noteworthy. At the time of his death, he had $45,000 invested in Nevada Copper Belt Railroad Company stock and $50,000 in its bonds. He was also a director of the railroad. They served not only the mines in the area but the increasingly profitable farming being done in those counties in the region immediately east of Carson City. The road began at Wabuska and extended to the mine and smelter and then on to Mason and on into the Smith Valley. The passengers and freight as well as the ore made it a profitable carrier.

Utah-Idaho Central Railroad

Reflecting an often repeated pattern, Utah's early agricultural development was followed by a period of rapid railroad expansion. Railroads were established to bring crops to market, link isolated populations, and boost certain areas for outside investment. The Utah-Idaho Central Railroad played a small but typical role in that period.

Stimulated by the success of his Ogden Rapid Transit Company, David Eccles decided to establish a similar system in Cache Valley. Although Eccles was beaten to the punch by a Mr. Mahler from the East, the Logan commissioners soon decided that Mahler's only interest was in reselling the franchise he had been granted, and in 1909 they reconsidered the matter, granting the franchise to David Eccles. The city line of the Logan Rapid Transit company was soon completed; its success prompted an appeal for a Smithfield-to-Providence franchise.

Three weeks after the Logan Rapid Transit petition a group of Logan men headed by M. J. Golightly requested a similar franchise. The Commissioners vacillated on the matter, first granting the franchise to the Golightly group, subsequently retracting it in favor of Eccles, and then granting franchises to both. Finally Eccles began construction of his line, completing the entire Smithfield-Providence section by October of 1912. The line was designed to serve students of the Utah State Agricultural College (now Utah State University), and averaged $10,000 in yearly earnings.

Meanwhile, the Golightly group had planned an interurban line running from Alexander, Idaho, to Ogden. The railroad was to be financed by approximately $5 million worth of bonds to be sold in France. The outbreak of World War I in 1914 put an end to Golightly's dream.

Two years after David Eccles' death, the Ogden and Logan Rapid Transit companies were combined around the Ogden and Northwestern Railroad and a new corporation, the Ogden, Logan, and Idaho Railway Company, was formed. After some indecision a route north from Brigham City, over Collinston hill, and through Mendon and Wellsville was chosen. Construction was begun during the summer of 1915 and completed on October 14th of the same year. The new railroad linked Preston on the north with Ogden and more distant points on the south.

Although its first few years were moderately successful, the railroad soon began a long period of decline. The original articles of incorporation were amended in 1918, renaming the company "the Utah-Idaho Central Railroad Company," fostering the hope that the line would be extended deeper into Idaho. Increasing costs led to very small profit margins despite record revenues in 1919. To combat this situation it was decided to divest the company of all its local street railway holdings. In 1920 Brigham City street service was discontinued, and the Logan, Ogden, and canyon lines were separated to form the Utah Rapid Transit which, in 1936 went into receivership.

Despite its drastic surgery, the parent Utah-Idaho Central Railroad was unable to reverse its losses. In 1926 it faced a matured interest of almost $500,000 on its bonds and was forced into receivership by a committee of bondholders. At this time control of the railroad was taken away from the Browning-Eccles interests and placed in the hands of a group of St. Louis promoters including M. E. Singleton and A. B. Apperson.

In an attempt to pare expenses to a minimum, buses were placed in operation in Logan and between Logan and Ogden. The Company's debt was reduced and by 1927 all interest charges were fully paid. Nevertheless, prospects for the future were glum and in 1939 George S. Eccles repurchased the Singleton holdings in his capacity as trustee for the Eccles-Browning bondholders. After the subsequent reorganization, the corporation's recorded book value of $5.6 million was restated at a more realistic $1.6 million. Its more believable financial report permitted the company to obtain loans from the Reconstruction Finance Corporation and First Security Corporation.

These two loans placed the railroad in a position to provide service during World War II. Profits were never realized, however, partly because of U. I. C.'s short line status and partly because of its inability to compete with larger railroads for tank cars and large orders. The prosperity of the war period largely bypassed U. I. C. and left it in the position of depending on low-revenue freight such as coal and sugarbeets. Several managers tried their hand at reversing the trend and eventual ownership of the road passed to the Amalgamated Sugar Company. By neglecting regular repairs and equipment replacement, the administration minimized losses for several years, but by November of 1946 the board of directors was forced to apply to the Interstate Commerce Commission and the Utah Public Service Commission for permission to abandon the railroad. The wire was scrapped by a Chicago firm; the Ogden buildings were divided between The Church of Jesus Christ of Latter-day Saints and the Ogden Transit Company.

Some of the right of way was sold to the Bamberger line. The U. I. C. rails which had been so happily welcomed in Cache Valley as economic saviors for the farming communities ended their career on Brazilian coffee plantations in South America.

C. Beet Sugar Refineries

Utah Sugar Company, Lehi

The Lehi sugar plant was the third beet sugar factory in the United States and the first one to use American-built machinery. It was the first plant operated by the Utah Sugar Company, which grew to be the Utah-Idaho Sugar Company.

Supported and sponsored by The Church of Jesus Christ of Latter-day Saints, the Lehi plant was built with money solicited from wealthy churchmen. When Eccles was invited to subscribe either $5,000 or $7,500, he replied that he would like to get by with the lesser figure. Contributing more out of loyalty to the Church than for any profit he might gain, he was even hopeful for an immediate offer to sell his stock for half of what he paid for it. The company amassed some $600,000 from a general appeal put out by the Church but still found itself $100,000 short enough to start operations. This money was obtained by a loan from Wells Fargo Bank of San Francisco, secured by endorsements from prominent Utah capitalists. Eccles was among those who endorsed the notes, again out of a sense of loyalty to the Church. The raising of funds for starting was completed in 1891.

The machinery for the sugar plant was built and installed by E. H. Dyer and Company, which had previously built factories in Alvarado and Watsonville, California. The first three years of the Lehi operation seemed to confirm Eccles' initial pessimism. The company lost money and there was fear that perhaps it never would make a profit. Eccles, however, ironically saw the possibilities of the success of the venture and purchased stock from less optimistic stockholders. The company declared its first dividend in 1894. From 1896 to the middle of 1899 Eccles received a $42\frac{1}{2}$ percent dividend on his investment. By 1899 annual production of the plant reached 135,000 hundred pound bags of sugar from 53,000 tons of sugarbeets.

David Eccles was elected to the board of directors in 1897 and remained there until the competition with other sugar companies with which he became affiliated created a division of interest.

The Lehi plant operated for thirty-four years, from 1891 to 1924, after which its equipment was transferred for use in other plants owned by Utah-Idaho Sugar Company. The plant was finally dismantled in 1939. David Eccles' investment in U and I Sugar at the time of his death was valued at $300,000.

Ogden Sugar Company

Soon after his election to the board of directors of the Lehi sugar concern, David Eccles was appointed to consider the question of building a factory in Ogden. The city of Ogden offered an inducement of $100,000 to the company if they would open in the area. Disappointed at the Utah Sugar Company decision not to expand into Ogden, Eccles organized in 1897 the Ogden Sugar Company as a separate concern. By the end of 1897 more than $250,000 had been raised from five hundred subscribers. Eccles hoped to get as many people as possible to subscribe, and thus engendered a personal interest in the business by farmers, consumers, and businessmen. David Eccles was elected president of the company; Thomas D. Dee was named vice-president; H. H. Rolapp, secretary; and James Pingree, treasurer. Joining Eccles on the board of directors were Hiram H. Spencer, Joseph Clark, George Q. Cannon, John R. Winder, Joseph Scowcroft, Fred J. Kiesel, and E. P. Ellison.

The Utah Sugar Company in Lehi willingly gave technical assistance. The $400,000 factory, capable of processing about 350 tons of beets daily, was constructed by E. H. Dyer and Company, and was in operation by October 1898. Meanwhile farmers had agreed to plant enough sugarbeets for the first season's production of sugar, which totaled more than 30,000 hundred-pound sacks. Within two years the plant was producing more than 60,000 bags annually.

Eccles and associates later built factories at LaGrande, Oregon, and Logan, Utah. When Henry O. Havemeyer of the American Sugar Refining Company, the principal producer of cane sugar in the United States, decided in 1902 to acquire a network of beet sugar companies as well, he negotiated with Eccles and associates to buy a controlling interest in the Lehi, Ogden, LaGrande, and Logan factories. Eccles proved to be an expert bargainer and was able to dispose of half the stock in the four companies for more than their total investment. After the sale which left Eccles and associates in managerial control, Eccles consolidated the Ogden and Logan factories into a single company known as the Amalgamated Sugar Company. As a result of this merger, Ogden Sugar Company investors received a 300 percent return on their original investment in just four years.

When American Sugar and Refining Company was forced to reduce its holdings in Amalgamated in 1912, Eccles began negotiations to repurchase their shares, but these were cut short by his death. Amalgamated continues as a vibrant force in the beet sugar industry, but the Ogden plant was closed in 1930. Dismantled in 1941, the equipment was installed in a new factory at Nampa, Idaho.

Oregon Sugar Company, LaGrande

The Oregon Sugar Company was incorporated on February 12, 1898 by David Eccles, C. W. Nibley, and George Stoddard. The first directors of the company included David Eccles, Thomas R. Cutler, C. W. Nibley, George Stoddard, and William Eccles. The first sugar factory built in Oregon or anywhere else in the Northwest, the Oregon Sugar Company plant was the tenth to be built in the United States. It was an exact duplicate of the Ogden factory. As Eccles contracted with the various firms for machinery and building materials, he bought for both factories at once, achieving substantial savings.

Although Oregon seemed to have an ideal climate to produce good quality sugarbeets, Oregon farmers were not as willing to produce beets as farmers in Utah. The year's production was less than 20,000 bags, hardly enough to be profitable. The production continued to be disappointingly low. Oregon farmers did not have the labor supply (not as many children) and preferred to grow wheat (not an attractive alternative in arid Utah). In 1899, less than 12,000 tons of beets were processed, and in 1900 only 9,000. The promoters of the company had hoped by then to be receiving somewhere around 50,000 tons of beets, considering 40,000 to be essential for a profitable operation.

Formally absorbed into the Amalgamated Sugar Company in 1902, the LaGrande factory struggled along for almost ten more years. The factory was relocated at Burley, Idaho, in 1912.

Logan Sugar Company

Logan and Cache Valley had sufficient population that the manpower problems which plagued the Oregon Sugar Factory would not endanger a successful operation. Before he would sponsor the building of the Logan factory, however, Eccles required a commitment from local farmers to produce a certain acreage of beets. At its opening, the factory had 15,000 tons in the shed waiting to be processed — more than LaGrande had ever had in a total season.

In December of 1900 David Eccles and associates made contracts with the E. H. Dyer Company and began construction of the $500,000 factory. Incorporators of the Logan Sugar Company were David Eccles, Thomas D. Dee, Hiram H. Spencer. Henry H. Rolapp, William Eccles, Charles W. Nibley, and George Stoddard, with Eccles as president.

The factory in Logan was an immediate success. The first year it paid a dividend of 15 percent. The sugar production of the plant more than doubled the first year poundage at the Ogden plant. On July 2, 1902, the Logan and Ogden factories were consolidated under the name Amalgamated Sugar Company. The officers of the new company were David Eccles, president; Thomas Dee, vice-president; H. H. Rolapp, secretary; C. W. Nibley, treasurer. Eccles, Dee, Rolapp, Nibley, Spencer, Kiesel, Ellison, Stoddard, Scowcroft, Clark, and Adam Patterson were the directors of the company.

The Logan plant continued to operate until 1926; it was dismantled in 1936. In twenty-five years of operation the factory processed 1.5 million tons of beets and produced 3.5 million hundredweight bags of sugar. In a peak year, 1920, the plant used 100,000 tons of sugarbeets.

Knight Sugar, Land & Investment Company

The estate settlement of David Eccles included 2,020 shares ($252,000) of stock in the Knight Sugar Company of Raymond, Alberta, Canada. The founder of the company was Jesse Knight, who had started his career as a miner in Utah and then moved into cattle and land interests in Canada. In 1902 Knight employed E. H. Dyer to build a 350-ton-a-day Raymond factory and have it ready for the harvest of the following year. The growing of beets in Canada was new and no one there had any experience in growing sugarbeets. The first year 8,000 bags were produced; the next few years were no better and the entire history of the plant in Canada was one of frustration. It was a repetition of the Oregon story: long distances, formidable climate, lack of labor; wheat and livestock were better alternatives. The plant was closed in 1913, and the equipment later removed to furnish a new factory in Cornish, Utah. This was in the heart of Cache Valley. The Amalgamated Sugar Company bought the factory in 1920 to avoid destructive competition with the Logan and Lewiston plants. The equipment was moved to Missoula, Montana, in 1928.

Lewiston Sugar Company

On June 2, 1903, C. W. Nibley and his associates organized the Lewiston Sugar Company, over the protests of both Amalgated Sugar Company and the Utah-Idaho Sugar Company. The new company's directors were C. W. Nibley, William H. Lewis, George C. Parkinson, Abraham O. Woodruff, Joseph Morrell, Rudger Clawson, William B. Preston, Joseph Howell, and Brigham H. Hendricks. Amalgamated and Utah-Idaho Sugar thought another sugar company would be detrimental to their established business and also a betrayal of the interests in the East (American Sugar Refining Company) which were associated with them. Nibley was an ex-partner with Eccles in lumber, and their disputes now carried over into sugar. Nibley apparently had trouble raising enough capital for the sugar plant, especially without the support of Eccles. Nibley sought support from the Sugar Trust but could not obtain it until Eccles relented and spoke on his behalf to Henry O. Havemeyer of the trust. Havemeyer's support was forthcoming.

As with other plants in the region, the Lewiston factory was constructed by E. H. Dyer at a cost of $525,000. The factory was successful, producing 12,000 hundredweight bags of sugar its first year from 14,000 tons of beets. By 1912, the year of Eccles' death, the factory was producing more than 175,000 bags of sugar. At that time Eccles owned $650,000 worth of stock in the company. The factory remained in operation until 1972, serving as a part of the Amalgamated Sugar in the years after 1914.

Burley Sugar Factory

In the fall of 1911 the Amalgamated Sugar Company relocated the LaGrande, Oregon Sugar Factory in Burley, Idaho. The first year of operations at Burley produced 62,539 bags of sugar from 21,121 tons of beets purchased, greater than even the peak year of operation of the LaGrande factory. The factory was closed in 1948.

Amalgamated Sugar Company

After his affiliation with the Lehi Sugar Company proved successful, David Eccles went on to spearhead the organization of other sugar companies, the first of which was the Ogden Sugar Company. Other factories were located in LaGrande, Oregon; Logan and Lewiston, Utah; and Burley, Idaho.

The sugar refining industry of the United States was dominated by the American Sugar Refining Company, less flatteringly referred to as the Sugar Trust, which owned or controlled some 98 percent of the nation's sugar refining capacity. The ASR desired to expand into the beet sugar industry and exerted significant pressures on the companies to sell. In early 1902 the Utah Sugar Company (Lehi) owners sold 51 percent of their stock to ASR. ASR treated the new subsidiary well, local control continued, and a reasonable price was paid for the stock. In June of 1902, David Eccles and associates sold ASR half of the stock in the three sugar companies, Ogden, LaGrande, and Logan. The price paid by Henry O. Havemeyer, president of ASR, for his half of the stock probably exceeded the total investment in the three sugar companies. Pleased with the price, Eccles and associates began consolidation of the Logan and Ogden factories under the name Amalgamated Sugar Company. The presidency of the new company was retained by David Eccles and the other officials and directors were: Thomas Dee, vice-president; H. H. Rolapp, secretary; C. W. Nibley, treasurer. Eccles, Dee, Rolapp, Nibley, H. H. Spencer, Fred J. Kiesel, E. P. Ellison, George Stoddard, Joseph Scowcroft, Adam Patterson, and Joseph Clark were directors. The LaGrande, Oregon factory was formally absorbed into the Amalgamated Sugar Company a few days later, and other factories were added as years went on. Eccles' investment in 1912 was valued at $650,000.

In 1905 the beet leafhopper or white fly (Eutettix tenellus) made its first appearance in the fields of the Amalgamated Sugar Company suppliers. This menace seriously affected operations at all Amalgamated factories. The total production of sugar dropped 30 percent from the 1904 level when only three factories were being operated. However, the 1906 production jumped back to the 1904 level and sugar production continued to increase until 1907, when the company reached a new high of 325,000 bags. In 1909 the three Utah facilities were expanded, and in 1911 the company's sugar production topped the half-million bag total.

Beginning in 1911 and continuing through 1912 and 1913, the American Sugar Refining Company was involved in several actions by the Justice Department to break up their control of the American sugar industry. In the fall of 1912 David Eccles began negotiations with the ASR to purchase part of their stock in the Amalgamated Sugar Company, but these negotiations were cut short by Eccles' death in December of 1912. With the prodding of C. W. Nibley, the trusts' interests were purchased by The Church of Jesus Christ of Latter-day Saints in 1914. The next year Amalgamated absorbed the Lewiston Sugar Company. The company continues as a prime influence in the beet sugar industry with large plants in operation at Rupert, Twin Falls, and Nampa, Idaho, and Nyssa, Oregon.

D. Food Processing Establishments

Utah Condensed Milk Company

The first settlers in Cache Valley, Utah-Idaho, brought forty-one cows with them, inaugurating the region's most productive industry. Since the valley was not adjacent to a large metropolitan area and milk could not be shipped long distances, enterprising dairymen, many of them Scandinavians, erected a string of creameries. Shortly after the development of evaporated milk H. B. Rackliff, an easterner connected with the industry, visited Cache Valley to interest them in building a factory. This was in 1902. After visiting some factories and other investigation, the farmers and townspeople under the leadership of Marriner W. Merrill subscribed for stock in the newly-formed Utah Condensed Milk Company. A plant was built at Richmond; at the time it was the largest milk factory in the West and only the third built. Its product was named for the sego lily, whose bulbous root had on more than one occasion saved the Mormons, as it had saved the Indians, in time of famine. The factory commenced operation in 1904.

David Eccles' role in the company was probably brought about through his long-time association with Marriner Merrill and other Logan and Cache Valley acquaintances. In 1908 David Eccles organized the Richmond State Bank and was its leading shareholder and president. The bank and company had an agreement which would allow participating farmers to borrow money by making a note on the milk company. Later, the milk company would just deduct payment out of the farmers' milk checks and pay the bank. The Richmond bank came to own shares in the factory as some farmers used their stock as collateral and then failed to repay the loan. Ultimately, the bank owned a significant portion of the stock in the milk company. At the time of his death Eccles himself owned 600 shares worth $10,000. He also served as a director.

After Eccles' death his sons, especially Marriner Eccles, spurred the company through its greatest period of growth. In 1928 the firm was sold to Pet Milk. Pet Milk continues to market its product in the west under the Sego brand.

Utah Canning Company

The first canning company in Utah was the Utah and Colorado Canning Company which was started by Isaac N. Pierce, A. C. McKinney, and Robert Lund in 1888. The plant was a small shack which produced three hundred cans of tomatoes the first year and greatly increased its production in following years until the company went bankrupt with the Panic of 1897.

On January 28, 1897 the articles of incorporation of the Utah Canning Company were filed by Eccles' associate Thomas D. Dee, Isaac N. Pierce, George H. Matson, and James Taylor. With a capital stock of $12,000 and with loans from David Eccles and the First National Bank of Ogden, the company enlarged the old Utah and Colorado Canning Company factory to a capacity of 1,200,000 cans per year and employed about one hundred people. Thomas Dee served as president, Pierce was vice president, E. W. Watson was secretary, and Matson was treasurer. By 1904 Utah Canning Company was one of the largest of the seventeen canning factories operating in Utah. Their tomato production in that year amounted to more than 45,000 cases. At a time when the company was unable to repay its loans, David Eccles purchased fifty shares (par value $100), and at the time of his death he held these shares, which by then were valued at $25 each.

Continuing after Eccles' death to expand, Utah Canning Company merged in 1960 with the Pleasant Grove Canning Company to form Utah Packing Company, creating a multi-million dollar concern which became the largest independent packer in the Intermountain area.

Ogden Milling and Elevator Company

The Ogden Milling and Elevator Company consisted of three large flour mills, each of which had operated individually before being purchased by David Eccles and his associates in 1886. The earliest of these mills, the Farr Mill on Washington Boulevard, was destroyed twice by fire before its four stories were rebuilt out of brick and rock. When the mill was purchased by David Eccles and Joseph Clark it operated under the name "Advance Roller Mill." A second mill was originally built by Chauncey W. West in 1866, and operated as the Weber Mill. Upon the death of West in 1870, the mill was purchased by William Jennings, who sold it to D. H. Peery in 1872. Ten years later the mill was destroyed by fire. Peery, in company with James Mack, built a new $50,000 mill on the same site, choosing "The Phoenix Mills" as the name for the new establishment. A third mill, the Stevens and Stone Mill, constructed in 1883, was renamed the Eagle Mills, and in 1886 was leased to George A. Lowe.

In 1888 these three mills were consolidated as the Ogden Milling and Elevator Company with a capital stock of $200,000. The owners were David Eccles, Joseph Clark, James Mack, D. H. Peery, W. S. Stone, L. S. Hills, J. W. Abbott, and George A. Lowe. James Mack was chosen president, W. Abbott, secretary and treasurer, and Joseph Clark, manager. In 1890 the company expanded its milling capacity of five hundred barrels per day, and marketed its product throughout Utah, Idaho, Wyoming, Nevada, Montana, and Texas. The Eagle Mills were sold sometime before 1892 and the Taylor Mills, just south of Ogden, were purchased. This mill had been built in 1853 by Daniel Burch, and was purchased five years later by Apostle John Taylor.

Under the leadership of Joseph Clark and David Eccles, Ogden Milling & Elevator continued to expand, shipping as much as ten million pounds of flour outside the United States in 1902. The company purchased 30,000 bushels of wheat in Utah, mostly from Cache or Weber counties. The company terminated shortly after Eccles' death in 1912. His investment at that time was valued at $32,000.

Shupe-Williams Candy Company

Concurrent with the birth of Utah's sugar industry was the advent of the candy business, one notable undertaking being the Shupe-Williams Candy Company of Ogden, Utah. The company's first president and manager, William R. Williams, was involved, at the age of twenty-three, in a partnership with Daniel W. Shupe and John Pawlas. Pawlas soon withdrew and shortly after the firm's incorporation in 1900 the death of Daniel Shupe left Williams sole owner of the growing concern. Ogden-born William Williams displayed his entrepreneurial skill as the Shupe-Williams Candy Company marketed chocolates, bon bons, and other confections in Utah, Wyoming, Idaho, Oregon, Nevada, Colorado, the Northwest, the Pacific Coast, and Hawaii. The company employed some two hundred people as well as fifteen traveling salesmen.

David Eccles' interest in the Shupe-Williams Candy Company came about as a product of the necessarily symbiotic relationship between his Ogden banks and his Ogden sugar factory with this large user of his services. At his death Eccles' estate listed two hundred shares of Shupe-Williams in his name, amounting to $23,000 worth of company stock.

E. Construction

Utah Construction Company

The growth of the Utah Construction Company from a small extension of a grocery business to an international giant with interests in mining, construction, and real estate closely parallels the economic growth and development of the western United States.

Four brothers of the Corey family, George L., Charles J., Amos B., Warren W., and a half-brother, J. E. Spaulding, were the original founders of the company. Both the Coreys and the Spauldings were early Utah pioneers, the Spauldings having arrived in 1847 in Brigham Young's wagon company and the Coreys a few years later in the early 1850's. After settling in Uinta, a small town south of Ogden of only twenty families, the brothers were prompted into the grocery business by the accelerating railroad boom of 1868-1869 and the relatively greater opportunities of merchandising over farming. As long as Uinta was the railroad shipping terminal everyone prospered, but with the completion of the Utah Central Railroad from Ogden to Salt Lake City in 1870, the boom ended.

After several bleak years the Corey grocery and supply business was moved to Ogden where, a short time later, the brothers first entered the construction business by bidding on and winning a contract for the excavation work, road bed, and track of the Oregon Short Line Railroad running from Granger, Wyoming to Huntington, Oregon, a total length of about 550 miles. During the years following this first contract, the Corey brothers accepted contracts on railroads throughout the western United States. Crews of up to five hundred were employed under the supervision of four of the five brothers. The fifth remained in Ogden to supervise the grocery business, which thrived by outfitting the construction firm. In 1887, in a move which was to have far-reaching importance to the fledgling Corey Brothers Construction Company, Edmond O. (married to a Corey sister) and

William H. Wattis were made full partners in the firm. The Wattis brothers eventually became the driving force in the company. The growing firm provided much needed employment for Utah's settlers who, in turn, provided a standard of order, cleanliness, and work that was exemplary in the railroad construction business.

In 1893 Corey Brothers and Co. accepted a contract for a railroad between Astoria and Portland, Oregon. Because of a general business depression that year, the railroad was unable to meet its obligations and the heavily committed construction company found itself in financial difficulty. W. H. Wattis appealed to David Eccles who, through the First National Bank of Ogden, was able to provide adequate financing. Shortly after finishing the Astoria-Portland contract, Wattis returned to First National of Ogden seeking operating funds for a ten-mile project on the Columbia River. Through mortgages, the funds were made available, and after the project was completed, the construction company was able to liquidate its debt to First National.

During the next few years the company was forced, on several occasions, to secure financing from First National of Ogden. Sensing management problems, David Eccles and Thomas Dee encouraged a reorganization. Eccles, who had great faith in W. H. Wattis, used his power as head of the creditor bank to send Wattis to Nevada with instructions to terminate work on the existing contracts in order to minimize impending losses. Wattis was able to persuade Eccles to carry the company through with his personal funds. In 1900 the company was reorganized as the Utah Construction Company with a total capital of $200,000. Eccles received one-third of the stock, his associates Thomas Dee and James Pingree one-sixth each, and the Wattis brothers the remaining third. The Corey brothers were moved into less critical positions.

After several good years Utah Construction was in a position to bid on the largest railroad contract ever let west of Chicago — construction of the Western Pacific Railroad line from Salt Lake City to Oroville, California. Eccles used his personal reputation in aiding the relatively unknown company to secure the immense contract. The building of the railroad occupied five years and entailed the overcoming of financial as well as engineering difficulties. At one time, because of a fund shortage during the Panic of 1907, the directors of Western Pacific began to slow down the construction. Utah Construction's crews were cut by 25 percent and later by a full 60 percent. For operating funds the company was dependent on percentages paid for completion of each segment of the track, but Eccles and Wattis were able to resolve the difficulty by arranging a compromise with railroad officials. At another time, two checks totaling $225,000 were deposited in a bank that failed the following day. Eccles personally gave $100,000 and donated another $125,000 of Ogden First National's undivided profits to cover the loss. When the project was completed it was hailed as one of the great engineering marvels of modern times and Utah Construction was able to liquidate all its obligations. The net worth of Eccles' Utah Construction stock was valued at $705,000 in 1912.

Shortly before David Eccles' death, Utah Construction diversified by buying into Vineyard Land and Livestock Company. This company was weakened at the death of John Sparks, ex-governor of Nevada and one of the firm's founders, and because of quarrels between his successors, the company was offered for sale. Adam Patterson, an Ogden businessman, interested Eccles in the holdings, and, at the time of his death in 1912, Eccles was serving as president of both the Utah Construction Company and the Vineyard concern. The immense Vineyard Ranch comprised some three million acres in the high green country of Idaho, Utah, and Nevada. Some 42,000 sheep, 50,000 cattle, and 3,000 horses were grazed in the summer; they wintered in the lower, desert areas. Excellent water rights made it possible to feed the cattle with hay grown on the ranch.

After completing the great Western Railroad project, Utah Construction continued its railroad work and also branched out into irrigation and dam work. Many of its contracts were sub-contracted to other firms, thus giving rise to a whole generation of Utah contractors. Eccles and the Wattis brothers proved to be an efficient team.

When Eccles died, the transfer of his assets required payment of a large inheritance tax. To raise the necessary cash, his son, David C. Eccles, sold his father's personal interest in Vineyard Land and Livestock Company, valued at $312,000, to Utah Construction. Eccles' ownership in Utah Construction reverted to the Eccles Investment Company.

In the 1930s under Marriner Eccles' leadership, Utah Construction formed the nucleus of the six-company consortium that built the $49 million Boulder Dam (later renamed Hoover Dam). Later, the same group built such large projects as the Grand Coulee Dam and the Bonneville system. When the consortium was dissolved, Utah Construction had become one of the world's largest construction firms.

Under Marriner Eccles' guidance that firm shifted its emphasis from construction to the higher-profit mining industry, becoming the Utah Construction and Mining Company and eventually selling its construction division to the Fluor Corporation for $10,750,000. Now incorporated as Utah International, Inc., and the key holding company in the network of firms owned by the Eccles family, it is one of America's largest industrial corporations — with a story to warm the heart of any village groceryman.

United Order Manufacturing and Building Company

Founded in Cache Valley in 1875, the United Order Manufacturing and Building Company was an outgrowth of the Mormon belief in consecration, but was operated as a joint stock company as a community enterprise. The Logan Second Ward of The Church of Jesus Christ of Latter-day Saints founded the company from two firms, the Card and Sons Saw Mill and P. N. Peterson and Sons Planing Mill. The original name, "The Second Ward Manufacturing and Building Company of Logan," was later changed to the United Order Manufacturing and Building Company. On January 10, 1876, the articles of association were approved with Henry Ballard, bishop of the ward, president; P. N. Peterson, vice president; C. O. Card, manager; J. E. Hyde, secretary; C. W. Card, treasurer. C. W. Nibley and J. M. Wright were additional members of the board.

The cooperative acquired machinery from eastern firms to produce items necessary for pioneer life, and created employment for people in the ward. During the first spring of the company's existence, the cooperative built a company store, the U. O. Store, which, for a time, did the largest retail business of any store in Cache Valley. In 1877 the Third Ward of Logan combined its cooperative dairy with the company, adding another line of goods. The company prospered and built several new structures in Logan, including the Cache County Court House; sold large quantities of furniture, butter, cheese, and other retail items; and supplied 50,000 ties for the Oregon Short Line.

Despite the early success the company ran into financial difficulties in 1882-1883. C. W. Nibley and Thomas Cardon approached David Eccles for assistance. Eccles bought a half interest in the concern and gave good advice as a director. The company began to pay regular dividends of 15 percent on capital stock. The company remained productive until 1909, when it was sold to George Cole and Sons.

Eccles Building

The Eccles building was originally constructed by the Utah Loan and Trust Company on Washington and Twenty-Fourth street in Ogden at a cost of $340,000. This company was doing a general banking, mortgage, loan, real estate, and fire insurance business. With a capital of $200,000, Utah Loan also operated a branch bank in Brigham. Many of David Eccles' friends and associates were involved in the company, including N. C. Flygare, John Watson, Joseph Barton, F. M. Shurtliff, H. H. Rolapp, and Matthew Browning. In March 1893 the Ogden bank's impressive building was burned by fire. David Eccles bought the gutted building at a cost of some $100,000, refurnished and rebuilt part of the burnt structure, and began using it as an office building for his firms and others. It became a choice location for insurance offices, barber shops, medical and law offices, and commercial outlets; the Weber Club rented the fifth floor.

In 1911 another fire completely destroyed the building. The estimated loss of the blaze to Eccles himself was set at $250,000 and total estimates of damage went as high as $750,000. Eccles surveyed the damage and formulated plans to rebuild a modern eight-story structure on the site. Litigation concerning the south wall between David Eccles and the Commercial National Bank delayed the proposed construction until sometime after Eccles' death in 1912. The building was constructed later, and is still (1975) standing — a center of Ogden business and professional endeavors.

F. Banks and Insurance Companies

Deseret National Bank

It was the practice of the Deseret National Bank to involve the leading businessmen of the region as its directors. As a result of his growing fortunes as a banker and businessman David Eccles became a director of Deseret National in 1904.

The history and growth of the Deseret National Bank and Deseret Savings Bank are a mirror of Utah's progress. William H. Hooper and Horace S. Eldredge were business partners who had engaged in several mercantile pursuits in Salt Lake City in the 1860s. In 1869, inviting their bookkeeper, Lewis Hills, to be a partner and cashier, they opened a small bank with a capital of $40,000. The bank prospered and on September 1, 1871 was reorganized, its capital expanded to $100,000. Brigham Young was named as its president, but Hooper, Eldredge, and Hills continued a large portion of the ownership and management. On November 1, 1872 the Bank of Deseret obtained a national charter and became Deseret National Bank, with a capital of $200,000. The bank, referred to as "the financial handmaiden of the Mormon Church," continued to maintain strong ties with the Church throughout its early history.

Because of its Mormon ownership, Deseret National endeavored to establish other banks of a like cast in Utah. The Ogden First National Bank was begun by these men and they also assisted in founding Thatcher Brothers Bank in Logan and the First National Bank of Provo. David Eccles' first involvement with the Deseret National came as a result of his early involvement in the Ogden and Logan banks.

Because of the failures of other banks, Deseret National became the oldest national bank in Salt Lake City and one of the largest in the Mountain West. Many of the smaller banks in Utah and Idaho depended on it for support and security. In 1889, because of the amount of savings and loan business, the Deseret Savings Bank was formed with a capital of $100,000 and shared the same premises. By 1906 Deseret National Bank had deposits of $3.5 million.

The appraisers of David Eccles' estate announced that he held 117 shares in Deseret National with a par value of $312, and seventy shares in Deseret Savings valued at $75,250. His combined holdings totalled well over $110,000.

The banks continued normal operations until the Great Depression of the 1930s. During that difficult time Deseret Savings Bank failed and Deseret National was forced to make a "midnight consolidation" with the National Copper Bank, which was controlled by First Security Corporation. The Deseret National charter was used for the new consolidated bank established by First Security.

First National and First Savings Banks of Ogden

In 1881 the directors of the Deseret National Bank in Salt Lake City organized a national bank in Ogden. Horace S. Eldredge was first president; William Jennings, vice president; John Taylor, William H. Hooper, John Sharp, and Feramorz Little were directors. These were joined by S. W. Sears, manager of ZCMI in Ogden; N. C. Flygare, also connected with Ogden ZCMI and a member of the Ogden City Council; and Hyrum S. Young, son of Brigham Young, as cashier. Young had been assistant cashier of the Deseret National.

The first home for the new bank was the corner of the Ogden ZCMI where the bank opened on January 3, 1882. The capital stock was originally placed at $100,000, increased in 1883 to $150,000, at which time David Eccles was elected to the board.

David Eccles became president of the Ogden First National Bank in 1894, and when the Ogden Savings Bank was organized in 1900 to take over the savings department he also became president of that institution. The two continued operations in the same building and served as "sister banks." Eccles was an astute banker, although he manifested a pronounced dislike for "paper business." He never would maintain an office in the bank, preferring to locate down the street in the Eccles Lumber Company. He also would never accept a salary for serving as president of the two institutions, saying that he received his pay through the dividends the banks paid. Eccles was constantly concerned about the bank's integrity and financial standing. Twice during his presidency of the bank, the directors pushed for liquidation of assets to protect themselves in the face of panics and depressions. David Eccles each time refused to follow. He personally helped finance the bank through these lean periods, and the bank owed its financial reputation to the economic responsibility of David Eccles.

In 1912, when David Eccles died after having provided the crucial direction of the banks for almost twenty years, his holdings in the two banks were valued at $270,000. Although this stock went initially into David Eccles and Eccles Investment companies, as family holding companies, these shares came to be owned exclusively by the second family. First National Bank of Ogden is now the parent charter bank of First Security Corporation, largest financial system in Utah and Idaho.

Thatcher Brothers Banking Company

Thatcher Brothers Bank of Logan, Utah began in 1883 when, some two years after organizing the Ogden First National Bank, the directors of the Deseret National Bank of Salt Lake City advanced a significant amount of cash to the Thatcher brothers, Aaron, Moses, and John, to enable them to begin a bank in Logan. All of the original organizers of the bank were connected with the Utah and Northern Railroad which had just been completed from Ogden to Dillon, Montana. Of its original $58,500 capital, $23,000 came from Deseret National. In 1888 the bank was incorporated as the Thatcher Brothers Banking Company, with a capital of $100,000. The new bank was closely tied to Deseret National and Mormon Church circles in Salt Lake City, several of its directors were married to daughters of Brigham Young, and Moses Thatcher was serving as a member of the Quorum of the Twelve Apostles.

A reflection of the close connection among the Deseret, Ogden, and Logan banks is found in the involvement of David Eccles in all three. In 1900 Eccles owned ten shares in the Thatcher bank; in 1904 was elected to its board of directors; and later declined its presidency.

In 1912 when the bank and the opera company quartered above it were destroyed by fire, temporary offices were established in a building owned by Eccles.

Upon Eccles' death, his position as a director was assumed by his son Marriner S. Eccles. Marriner took every available chance to increase his stock and eventually controlled the major portion of the bank through the Eccles Investment Company. A new building was erected to house not only the bank but also the Eccles Hotel. By the early twenties, the original Thatcher owners had faded out of the picture.

The Thatcher Bank's prosperity rested on the agricultural productivity of the surrounding region. Wheat, sugarbeets, peas, and the dairy industry all contributed to this prosperity and helped attract such large employers as California Packing Company (now Del Monte), Amalgamated Sugar, and Utah State University. This base helped push the bank's total resources to more than $2.2 million in the mid-twenties. Incorporated into the First Security Corporation in 1928, the bank easily survived the depression of the 1930s, and has continued to expand.

Burley State Bank

David Eccles founded the first bank in Burley, the Burley State Bank, in 1906. He was interested in the region because of its sugarbeet production possibilities; in 1906 he envisioned locating a sugar factory there, though he did not build it for another six years. Eccles was the first president of the bank, although most of the supervision of the actual banking operations was handled by local people. M. S. Browning, a longtime Ogden partner, joined Eccles in the enterprise. When Eccles died in December of 1912, his estate listed holdings of forty shares in the Burley State Bank with a value of $4,000. M. S. Browning succeeded Eccles as president, and later he was in turn succeeded by L. R. Eccles.

In the center of an expanding agricultural area, Burley had four banks by 1920 — more than justified under normal circumstances. Three of the four banks, including the Burley State Bank, failed during the depression of 1921.

State Bank of Brigham City

In the fall of 1890 O. G. Snow opened the first bank in Brigham City, the Bank of Brigham City. A year later Snow and John T. Rich formed a partnership to run the bank, the name remaining unchanged. In 1891 the Utah Loan and Trust Company of Ogden established a bank in the community. In the summer of 1892 Rich and Snow purchased the other bank and occupied its quarters. Later Snow sold his portion of the Bank of Brigham City to his partner John Rich, who continued to operate the bank until its reorganization.

David Eccles and M. S. Browning and their Ogden associates, along with several local businessmen, reorganized the bank in 1906, changing the name to The State Bank of Brigham City. Eccles served as president of the institution, although Browning presided over most of the board meetings. Eccles was the largest shareholder with thirty-five shares, valued at $7,000, and Browning had twenty-five. At the time of the reorganization, the bank's deposits were $276,000; by 1911 deposits had increased to $500,000. After Eccles' death, Browning assumed the presidency. The State Bank merged with another Brigham City bank in 1922 to form Security State Bank. This bank later became part of the First Security System.

State Bank of Richmond

David Eccles helped establish the first bank in Richmond, along with Moses Thatcher, M. S. Browning, Adam Patterson, and Newell Bullen. The bank was capitalized for $25,000 when it was incorporated in 1908. As the largest stockholder, with fifty shares, Eccles became president. The board of directors was made up of men representing Ogden, Logan, and Richmond interests, with three men from each area serving on the nine-member board.

In 1904 the opening of the Utah Condensed Milk Company plant in Richmond assured a ready market for the farmer's milk production. The Richmond State Bank worked closely with the plant, enabling the farmers to obtain agricultural financing and credit. The plant's need for banking services is probably one of the reasons for the establishment of the bank. The bank's assets of $59,000 doubled by 1910, and continued to increase. By 1920 assets were in excess of $188,000. After Eccles' death in 1912, Marriner S. Browning assumed the presidency. The Richmond State Bank later became one of the network of First Security Bank serving Utah, Idaho, and Wyoming.

Hyrum State Bank

David Eccles, M. S. Browning, and H. E. Hatch organized the Hyrum State Bank and filed articles of incorporation on August 26, 1908. The bank was set up in typical Eccles fashion: although Eccles and his associates controlled it with 126 of the 250 shares, many local people purchased one, two, or three shares. J. P. Corry was the first cashier and he generally supervised the bank's operation. Eccles was elected a director and made president of the bank although he was more aptly characterized as "investor and silent partner."

The bank immediately prospered but it was not until 1910 that it got its full $25,000 authorized capital. It maintained close relations with the Thatcher Brothers Bank in Logan and also the Ogden First National, with both of which Eccles was involved. The bank paid good dividends, although it followed Eccles' policy of retaining a substantial part of earnings. Marriner Eccles worked in the bank along with Orval W. Adams for a short length of time. After Eccles' death in 1912, the bank continued in operation, with Matthew Browning succeeding Eccles to the presidency.

Home Fire Insurance Company

In the fall of 1886 the Home Fire Insurance Company, one of the initial fire insurance ventures of the western United States, was incorporated with a capital stock of $200,000, half of which was paid. The officers and directors that were elected at the first meeting were retained for a number of years. They consisted of Heber J. Grant, president; James Sharp, vice president; Elias A. Smith, secretary and treasurer; H. J. Grant, John C. Cutler, John Henry Smith, James Sharp, Philo T. Farnsworth, Thomas G. Webber, George Romney, David Eccles, and Henry Dinwoodey, directors.

The year 1893 — a year of depression and panic — was a difficult one for insurance entrepreneurs and especially difficult in Utah because of the extensive fires that took place that year. Nevertheless, Home Fire Insurance Company presented its stockholders with a profitable year. Whereas there were thirty local insurance institutions west of Denver at the time Home Fire Insurance was founded, by the late 1890s there remained only three. The success of Home Fire was partly a result of the willingness of the people to invest in a "home" institution and partly a result of wise management and investment on the part of the company's officers and directors. One result of the continued growth of the company was its branching to other states. Offices were established in Utah, Arizona, Idaho, Wyoming, Washington, Montana, California, and parts of British Columbia. David Eccles' investment in this company, of which he was a long-time director, was valued at $45,000 at the time of his death. By the time of Eccles' death in 1912 the Home Fire Insurance Company was reportedly the only insurance business in the million dollar class between Chicago and the West Coast.

G. Land and Livestock Projects

Promontory-Curlew Land Company

When the Union Pacific and Central Pacific Railroad companies began building the transcontinental line, the United States government made a series of land grants to the two companies. Each company was to receive all the odd numbered sections extending twenty miles on either side of its tracks. Under this system, the Central Pacific received alternate sections of a tract of land beginning west of Corinne, Utah, running some sixty miles west to Kelton, Utah, and north beyond the Idaho border. Eventually the 400,000 acres in the grant became the personal property of Charles Crocker, one of the founders of Central Pacific.

Upon Crocker's death, two companies, the Promontory Ranch Company and the Curlew Ranch Company, were organized to handle the vast stock ranches then operating on the tract. The Crocker holdings included most of the water resources of the entire area and thus it was nearly impossible for the owners of the even numbered sections to use their land to good advantage. Nonetheless the Crocker interests refused to sell any portion of the land in small parcels. Late in 1908 Congressman Joseph Howell of Wellsville and Logan and David Eccles proposed the purchase of all the Crocker holdings in Utah and Idaho. The Promontory-Curlew Land Company was formed with Eccles as president, Joseph Howell as vice president, and another prominent Richmond and Logan man, Herschel Bullen, Jr., as secretary. H. E. Hatch was the first treasurer of the company and the remaining members of the board of directors were M. S. Browning, Oleen N. Stohl, and S. A. Langton. In July 1909 the newly formed company purchased the 400,000 acre tract, printed a glowing brochure praising the soil, climate, and boundless opportunities of "this world of grizzled sage." Grazing land was offered at $1 to $2.50 an acre, dry farm wheat land at $10 per acre, and 2,000 acres of irrigated land at $45 to $55 an acre. The virtual indestructibility of dry farm wheat was emphasized along with the coming prosperity of the region.

The 1910 appraised value of the Promontory-Curlew holdings totaled $1,651,472; $41,275 in the townsite of Howell, $135,000 in irrigated land, and $1,475,197 in dry farm grazing land. Eccles' part in the purchase had been $25,000 and early in November of 1910 the land company returned his original investment, less $200 for a lot in Howell. The Eccles investment in Promontory-Curlew was valued at $55,000 in 1912.

Eventually more than half of the original 400,000 acres was sold to new settlers and the parties involved in the original speculation realized a profit.

Bear River Irrigation Company and Ogden Waterworks

In 1883, 52,000 acres of the land granted to the railroads in payment for the construction of their lines were sold to Alexander Toponce and John W. Kerr for $1.25 an acre. From this start the Corinne Mill, Canal and Stock Company was formed. In 1888, after being offered a contract by John W. Kerr, John R. Bothwell became interested in the Bear River Valley and the great possibilities that he saw for the valley if properly irrigated. In partnership with John W. Kerr and Alexander Toponce, Bothwell planned a giant irrigation enterprise. By interesting Samuel M. Jarvis and Roland R. Conklin of Kansas City in their enterprise, he obtained the financial backing of the Jarvis & Conklin Mortgage and Trust Company. On September 25, 1889 the Bear River Water Works and Irrigation Company was incorporated with a capital stock of $2.1 million. At the same time the rights of Ogden River were sold to John R. Bothwell along with the reservoir and distributive pipe system of Ogden City. Later it appeared that Bothwell was only acting as an agent for the Jarvis-Conklin Mortgage and Trust Company in his purchase of the Ogden City Waterworks.

During the fall of 1889 the Bear River Water Works and Irrigation Company commenced building canals, dams, and tunnels. Although possibilities were apparent, the depression of the 1890s brought about the company's bankruptcy in 1893. In 1894 the Bear

River Water Works and Irrigation Company was reorganized under the name of Bear River Irrigation and Ogden Water Works Company, with a capital stock of $2.4 million.

Over a number of years the question of the ownership of the Ogden City waterworks system had been a point of controversy. Later it became apparent that through Bothwell, Jarvis, and Conklin people had purchased a large share if not a majority of the stock of the system. After a time the city commission decided that the municipality should purchase the system immediately, but the Jarvis and Conklin people would not sell. Still later a group of Ogden businessmen headed by David Eccles bought the Ogden City waterworks for an amount which would be paid in the bonds of the new company. On October 12, 1900 it was announced in the *Ogden Standard* that the transaction was for the most part completed. The men involved in the new company, besides Eccles, were Thomas D. Dee, who served as president E. P. Ellison, Jr., vice-president; George H. Matson, secretary; H. H. Spencer, treasurer; and C. H. Kircher, manager. At this time Eccles and his associates also bought the Ogden City Street Car Line and were in possession of the Bear River Canal.

The city bought the waterworks from Eccles and his partners in 1908 for $450,000. With that purchase the city received 31,256 feet of arterial piping, 167,421 feet of distributive piping, 117 fire hydrants, and a 6,500,000 gallon reservoir.

After experimentation with the possibilities for beet sugar growth in the Bear River Valley, David Evans and George Austin, agents of the Utah Sugar Company, purchased one fourth of the stock of the Bear River Irrigation Company. These purchases continued until the combined value of the lands and canals owned by Utah Sugar Company in 1902 totaled approximately $3 million. A beet sugar factory was built at Garland and became one of the key producers in the Utah-Idaho sugar network. David Eccles apparently acquired Utah-Idaho stock in the exchange.

Austin Brothers Association

The John Austin family, immigrants to Utah, began farming in the area around Lehi. They became prominent in the industries of that area, participating extensively in the old Lehi plant of the Utah-

Idaho Sugar Company. Several sons of Austin became superintendents of sugar production at various U & I factories. George Austin became the agricultural supervisor for all the factories. Pioneers in the early growing and testing period of the sugar industry, their success prompted their involvement in other enterprises.

The Austin Brothers Association, sheep growers and dealers in wool, was organized in 1903 with the following officers: Mark Austin, president; Heber Austin, vice president; George Albert Smith, secretary and treasurer; and Thomas H. Austin, general manager. The enterprise with its $150,000 capital was a leader in the livestock business. The company owned some 15,000 acres of grazing land and 35,000 sheep. The brothers also owned another livestock company, the Austin and Sons Livestock Company. This, formed in 1907 with a capital of $106,000, had some 40,000 acres of land on which some 15,000 sheep grazed.

The sheep industry was subject to its own booms and depressions. In 1909, there was a boom period, while just two years later, in 1911, hard times struck again. The profit margin in the industry was small and the prices for wool and mutton goods were constantly fluctuating. The Austin brothers, however, were able to maintain profits through both these periods because of their careful and efficient management.

David Eccles joined the board of the Austin Brothers Association of directors in 1912. He was an extensive owner in both the Austin Brothers Association and the Austin and Sons Livestock Company; the value of his stock amounted to $64,000 in 1912.

Vineyard Land and Livestock Company

See Utah Construction Company.

H. Other Enterprises

Black Hawk Coal Company

Hiawatha, Utah, a small township in the area where the famous Black Hawk War once took place, was originally the site of good grazing land for sheep and cattle. However, overgrazing caused severe erosion which destroyed the vegetation on the hillsides. Upon the discovery of coal in the area, Fred A. Sweet opened two mines near Hiawatha on the middle fork of Miller Creek. In 1909 the Consolidated Fuel Company built the first railroad into the area, chiefly for the purpose of shipping the coal out to the surrounding communities.

In Utah 1910 proved to be a record coal year. The previous annual record for coal production was exceeded by more than 250,000 tons during that year. In 1911, however, a shortage of railroad cars and a lessening in the demand for coal caused the market to slow down slightly.

The Black Hawk Coal Company was organized in 1911 by David Eccles, H. H. Rolapp, George H. Tribe, M. S. Browning, Heber Scowcroft, Daniel Heiner, and James Anderson. The company's operations were located between Hiawatha and Mohrland along the railroad route, and 125 men were employed by the enterprise.

Although the original operations in the coal mines were extremely primitive, the mines were well planned and the initial building had been successful. Later on such modern developments as room and pillar methods and undercutting machines were used in the mines of Sweet and Eccles.

In 1912, William G. Sharp, president of the United States Smelting, Refining and Mining Company, purchased the Black Hawk property from David Eccles and his business partners. Following Sharp's purchase, certain business transactions took place after which the Black Hawk Mine ended up as the property of the United States Fuel Company. There is some discrepancy as to the actual date of this transaction since some sources list it as having taken place in 1912, while others place it in 1914.

The Black Hawk Mine was operating well. However, railroad facilities were needed in order to distribute the coal more quickly from the Black Hawk camp to the purchasers. Finally, in 1914 the Utah Coal Route was built which connected with the main line of the Denver and Rio Grande Western Railroad at Martin Junction, thus improving the marketability of the firm's product.

Lion Coal Company

Shortly before his death in 1912 David Eccles founded the Lion Coal Company, which began operations four miles outside of Rock Springs, Wyoming. The original work commenced on 600 acres of what was described as the best coal land in the district. Getting in on what was basically the ground floor of the coal industry, Eccles and his Ogden business associates developed the dormant land into a busy mine that became one of the principal suppliers for the Ogden area.

To establish an efficient method of transportation for the coal, Eccles supervised the building of a railroad line which connected the mines and the Union Pacific Railroad. The line was completed in late 1912, at which time the company was able to start shipping coal.

In 1917 a particularly cold winter coupled with tie-ups on the railroad lines caused a severe coal shortage in Utah and Idaho. By continuing good service in this time of crisis, the Lion Coal Company grew in range and influence.

In 1919 the Eccles holdings at Rock Springs, valued at $2 million, were merged with the W. H. Wattis mines in Carbon, County, Utah, valued at $1.5 million, under the Lion Coal Company name. The Wattis camp, located about twenty miles from Price, Utah, began initial mining operations in 1916 after John M. Browning and W. H. and E. O. Wattis had purchased 160 acres from the United States government and began development. The combined interests were officially incorporated by David C. Eccles, W. H. Wattis, E. O. Wattis, Joseph Scowcroft, M. S. Browning, and J. M. Browning. D. H. Pape and J. T. Hill, formerly with the Eccles company for a number of years, served as manager and sales manager of the new corporation.

After the two mines were combined in 1919, business continued to grow. The company experienced particularly good years during World War II.

Consolidated Implement Company

The Consolidated Implement Company had its beginning in 1872 under a different name when Barnard White, Lester Herrick, and W. W. Burton created a general merchandise and implement company. The business operated successfully for a number of years, and then underwent a change in organization as Herrick withdrew from the firm and additional stockholders came in. The name was changed to the Consolidated Implement Company (some sources list it as the Consolidated Machine Company). The firm was operated with branches at Salt Lake City, Logan, and Milford, Utah, their trade reaching throughout the states of Utah, Idaho, Nevada, and Wyoming. Moses Thatcher was president of the company with Barnard White, vice president; W. W. Burton, director, and J. F. Burton, manager. David Eccles later acquired stock in the concern.

In 1883 George T. Odell, Joshua F. Grant and Heber J. Grant combined their efforts and established a vehicle and implement business under the name of Grant, Odell and Company. This partnership was later incorporated, and the name was changed to Co-operative Wagon and Machine Company, Inc.

The two firms, dealing in approximately the same type of merchandise and with the same type of consumer, arranged a merger in 1902. At that time each company was valued at approximately $750,000. Thus the new Consolidated Wagon and Machine Company began with a capitalization of $1.5 million. Joseph F. Smith was president; W. S. McCornick, vice president; Melvin D. Wells, secretary; Frank F. Snow, treasurer; and George T. Odell, general manager. Serving as directors along with these officers were George A. Snow, George Romney, H. B. Pout, Gilbert G. Wright, James H. Moyle, Lewis S. Hills, Heber J. Grant, C. S. Burton, and John Henry Smith.

At the time of his death in 1912 David Eccles owned 476 shares of stock in the Consolidated Wagon and Machine Company, which was worth approximately $47,600. The business went bankrupt during the depression of the 1930's.

Ogden Furniture and Carpet Company

In June of 1901 the Ogden Furniture and Carpet Company was incorporated with Thomas D. Dee as president; Hiram H. Spencer, vice president; James Pingree, secretary and treasurer. David Eccles and Egbert Stratford were the remaining members of the board of directors. The company purchased the stock of E. Stratford and Sons and immediately began business in a showroom situated on Washington Avenue in Ogden.

The company was capitalized at $100,000 and soon had erected the largest warehouse in Ogden. Salesmen were dispatched to begin selling the firm's complete line of household furnishings. The company prospered, as did most of David Eccles' undertakings, and he remained the largest single stockholder until his death in 1912.

Blacksmith Fork Power and Light Company

In 1910 David Eccles and his associates began formulating plans for an interurban electric railroad line which would connect Salt Lake City with Ogden, Brigham City, Wellsville, Hyrum, Logan, Smithfield, and Richmond, Utah, and Franklin, Idaho — a distance of about 120 miles. To provide power for the new line, to be completed by the end of 1913, the Blacksmith Fork Power Company was reorganized in 1911, with the following officers: M. S. Browning, J. I. Shepard, A. B. Irvine, H. C. Parker, D. C. Budge, Joseph J. Cannon, and Alfred Budge. The Ogden and Logan Rapid Transit Company continued to hold the controlling stock in the Blacksmith Fork Power Company. The plant was located at the mouth of Blacksmith Fork Canyon, southeast of Hyrum's city power plant. With a generating capacity of 4,000 horsepower, the plant valued at $250,000 was leased to the Utah Power and Light Company in 1913 prior to its completion. The plant was operated until 1958.

High Creek Power and Light Company

The year 1910 found four electric power companies trying to establish themselves in Cache Valley: namely, the Telluride, Hyrum, Logan City, and High Creek power companies. The initial action on the High Creek enterprise involved D. C. Budge, M.D., of Logan, four of his associates, and two apparent swindlers. These two men convinced Budge and his friends that there was a location just north of Richmond, Utah on High Creek that would be ideal for a power plant.

Although Budge was led to believe that all he would be required to furnish for the partnership would be $100 and his own personal influence, he found that he had been alarmingly misled. Instead of twenty-two second feet of water available for use in the power plant as he had previously been told, he found there were only eight second feet. Furthermore, Budge learned that standing idle at the Richmond site was $80,000 worth of heavy equipment which had yet to be paid for.

At this point David Eccles heard of the situation in which his friend, Budge, found himself. With his business knowledge he was able to have the promoters dismissed and the other five men liberated from the $80,000 note which they had each signed. Thereupon, Eccles became a partner in the endeavor.

After that time the venture was under the direction of C. R. Slusser, Alfred Budge, Joseph Monson, J. I. Shepard, K. C. Schaub, and D. C. Budge. Some $75,000 worth of capital stock was issued in which Eccles initially held 1,000 shares at $10 each. The new board of directors surmised that since High Creek had proven to lack sufficient water, an alternate location would need to be chosen, and the power plant was ultimately built on the Cub River east of Franklin.

The climax to the construction of the plant on the banks of the Cub River occurred when the waterwheel was arduously delivered in March of 1907, finally readying the structure for operation. The plant serviced such small surrounding communities as Preston, Franklin, and Fairview, Idaho, and Lewiston, Richmond, Smithfield, and Hyde Park in Utah.

On December 20, 1913 the High Creek Power and Light Company announced its consolidation with the Utah Power and Light Company, a company still serving Utah and Idaho.

Grand Opera House Company

Prior to 1880 Ogden's cultural offerings had been limited to the small Union Opera House. In May 1890, motivated both by civic pride and economic considerations, David Eccles, who had recently completed a two-year term as mayor; J. M. Browning, who would serve as mayor from 1900 to 1901; M. S. Browning; and Joseph Clark formulated a project to provide Ogden with a first-class opera house. Originally Eccles and Clark each took a one-fourth interest with the two Brownings picking up the remaining half. However, when the cost of the project increased unexpectedly and the Brownings proved unable to carry their one-half interest, Eccles took an additional fourth interest from them.

The building was erected on a plot of land owned by the Browning family and located in the center of Ogden at the junction of all the street car lines (which Eccles later purchased). Styled in a rather eclectic Romanesque-Moorish-Turkish manner, the opera house consisted of a five-story mercantile and office building on Washington Avenue with an entrance connected with another building farther back in the block which housed the Grand Opera House proper. Tickets were purchased in a mirror-spangled box office from which the opera goer passed to a foyer decorated with Moorish arches, oriental draperies, and ornamental brass work. Two sweeping oak stairways led upwards to the balcony and family circles. Above this first gallery was another, even larger gallery. The auditorium and galleries were furnished with automatic folding chairs finished in blue plush. Such "modern" conveniences as forced air heating and cooling systems and electrically controlled exits were provided. At the time of its completion, the Ogden Grand Opera House was probably one of the most elegant buildings between Chicago and California.

At the time of the opera house's formal opening on December 28, 1890, newspapers hailed the occurrence as marking "the turning point in the transition from village to cityhood"; visitors and important local personages lent their presence; and Emma Abbott, one of the leading actresses of the day, "tripped gaily upon the stage and received another rapturous greeting" in her role as Elvira. At the close of the night's festivities, the opera house's four promoters were brought on stage to receive the audience's applause.

Despite Miss Abbott's untimely death of pneumonia six days after the grand opening, the opera house prospered for many years, often being filled to its capacity of 1,750 persons. Ogden's status as the central transfer point between East and West encouraged many top opera and theatrical companies to stop there as they journeyed between larger cities. In addition to its regular program of musical comedies, operas, and variety shows, the Grand Opera House also served as a popular meeting place for local citizens and as the scene of many school and civic productions.

The facility continued under its original ownership for many years, with Joseph Clark serving as manager. David Eccles' personal appointment books show that he frequently went to the theatre, often as host to important guests. The Grand remained the premier theatre of Ogden for many years, and later, with the coming of movies, it was adapted to that type of entertainment. Now known as the Orpheum Theatre, it continues to supply diversion for the people of Ogden.

Bibliography

The principal sources for the life and business affairs of David Eccles are the manuscript holdings of Mrs. Royal Eccles (Cleone) in Ogden, Utah; the manuscript holdings of the Historical Department of The Church of Jesus Christ of Latter-day Saints, in Salt Lake City; and the David Eccles Collection in the Utah State University Library in Logan. With the recent untimely death of Mrs. Eccles, her collection is now in the hands of her son, Justin Eccles, also in Ogden. The Royal Eccles Collection in the possession of Justin Eccles includes letters written to and by David Eccles, diary and memoranda books kept by David Eccles, newspaper clippings, photographs, account books and business records in considerable volume, responses to a questionnaire mailed by Royal Eccles asking information about his father, records of interviews conducted by Royal Eccles in the 1930's with several dozen business associates of David Eccles, and other memorabilia. David Eccles' materials in the possession of Mrs. Nora Eccles Harrison have included a lengthly taped interview with her mother, Mrs. Ellen Stoddard Eccles; a movie of the life of Mrs. Eccles; copies of published sketches of David Eccles; and collections of family stories. All of these have been made generously available to the writer of this biography. I have also been provided with genealogical and biographical materials by the Eccles Family Association, whose current president is Stewart

B. Eccles. Of particular value is a typescript compilation entitled "Dates and Data Concerning the Life of David Eccles," copy given to the writer. Various members of the family have granted interviews and otherwise contributed toward the body of information out of which this biography has been written.

The holdings of the Historical Department of the Church include files on William and David Eccles containing letters and reminiscences, records of the wards and branches to which William and David belonged, files on many of David Eccles' associates, and files on many of the businesses with which David Eccles was connected. The files I have accumulated in preparing this biography are deposited in the Leonard J. Arrington Collection in the LDS Church Archives under the heading "David Eccles Research Files."

Both the Utah State University Library and the Western Americana Collection of the University of Utah Library have minute books, stock books, and other records of many of the David Eccles enterprises. We have used microfilms of the Ogden and other newspapers in the Utah State University Library and Ogden Public Library.

The following interviews with and letters from friends of David Eccles are in typescript in the Royal Eccles Collection in Ogden, photocopies in the David Eccles Research files, Church Archives, Salt Lake City:

Joseph Barton	October 21, 1929
C. L. Becker	November 6, 1929
A. P. Bigelow	November 6, 1929
D. C. Budge	November 13, 1929
Reed Bullen	July 31, 1971
	(by Leonard Arrington)
Thomas Cunningham	September 18, 1929
J. C. Doon	October 14, 1962
Cleone Eccles	June 17, 1971
	(by Leonard Arrington)
E. D. Ellison	December 5, 1929
Joseph B. Evans	August 16, 1929
W. C. Geddes	January 5, 1946
Heber J. Grant	October 28, 1929
John P. Holmgren	March 13, 1942
Homer C. Hutchinson	December 31, 1930

N. A. Lockwood   March 6, 1930
John H. Moyes   November 11, 1934
Sumner P. Nelson   September 23, 1929
John Pingree   October 23, 1929
O. D. Romney   November 1, 1929
John Watson   September 20, 1929
W. H. Wattis   ca. September 1929

General published sources and scholarly studies of value include:

Abdill, George B. *Pacific Slope Railroads: From 1854 to 1900*. New York, 1954.
Adams, Kramer. *Logging Railroads of the West*. New York, 1959.
Alfred, L. Lomax. *History of Wool and the Woolen Textile Industry in Oregon, 1811-1875*. Portland, 1941.
Andrews, Ralph W. *Glory Days of Logging*. New York, 1956.
────────. *This Was Sawmilling*. New York, 1957.
Anderson, Nels. *Desert Saints: The Mormon Frontier in Utah*. Chicago, 1942.
Arrington, Leonard J. "Bankers Extraordinary: A History of First Security Corporation, 1928-1973," unpublished manuscript in possession of the author, Salt Lake City, Utah.
────────. *Beet Sugar in the West: A History of the Utah-Idaho Sugar Company, 1871-1966*. Seattle, 1966.
────────. *Great Basin Kingdom: An Economic History of the Latter-day Saints, 1830-1900*. Cambridge, Mass., 1958.
Bachman, J. R. *Story of the Amalgamated Sugar Company*. Caldwell, Idaho, 1962.
Bancroft, Hubert Howe. *History of Oregon*. 2 vols. San Francisco, 1888.
────────. *History of Utah*. San Francisco, 1889.
────────. *History of Washington, Idaho, and Montana, 1845-1889*. San Francisco, 1890.
Beal, Merrill D. *A History of Southeastern Idaho*. Caldwell, Idaho, 1942.
────────. *Intermountain Railroads: Standard and Narrow Gauge*. Caldwell, Idaho, 1962.
Beal, Merrill, and Merle Wells. *History of Idaho*. 3 vols. Chicago, 1959.

Berrett, William E. *The Restored Church.* Salt Lake City, 1961.
Blair, George E., and R. W. Sloan. *Mountain Empire Utah.* Salt Lake City, 1904.
Bowles, Samuel. *Across the Continent: A Summer's Journey to the Rocky Mountains, the Mormons, and the Pacific States.* Springfield, Mass., 1865.
Buchanan, Frederick S. "The Emigration of Scottish Mormons to Utah, 1849-1900" Master's thesis, University of Utah, 1961.
Codman, John. *The Mormon Country.* New York, 1874.
Dwyer, Robert Joseph. *The Gentile Comes to Utah.* Washington, D.C., 1941.
Eccles, Marriner S. *Beckoning Frontiers: Public and Personal Recollections.* Sidney Hyman, ed. New York, 1951.
Ellsworth, S. George. *Utah's Heritage.* Salt Lake City, 1972.
Ericksen, Ephraim Edward. *The Psychological and Ethical Aspects of Mormon Group Life.* Chicago, 1922.
Esshom, Frank. *Pioneers and Prominent Men of Utah.* Salt Lake City, 1930, esp. p. 854.
Ferrell, Mallory Hope. *Rails, Sagebrush, and Pine: A Garland of Railroad And Logging Days in Oregon's Sumpter Valley.* San Marino, California, 1967.
Flower, Fred G., ed. *Descriptive Illustrated Review of Ogden City and Utah Territory, 1890.* Ogden, 1890.
Furniss, Norman F. *The Mormon Conflict 1850-1859.* New Haven, 1960.
Galbraith, John Kenneth. *The Scotch.* New York, 1966.
Garnsey, Morris E. *America's New Frontier: The Mountain West.* New York, 1950.
Gates, Charles M. and Dorothy O. Johansen, *Empire of the Columbia: A History of the Pacific Northwest.* New York, 1957.
Ghent, W. J. *The Road to Oregon: A Chronicle of the Great Emigrant Trail.* New York, 1934.
Glover, Janet R. *The Story of Scotland.* London, 1960, p. 317.
Haldane, Elizabeth S. *The Scotland of Our Fathers: A Study of Scottish Life in the Nineteenth Century.* New York, 1934, p. 260.
Hiatt, Isaac. *Thirty-one Years in Baker County.* Baker, Ore. 1893.
History of Ogden. Utah Historical Records Survey Project. Ogden, 1940.

Horne, J. Arthur. *Latter-day Saints in the Great Northwest*. Seattle, Wash., 1968.
Hunter, Milton R., ed. *Beneath Ben Lomond's Peak: A History of Weber County, 1824-1900*. Salt Lake City, 1966.
Idaho's Mineral Industry: The First Hundred Years. Idaho Bureau of Mines and Geology, Bulletin No. 18. Moscow, Idaho, 1963.
Jenson, Andrew. *Encyclopedic History of The Church of Jesus Christ of Latter-day Saints*. Salt Lake City, 1941.
Kotter, Richard E. "An Examination of Mormon and Non-Mormon Influences in Ogden City Politics, 1847-1896." Master's thesis, Utah State University, 1967.
Larson, Gustive O. *The "Americanization" of Utah for Statehood*. San Marino, California, 1971.
Mackenzie, Agnes More. *Scotland in Modern Times*. London and Edinburgh, 1942.
Malmquist, O. N. *The First 100 Years: A History of the Salt Lake Tribune, 1871-1971*. Salt Lake City, 1971.
Mulder, William. *Homeward to Zion: The Mormon Migration from Scandinavia*. Minneapolis, Minn., 1957.
Neff, Andrew L. *History of Utah, 1847 to 1869*. Salt Lake City, 1940.
Nibley, Charles W. *Reminiscences of Charles W. Nibley, 1849-1931*. Salt Lake City, 1934.
O'Dea, Thomas F. *The Mormons*. Chicago, 1957.
Pomeroy, Earl. *The Pacific Slope: A History of California, Oregon, Washington, Idaho, Utah, and Nevada*. New York, 1965.
Rich, Russell R. *Ensign to the Nations: A History of the Church from 1846 to the Present*. Provo, Utah, 1972.
Ricks, Joel E., ed; Everett L. Cooley, assoc. ed. *The History of a Valley: Cache Valley, Utah-Idaho, 1856-1956*. Logan, Utah, 1956.
Roberts, B. H. *A Comprehensive History of The Church of Jesus Christ of Latter-day Saints: Century I*. 6 vols. Salt Lake City, 1930.
Route of the Oregon Trail in Idaho. Idaho Department of Highways. Boise, 1967.
Smith, Joseph Fielding. *Essentials in Church History*. Salt Lake City, 1950.
Smout, T. C. *A History of the Scottish People, 1560-1830*. New York, 1969.

Sutton, Wain, ed. "David Eccles," in *Utah: A Centennial History.* III, 25. Chicago, 1950.
Taylor, Fred G. *A Saga of Sugar.* Salt Lake City, 1944.
Taylor, P.A.M. *Expectations Westward: The Mormons and the Emigration of their British Converts in the Nineteenth Century.* Edinburgh, 1967.
Tullidge, Edward W. *History of Northern Utah and Southern Idaho* In *Tullidge's Histories,* Volume II, Salt Lake City, 1889.
Warrum, Noble, "David Eccles," and "Ellen Eccles." In *History of Utah Since Statehood* II, 50-56; IV, 350-51. 4 vols., Chicago, 1919.
Whitney, Orson F. *History of Utah.* 4 vols. Salt Lake City, 1892-1901.
Winther, Oscar O. *The Great Northwest: A History.* 2nd ed., New York, 1956.
Young, Kimball. *Isn't One Wife Enough?* New York, 1954.

Notes and References

In referring to the collections described in the bibliography and in footnotes, the following abbreviations are used:
- HDC: Archives of the Historical Department of The Church of Jesus Christ of Latter-day Saints, 50 East North Temple Street, Salt Lake City, Utah.
- REC: Royal Eccles Collection in the possession of Justin Eccles, 2508 Jackson Street, Ogden, Utah.
- USU: Royal Eccles Collection in the Special Collections Division of Utah State University Library, Logan, Utah.

Index

- A -

Aarhus, Denmark, 168
Abbott, Emma, 272
Abbott, J. W., 249
Adams, Charles Francis, 87, 218, 228
Adams, Orval W., 261
"Advance Roller Mill," 249
Albany, New York, 52
Alberta, Canada, 122
Alexander, Idaho, 237
Almy, Wyoming, 44
Amalgamated Sugar Company: incorporated, 2, 116, 206, 241, 243; in antitrust suit, 123; Eccles president of, 145; worth of, 182; operations of, 185; holdings of, 186, 238, 243, 244; debt free, 201; history of, 245-246
American Sugar Refining Company, 115, 241, 242, 244; in antitrust suit, 123; connection with Amalgamated Sugar, 245-46
Anderson and Sons Lumber Company, 226
Anderson, Anthon, 226, 227
Anderson, Edward H., 72, 226
Anderson, James, 267
Anderson Lumber Company: Eccles' interest in, 122, 129, 215; history of, 206, 225-27
Anderson, Robert, 226
Anti-Polygamy Law (1862), 187

Apperson, A. B., 238
Armstrong, James C., 142
Astoria, Oregon, 252
Austin and Sons Livestock Company, 266
Austin Brothers Association, 122, 206, 265-66
Austin, George, 171, 265, 266
Austin, Heber, 266
Austin, John, 265
Austin, Mark, 266
Austin, Oregon, 92, 121, 225
Austin, Thomas H., 266
Australia, 109
Augusta Victoria, 168

- B -

Bamberger Line, 239
Ballard, Henry, 254
Baker City Electric Light Company, 94
Baker, Oregon: Eccles mill at, 88, 89, 217, 218, 223; Eccles workers assembled at, 89; mission headquarters in, 94; Eccles children born in, 111; railroad connections at, 215; timber to and from, 228, 229
Ballantyne, J. T., 213
Ballantyne, Richard, 20
Banking, 124, 207, 256-61
Barnes, A. R., 182
Barnett, Josiah, 236
Barton, Joseph, 255
Bear Lake Divide, 46, 211

282 / INDEX

Bear River, 68
Bear River Canal, 265
Bear River Irrigation and Ogden Water Works Company, 206, 264-65
Bear River Valley, 264, 265
Bear River Water Works and Irrigation Company, 264
Beaver Canyon, Idaho, 61, 84, 213-14
Beehive House, 164
Beet sugar, *See* sugar industry
Benson, Ezra T., 14
Bertha Eccles Community Art Center, 142
Bingham, "Aunt Mandy," 54
Black Hawk Coal Company, 117, 206, 267-68
Black Hawk War, 267
Blacksmith Fork Power and Light Company, 121, 206, 234, 270
Blue Mountains, Oregon, 33, 225
Boise Payette Lumber Yard, 227
Book of Mormon, 12
Bothwell, John R., 119, 264
Boulder Dam (Hoover Dam), 254
Bowen, Lewis, 21
Bowerman Lumber Company, 227
Boyle, John A., 72, 77
Bradley, Henry R., 236
Brigham City, Utah, 237, 238
Brimhall, Lila Eccles. *See* Eccles, Lila
Brimhall, Dean R., 145
Brown, Moroni, 215
Browning, John M., 194, 268, 272
Browning, Marriner, 261
Browning, Matthew S., 255; with banks, 259, 260, 261; with land company, 263; organizes coal company, 267, 268; with opera house, 272; with power company, 270
Bryan, William Jennings, 67
Budge, Alfred, 270, 271
Budge, D. C.: Eccles associate, 120; directs power company, 121, 270, 271; comments on Eccles, 132n, 138n, 175; physician, 200; urges Logan transit, 233
Buffalo, New York, 52
Bullen, Herschel, Jr., 263
Bullen, Newell, 260
Burch, Daniel, 249
Burley, Idaho, 1, 116, 243
Burley State Bank, 259
Burley Sugar Factory, 206, 245
Burns, Robert ("Bobby"), 130, 168
Burton, C. S., 269
Burton, J. F., 269
Burton, W. W., 269
Burton Walker Lumber Company, 227
Butler, Truman, 91
Button, F. H., 221

- C -

Cache County Court House, 255
Cache Valley, Idaho-Utah, 94, 120, 220, 247, 270-71
"Cache Valley Limited," 163
Caine, George E., 157
Caine, Marie Stoddard Eccles. *See* Eccles, Marie Stoddard
California, 35, 108, 116, 230, 232, 252
California Packing Company (Del Monte), 259
Campbell, A. G., 68
Canada, 23, 116, 122, 184, 244
Cane sugar, 117
Canning industry, 248
Cannon, Abraham H., 230-31
Cannon, George Q., 21, 68, 230, 241
Cannon, Joseph J., 270
Carbon County, Utah, 117, 191, 267
Card, Charles O., 254
Card and Sons Saw Mill, 254
Card, C. W., 254
Cardon, Thomas, 255
Caribbean, 117
Cascade Mountains, Oregon, 33, 235
Castle Garden, New York, 22-23, 51
Cavanaugh Lumber Company, 221
Central Pacific Railroad, 263
Charlie Buck, 20
Chenowith, Washington: sawmill near, 84, 217, 219, 221, 234
Cheyenne, Wyoming, 215
Chicago, Illinois, 23
Chicago World's Fair (1893), 168
Child Culture Club, 144
Children's Aid Society, 144
Childs, Warren, 49, 211
Childs, William, 89
Church of Jesus Christ of Latter-day Saints, The: W. Eccles joins, 11-12, 15; threatened by railroad, 41; in Utah political struggle, 67, 68, 136; organizes trade board, 74; discontinues plural marriage, 99-100; invests in sugar, 100-101, 103, 240, 246; in debt, 107; Eccles' commitment to, 2, 134, 135, 240; programs of, 144; Ellen Eccles active in, 154; encourages achievement, 195; prominent in Ore-

gon, 218; acquires buildings, 238; financial handmaiden of, 256
City of the Saints. *See* Nauvoo, Illinois
Civil War, 23
Clark, Joseph, 215, 241; with Amalgamated, 243, 246; purchases mill, 249; with opera house, 272
Clawson, Rudger, 244
Clear Creek, Oregon, 222
Cliff, Edward, 21
Coates and Clark Mills, 6
Cole, Erastus, 153-54, 168
Cole, George, 226
Cole, George and sons, 255
Columbia River, Oregon: Eccleses travel to, 33, 217, 221, 234
Columbia University, 156-57
Commercial National Bank, 255
Conklin, Roland R., 264
Conservation, 93
Consolidated Fuel Company, 267
Consolidated Implement Company: history of, 122, 206, 269-70
Consolidated Machine Company. *See* Consolidated Implement Company
Consolidated Wagon and Machine Company. *See* Consolidated Implement Company
Construction: companies listed, 208
Co-operative Wagon and Machine Company, Incorporated, 269
Cooperatives, 41, 42
Cope, George A., 187
Copenhagen, Denmark, 168
Corey, Amos B., 194, 251
Corey Brothers Construction Company, 108, 251
Corey, Charles J., 251
Corey, George L., 251
Corey, Warren W., 251
Corinne Mill, Canal and Stock Company, 264
Corinne, Utah, 68, 263
Cornish, Utah, 244
Corry, J. P., 261
Council Bluffs, Iowa, 52
Crocker, Charles, 263
Cross Lumber Company, 227
Cub River, 271
Cuba, 117, 169
Cunningham, Thomas, 23
Curlew Ranch Company, 263
Cutler, John C. (Utah governor), 171, 261
Cutler, Thomas R., 242
Cushnahan, Father, 105
Cynosure, 17, 19-20, 21, 63

- D -

Daughters of the Utah Pioneers, 144
David Eccles and Company, 58, 205, 212-13, 215
David Eccles Building, 119
David Eccles Company, 145, 190, 258
David Eccles Lumberyard, 214
Davidson, A. J., 221
Davidson, William F., 221
Davidson, L. M., 221
Davidson, P. S., 221
Day, John, 89
Dee, Oregon, 92, 121, 222, 235
Dee, Thomas: stockholder, 221; with Ogden Transit, 232-33; alderman, 69, 70; Utah Construction Company, 108, 252; Eccles partner, 215; finances building, 217; Utah Pacific director, 231; sugar interests, 241, 243, 246; with canning company, 248; with Ogden waterworks, 265; furniture company president, 270
Democratic Party, 67, 79
Denmark, 50, 54, 168
Denver and Rio Grande Western Railroad, 191, 268
Depression (1893), 89, 105
Depression (1930), 257
Deseret National Bank, 164; history of, 71, 103-104, 107, 171, 256-57
Deseret Savings Bank, 107, 171, 256-57
Detroit, Michigan, 23
DeVoto, Bernard, 194
Dickens, Charles, 18
Dillon, Montana, 213
Dinwoodey, Henry, 262
Dog Valley, Utah, 48
Douglas, Flora Eccles. *See* Eccles, Flora
Douglas, Orson, 145
Dower, 188
Dumbartonshire, Scotland, 5
Dwinnel, George W., 223
Dyer, E. H., and Company, 240, 241, 243, 244, 245

- E -

Eagle Mills, 249
Early, Charles, 221
Eccles, Albert (son of Margaret): contesting heir, 14n, 183
Eccles, Anna Vivian (daughter of Bertha), 111, 145
Eccles, Bertha Marie Jensen (wife of David): at mill camp, 56; marriage of, 66, 135; children of, 71, 111, 145,

284 / INDEX

226; comments on husband, 73, 197; in Ogden, 96, 163; travels of, 110, 117, 168-69; finances of, 126; homes of, 142-43; interest in arts, 142-43; generous, 144-45; active in community, 144; husband's death, 173, 177; in estate settlement, 183, 188. *See also* Jensen, Bertha Marie
Eccles, Bertha Olivia (daughter of Bertha), 71, 143, 145
Eccles, "Bud" (nephew), 92n
Eccles, David
──────, business enterprises of: *See* index entries for individual companies and Appendixes 1 and 2
──────, characteristics of: mathematical ability of, 90-91; inquisitive, 117; mind for detail, 123-124, 198; as corporate executive, 122; frugality of, 126-129, 199-200; generosity of, 129, 137-38, 167-68; unpretentious, 129-30; Scottish upbringing of, 130-32; enterprising spirit of, 131; word good, 132; working day of, 164; as employer, 167; not a speculator, 196; physical appearance, 197
──────, church involvement of, 2, 101-102, 104, 135, 137
──────, death of, 1, 172-73
──────, early life of: in Glasgow, 7; schooling of, 7-8, 28; young peddler, 7, 8; on the Plains, 25; in Salt Lake, 26; fells trees, 34; finds work in Ogden, 39; strikes out alone, 42; first property of, 43; loses share in sawmill, 48; responsibilities as youth, 196
──────, on education, 134, 146-47, 156-57
──────, financial involvement and operations, 184-86
──────, family life of: courtship and marriage of, 49-50, 55-56; courts Ellen, 65; marries Bertha, 135; third wife of, 141n, 183; children of, 111, 145, 157; with children, 146, 155; wants children to work, 156; manages two families, 163; visits missionary sons, 164
──────, funeral of, 177-80
──────, Grant, Heber J. comments on, 101-102, 130, 198, 201-202
──────, legal difficulties of, 93-94, 154, 220
──────, on money, 198
──────, Ogden alderman, 69-70
──────, Ogden mayor, 72-73, 75-77
──────, recreation and travel, 168-69, 197, 198
──────, Smith, J. F., comments on, 175, 179-80
──────, wealth of, 122, 181-83, 186
──────, wife praises, 56n
──────, on work, 198
Eccles, David Christen (son of Bertha), 59-60, 110-111; notified of father's death, 173; on father's health, 174; estate administrator, 183; president of David Eccles Company, 145; president Oregon Lumber, 220; raises cash, 253
Eccles, Ellen Stoddard (wife of David): at Scofield store, 71; in Oregon, 71, 86, 215; fashions own home, 86; kept marriage secret, 86, 100, 153; in Logan, 96; children of, 111, 154-55, 157; finances of, 126, 188, 190; travels, 132, 156; description of, 158; moves of, 163; attends Mayo Clinic, 200; at husband's funeral, 177; not an heir, 183. *See also* Stoddard, Ellen
Eccles, Ellen Stoddard (daughter of Ellen), 155, 157
Eccles, Emma Stoddard (daughter of Ellen), 111, 155, 157
Eccles, Flora (daughter of Bertha), 111, 145, 173
Eccles, George Stoddard (son of Ellen): born, 111, 155; works when young, 156; president First Security Corporation, 157; hears of father's death, 174; purchases Utah Transit, 233
Eccles, Gibson and VanNoy, 205
Eccles, Homer Gordon (son of Bertha): born, 111, 145
Eccles, Jessie Stoddard (daughter of Ellen), 111, 132-33, 155, 157
Eccles, John (brother of David), 7, 23, 211
Eccles, Joseph Merrill (son of Bertha), 96, 145, 173
Eccles, Laura (daughter of Bertha), 111, 145, 173
Eccles, LeRoy R. (son of Bertha), 60, 145, 173, 174, 259
Eccles, Lila (daughter of Bertha), 96, 117, 143-45, 156, 173
Eccles, Marie Stoddard (daughter of Ellen): husband of, 153, 156, 157
Eccles, Margaret Miller (grandmother of David): missionaries preach to, 11-12, 13
Eccles, Margaret (sister of David), 20

INDEX / 285

Eccles, Marriner Stoddard (son of Ellen): comments on mother, 64, 155; born, 96, 153; serves mission, 132; early jobs of, 156, 261; with Federal Reserve, 157; hears of father's death, 174; president Eccles investment Company, 190; comments on father, 198; directs lumber interests, 223-24, 226, 259; directs Utah Construction, 253-54; with milk company, 248

Eccles, Nora Stoddard (daughter of Ellen), 111, 155, 157, 174

Eccles, Royal (son of Bertha), 60, 144; lawyer, 145; schooling of, 146; in estate proceedings, 183, 184

Eccles, Samuel (brother of David), 20

Eccles, Sarah (sister of David), 20, 31-32, 36, 37-38, 43

Eccles, Sarah Hutchinson (mother of David): in Oregon, 30-34; in Salt Lake City, 26; witnesses healing, 37; feeds strangers, 38; later life of, 39n; wedding anniversary, 144; gave Eccles responsibilities, 195-96

Eccles, Spencer and Company, 205, 213-14

Eccles, Spencer Cattle Company of Beaver Canyon and American Falls, 214

Eccles, Spencer Mercantile Company Limited, 205, 214

Eccles, Spencer Stoddard (son of Ellen), 154, 156, 157, 227

Eccles, Stewart (brother of David), 34, 36, 39, 137, 212; purchases mill, 59; called on mission, 59, 213

Eccles, Vida (daughter of Bertha), 60, 145, 169, 173

Eccles, Willard L. (son of Ellen), 155, 157

Eccles, William (father of David): woodturner, 5, 27-28; marries, 6; blind, 6; Mormon convert, 11-12, 13, 14-15; family of, poor, 14; to emigrate, 16; in Salt Lake City, 26; in Oregon, 30-34; proselytizes, 36; in San Francisco, 35; later life of, 39n; death of, 111; wedding anniversary, 144; did not dominate, 195. *See also* William Eccles and Company

Eccles, William H. (brother of David): emigrates, 20; manages Telocaset plant, 84; manages Mount Hood Road, 92n; mill of, 137; Oregon operations of, 217, 221, 225, 242; with railway, 229; with Logan Sugar, 243

Eccles, William Jack (son of Bertha), 111, 145

Eccles and Quantrell: founded, 205

Eccles Building, 255

Eccles Hotel, 259

Eccles Investment Company: organized, 156, 190, 227, 253, 259. *See also* Utah International, Inc.

Eccles Lumber Company: 58-59, 186, 205, 214, 227, 257

Eckersley, Emma. *See* Stoddard, Emma

Eckersley, Alice, 63

Eckersley, Joseph, 63

Eden, Utah, 27, 29

Education, of David Eccles, 7-8, 44-45, 197; on Mormon emigrant ships, 20; of Bertha Jensen, 54; Eccles comments on, 134, 146-47, 156-57

Eldredge, Horace S., 256, 257

Elev, Denmark, 54

Elk Creek, Idaho, 61

Ellison, E. P., 116, 241, 243, 246, 265

Emerson, P. H., 75

Emery County, Utah, 191

Emigration, 17-18, 19-20, 51

Emigration Canyon, 54

Empress Theater, 172

Endowment House, 55-56, 64, 135

England, 17

Esmeralda Mine, 206

Europe: Eccles visits, 117, 156, 168-69

Evans, David: sugar agent, 265

Evans, Joseph B., 88, 89

- F -

Farnsworth, Philo T., 262

Farr Mill, Ogden, 248-49

Factory Act, (1833), Scotland, 3

Family, Mormon, 195

Fife, William, 27

First National Bank of Boston, 196

First National Bank of Ogden, 71, 176, 186; history of, 107, 257-58; loans of, 248, 252

First National Bank of Provo, 256

First Security Bank, 261

First Security Banking Company, 157, 261

First Security Corporation, 238; officers: 157; establishes banks, 257, 258, 259

Florence, Nebraska, 24

Flour mills, 248-49

Fluor Corporation, 254

286 / INDEX

Flygare, N.C., 215, 255, 257
Fort Hall, Idaho, 32-33
Franklin, Idaho: Eccles' family in, 153
Free Silver, 67
Funge, W. W., 76

- G -

Garff, Christian, 226
Gates, Emma Lucy, 171
Geddes, Margaret, 141n., 183
Geddes, William, 141n., 183
Genereau (Mr.), 146
George A. Lowe and Company, 211
Gentiles: not to be patronized, 42; in Utah political struggle, 67; percent of population, 68; hopeful of economic power, 68, 74; gain political control, 77
Gibbs, John, 21
Gibson and Eccles, 205, 211
Gibson, Eccles and VanNoy, 211. *See also* Gibson and Eccles
Gibson, Henry E.: manages mill, 46, 48, 49, 211; parts with Eccles, 57-58, 212; sells interests, 215
Gibson, John, 59
Glasgow, Scotland, 4, 5, 6, 168, 197
Golightly Company, 234
Golightly, M. J., 237
Grand Coulee Dam, 254
Grand Opera House Company of Ogden, the, 122, 143, 205, 271-72
Grand Ronde Lumber Company: 206, 219, 223, 224
Grande Ronde River, Oregon, 33, 224
Grande Ronde Valley, Oregon, 94
Grande Ronde Valley Lumber Company. *See* Grand Ronde Lumber Company
Granger, Wyoming, 251
Grant, B. F., 173, 196
Grant, Heber J.: comments on Eccles, 101-102, 130, 198, 201-202; Church financial agent, 103; appeals to Eccles, 136; escorts Eccles family, 174; in insurance, 261-62; implement business of, 269
Grant, Joshua F., 269
Grant, Odell and Company, 269
Grass Creek Coal Company of Utah, 122
Grasshopper plague, 29
Gray's Gulch, Idaho, 60. *See also* Wood River, Idaho
Great Salt Lake City. *See* Salt Lake City, Utah

- H -

Hagenbarth, F. J., 236
Haight, Horton D., 24
Hailey, Idaho, 212
Hall, Eccles and Company, 205, 215-16
Hall, Thomas F., 84, 216
Hall, William, 29, 54
Hannibal, Missouri, 23
Harriman, Henry, 183, 189
Harrison, Ellen Stoddard Eccles Merrill. *See* Eccles, Ellen Stoddard (daughter)
Harrison, Hugh, 157
Harrison, Nora Stoddard Eccles Treadwell. *See* Eccles, Nora Stoddard
Harrison, Richard, 157
Harwood, Spencer, 214
Hatch, H. E., 128, 175, 261, 263
Havemeyer, Henry O.: Eccles associate, 108-109, 241; sugar magnate, 115, 201; comments on Eccles, 132; Ellen Eccles meets, 156; purchases Utah sugar stocks, 244-45, 246
Havemeyer, Horace, 132
Haynes Spur, Oregon, 217, 219
Hedlock, Reuben, 12-13
Heiner, Daniel, 267
Hendricks, Brigham H., 244
Hermitage, Utah, 233
Herrick, Lester, 269
Herrold (cattle rancher), 118
Heywood, A. R., 174
Hiawatha, Utah, 267
Higgenbotham, Mrs. Samuel, 55
High Creek Power and Light Company, 206, 270-71
Hill, J. T., 268
Hills, Lewis S., 107, 249, 256, 269
Hoge, William L., 231
Home Fire Insurance Company, 205, 261-62
Home Lumber and Coal Company, 227
Homestead Act (1862), 219
Hood River: Timber interests near, 84, 91, 234-35
Hood River, Oregon: sawmill at, 89, 219, 221; railroad constructed to, 91; Eccles holdings at, 92, 216, 220
Hood River Railway Company, 91, 235
Hooper, William H., 256, 257
Hoover Dam, 254
Hopwood, William, 21
Hot Springs, Utah, 232
House of Commons, 18
Howell, Joseph, 64, 244, 263
Howell, Utah, 264

Hudson River, New York, 52
Huntington, Oregon, 215, 251
Huntsville, Utah, 50, 54, 233
Hutchinson, Homer C., 90
Hutchinson, Sarah: marries, 6, 13. *See also* Eccles, Sarah Hutchinson
Hyde, Frank A., 172
Hyde, J. E., 254
Hyde, Orson, 14
Hyrum State Bank, 261
Hyrum, Utah, 270-71

- I -

Idaho, 1, 32-33, 60-61, 84, 116, 153, 212-14, 216, 237, 243, 246
Illinois, 13, 15
Indians, 23, 31-32, 53
Industrial Revolution, 3
Inglis, John, 48, 59, 85, 91, 221
Inglis, Oregon: mill at, 91, 121, 220, 221
Interstate Commerce Commission, 238
Iowa, 52
Irvine, A. B., 270

- J -

Jacobs, Henry C., 178
Jacos Brothers Mill, 34
James, David, 46, 76, 211
Jarvis and Conklin Mortgage and Trust Company, 110, 119, 264
Jarvis, Samuel M., 264
Jennings, William, 249, 257
Jensen, Bertha Marie: at school with Eccles, 45; early life of, 50-55; crosses Atlantic, 51; courtship and marriage of, 49-50, 55-56. *See also* Eccles, Bertha Marie Jensen
Jensen, Christian (Christen), 50, 51, 54, 55
Jensen, Jens, 50
Jensen, Karen Peterson, 51
Jensen, Maren Anderson, 50
Jensen, Peter M., 54
John J. Boyd, 63
Jones, Emma Stoddard Eccles. *See* Eccles, Emma Stoddard
Jones, LeGrande, 157
John Day River, Oregon, 225
John Stoddard and Son, 215

- K -

Kelton, Utah, 263
Kenner, S. A., 76-77

Kerr, John W., 264
Kiesel, Fred J.,; in mayoral elections, 69, 70, 73, 77; sugar interests of, 241, 243, 246
Kingdom of God, 12, 68, 134
Kircher, C. H., 265
Knotty problems, *See* lumbering
Knox Doctrine, 3
Knight, Jesse, 116, 244
Knight Sugar Land and Livestock Company, 122
Knight Sugar, Land and Investment Company, 206, 244

- L -

LaGrande, Oregon, 105, 106, 116, 223
LaGrande Sugar Company. *See* Oregon Sugar Company, LaGrande
LaGrande Sugar Factory, 94, 205, 223
Langton, S. A., 263
Larson, Charles, 36, 38
Latter-day Saints' Millenial Star, 18
Lauder, Harry, 130
Leaser, Ernest, 172
Lehi Sugar Company, 205. *See also* Utah Sugar Company, Lehi
Lehi, Utah, 101-102, 265-66
Lewiston Sugar Company, 116, 137-38, 186, 206, 244-45
Lewis, William H., 244
Liberal Party: organized, 68; in Ogden elections, 69, 70, 73, 77; dissolved, 79
Liberty, Utah, 27, 29
Lion Coal Company, 118, 206, 268-69
Little, Feramorz, 257
Little Salmon River, 219
Liverpool, England, 17
Livestock: Eccles companies listed, 208-209
Livingstone Lumber Company, 227
Logan, Utah, 106, 270-71
Logan Canyon, Utah, 226
Logan Rapid Transit: constructed, 121, 206, 233-34, 237
Logan Second Ward, 254
Logan Third Ward, 254
Logan Sugar Company: consolidated, 115-16, 241; construction of factory, 127; Eccles visits, 132; history of, 206, 243; stock of, sold, 246
Logan Temple, 65
Los Angeles, California, 230, 232
Lost Lake Lumber Company, 91, 220, 221, 234
Lowe, George A., 249

Lumbering: in Oregon, 84, 88, 91;
  interests conflict with government, 85;
  lumberman's convention, 85, 213;
  equipment used in, 91-92, 212; problems of, 92-93; Timber and Stone
  Act, 93; Eccles profits from, 191,
  194; Eccles companies, 207, 211-226
Lumberman's Convention (Logan), 85,
  213
Lund, Robert, 231, 248
Lyon, John, 15

- M -

Mack, James, 249
Mahler, Mr., 237
Manhattan, 51
Manifesto (1890), 99-100. *See also*
  Plural marriage
Market Lake (Roberts), Idaho, 214
Martha Society, 144
Mason Valley, Nevada, 235, 236
Matson, George H.: with Ogden Waterworks, 248, 265
Mayo Clinic, 200
McCornick, W. S., 269
McCoy, D. F., 172
McCune, A. W., 107, 231
McDonough and Company, 75
McEwan, Oregon: road to, 218, 222, 229
McFarland, A., 184
McIntosh, Richard, 231
McKay, David O., 134, 179
McKinley, William (U.S. President), 177
McKinney, A. C., 248
McQuarrie, Robert, 70
Meacham, Oregon, 89, 219
Mendon, Utah, 237
Merrill, Ellen Stoddard Eccles. *See*
  Eccles, Ellen Stoddard (daughter)
Merrill, Marriner W., 247
Metoka, 13
Mexico, 169, 196
MIA (Mutual Improvement Association), 144
Michigan, 23, 146, 223
Middleton, C. F., 184
Milk, 247-48
Milford, Utah, 107, 230, 232
Miller, H. E., 235-36
Mimnaugh, C. H., 224
Mimnaugh, P., 223, 224
Mimnaugh, T. H., 224
Mining, 44, 109, 235, 267-68

Minnie Moore Mine, 235
Minnoch, Peter, 215
Missionaries (Latter-day Saint), 11,
  12, 135, 136, 164
Mississippi River, 13
Missouri, 23, 52
Missouri River, 23, 24, 52
Moench, Louis F.: professor, 45, 55, 134
Mohrland, Utah, 267
Monson, Joseph, 271
Montana, 116, 192, 213
Monte Cristo Mill, 58, 59
Monte Cristo Mountains, Utah,: sawmill near, 46, 211, 212
Moore, D., 71
Mormon Church. *See* Church of Jesus
  Christ of Latter-day Saints, The
Morrell, Joseph, 244
Mount Hood, Oregon, 217, 221
Mount Hood Lumber Company, 206,
  221
Mount Hood Railroad Company, 92,
  222
Mount Hood Railway, 2, 157, 234-35
Mountain States Implement Company,
  157
Moyes, Alec, 35
Moyes, Elizabeth Hutchinson, 6, 37
Moyes, James, 17, 29, 36
Moyes, John H., 7, 27, 29-30, 34-35
Moyes, Margaret, 29-30, 36, 38
Moyes, Robert, 7, 35
Moyes, Stewart, 29-30
Moyes, William, 35, 174
Moyle, James H., 269
Murphy, F. S., 223
Mutual Coal and Lumber Company, 227

- N -

Nampa, Idaho, 241, 246
National Copper Bank, 257
Nauvoo, Illinois, 13
Nebraska, 52
Nevada: Eccles interests in, 1, 118, 236;
  railroads in, 107, 230-31, 235-36, mentioned, 48, 211, 229
Nevada-California-Oregon Railroad,
  229, 230
Nevada Copper Belt Railroad Company,
  206, 235-36
Nevada Douglas Copper Company, 236
Nevada Douglas Mine, 122
New Orleans, Louisiana, 13
New York, 22-23, 51-52
Niagara Falls, 23, 52, 132

INDEX / 289

Nibley, Alex, 223
Nibley, Charles W., 228, 254, 255; Eccles' partner, 84, 87, 94, 216, 219; in Oregon, 86, 217; comments on Eccles, 87, 131-32, 175-76, 179; buys light company, 94; LDS Presiding Bishop, 173; Utah and Pacific treasurer, 231; sugar interests of, 242, 243, 244, 246; lumber interests of, 221, 223-24
Nibley-Channel Lumber Company, 224
Nibley-Hilgard Lumber Company, 221
Nibley, Jim, 89
Nibley, Merrill, 89
Nibley-Mimnaugh Lumber Company, 122, 206, 224
North American Trust, 232
North Platte, Nebraska, 52
North Powder, Oregon, 83, 86, 89, 205, 215, 219
North Powder Milling Company, 216
Northwestern States Mission, 94
Nyssa, Oregon, 246

- O -

Odell, George T., 269
Ogden, Logan and Idaho Central Railroad: formed, 233, 237
Ogden, Utah: observes Eccles' death, 1; Eccleses move to, 27: railroads in, 39, 237, 251; B. Jensen moves to, 54-55; Eccles mayor of, 67, 73, 75; Gentiles in, 68-69, 77; People's Party in, 69, 77; Eccles' legal residence, 100; sugar plant in, 105, 241; waterworks in, 120; lumberyard in, 212
Ogden and Hot Springs Railroad, 110, 206, 232, 233
Ogden and Logan Rapid Transit Company, 270. *See also* Logan Rapid Transit and Odgen Rapid Transit
Ogden Canyon, 43, 54
Ogden Chamber of Commerce, 74
Ogden City Street Car Line, 206, 265
Ogden Drama Club, 144
Ogden Daily Herald, 71, 72, 74, 136
Ogden Electric Street Railway Lines, 110
Ogden Fifth Ward, 137
Ogden First National Bank, 164, 256, 261. *See also* First National Bank of Ogden
Ogden Furniture and Carpet Company, 122, 206, 270
Ogden Gas Light Company, the, 75
Ogden Girl Scouts, 144

Ogden Investment Company, 118
Ogden Milling and Elevator Company: founded, 205n, 248-49
Ogden Opera House. *See* Grand Opera House Company of Ogden
Ogden Railway Company, 206, 232
Ogden Rapid Transit Company; history of, 110, 206, 232-33; successful, 186, 237; acquires buildings, 238
Ogden River, 43
Ogden Standard-Examiner, 1, 77-78
Ogden Sugar Company: founded, 105-106, 205; consolidated, 115-16; employees at Eccles' funeral, 177; history of, 241-42; stock of, sold, 246
Ogden Tabernacle, 177
Ogden Transit Company. *See* Ogden Rapid Transit Company
Omaha, Nebraska, 52
Opera. *See* Grand Opera House Company of Ogden
Oregon: Eccles moves to, 30-34, 85, 214; Ellen Eccles in, 71, 154; Eccles interests shift to, 85; Eccles interests effect, 94-95; poor sugar production in, 242-43; mentioned, 215, 217, 219, 222, 224-25, 235, 251-52. *See also* Baker, Columbia River, Hood River, Inglis, McEwan, Meacham, Mount Hood, North Powder, Nyssa, Parkdale, Perry, Pleasant Valley, Portland, Prairie City, Salem, Sumpter Valley, Telocaset, Viento, Whitney, Wolf Creek
Oregon American Lumber Company, 220
Oregon and Stoddard Sales Company, 223
Oregon Lumber Company: founded, 2, 84, 86, 205; parent company of, 84; history of 90n, 216-21; indicted, 93-94, 225; continues growth, 89, 91, 122, 234; Eccles president of, 145; Eccles works at, 156; shareholders, 228
Oregon Railway and Navigation Company: construction of, 215, 216, 235
Oregon Short Line, 215, 230; to Wood River, 61; to Baker, 83; to Logan, 163; timber to, 228; contract with Utah and Pacific, 231; Corey contract on, 251
Oregon Sugar Company, LaGrande: established, 105, 205; inefficient, 106, 242-43; consolidated, 115-16, 246; history of, 242-43; relocated, 245; stock of, sold, 246

Oregon Trail, 31
Orem, A. J. and Company, 236
Orem, Walter C., 236
Ormsby, Dr. O. C., 154
Oroville, California, 108, 252
Orpheum Theater, 272

- P -

Paisley, Scotland, 3, 5, 11-12, 169
Pakistan, 109
Panic: in 1893, 262; in 1897, 248; in 1907, 252
Pape, D. H., 268
Paris, Idaho, 216
Paris World's Fair (1900), 169
Parkdale, Oregon, 91, 235
Parker, H. C., 270
Parkinson, George C., 244
Patterson, Adam, 118, 243, 246, 253, 260
Pawlas, John, 250
Pearl, 219
Peery, Mrs. D. H., 55
Peery, David H.: in mayoral elections, 69, 70, 72; over Ogden Chamber of Commerce, 75; shareholder, 215; purchases mill, 249
People's Party: Mormons establish, 68; gets majority vote, 68; in Ogden, 69, 70, 72, 77; dissolved, 79; *Ogden Herald* organ of, 136
Perpetual Emigration Fund, 15, 16, 17, 35
Perry, Oregon, 223
Peru, 109
Pet Milk, 248
Peterson and Sons Planing Mill, 254
"Phoenix Mills," 249
Pierce, Isaac N., 248
Pingree, James, 108, 241, 252, 270
Pingree, John, 176
Pioche, Nevada, 48, 211
Pitts, William H., 21
Pleasant Grove Canning Company, 248
Pleasant Valley, Oregon, 89, 217, 219
Plural marriage: condoned by LDS Church, 65; laws regarding, 65, 186-188; Eccles practices, 86, 141n, 163, 183; secrecy of, 86, 153-54; discontinued, 99-100; some amnesty for, 154; and estate distribution, 186; in Utah and Idaho, 214
Pocatello, Idaho, 213
Polygamy. *See* Plural marriage
"Polygamy Central." *See* Sumpter Valley Railway

Pope and Talbot, 36
Portland, Oregon, 215, 252
Portneuf River, 214
Pout, H. B., 269
Poverty, plight of Eccleses, 15, 126
Powder River, 87
Prairie City, Oregon, 228, 229
Pratt, Orson, 12
Preston, Idaho, 237
Preston, William B., 244
Priesthood, Mormon, 135, 196
Primary Association, 154
Promontory-Curlew Land Company, 122, 206, 263-64
Price, Utah, 268
Puget Sound, Washington, 36

- Q -

Quantrell, A. D., 60, 61, 212
Quinney, Mrs. S. Joseph. *See* Eccles, Jessie
Quinney, S. Joseph: lawyer, 157

- R -

Rackliff, H. B., 247
Railroad: sparks Mormon cooperatives, 41; into Hood River, 91; equipment, 91-92; in Utah, 107; Eccles in, construction, 108, 191; Eccles, companies listed, 207, 228-240
Raleigh v. *Wells,* 188
Ramsey, O. N., 84, 216
Rank, W. M., 69, 70
Raymond, Alberta, Canada, 116, 244
Reconstruction Finance Corporation, 238
Reforestation, 93
Reformation (LDS), 14
Relief Society, 144, 154
Republican Party, 67, 79
Reno, Nevada, 229
Rice, Leonard G., 53
Rice, Wendsor, V., 236
Rich, Ezra, 174-75
Rich, John T., 260
Richmond State Bank, 206, 247
Richmond, Utah, 226, 247
Richards, Addison, 145
Richards, Franklin D., 69
Richards, Vivian Eccles. *See* Eccles, Vivian
Rigby, William F., 62
Rio Grande Western Railroad, 59, 191, 268
Riter, W. W., 171, 173, 176, 221
Roberts, Idaho, 214

INDEX / 291

Rock Springs, Wyoming, 268
Rocky Mountain Locusts, 29
Rolapp, Henry H., 221, 255, 267; with Amalgamated Sugar, 243, 246; sugar interests of, 241, 243, 246
Romney, Alonzo, 145
Romney, George, 217, 221, 262, 269; speaks at Eccles' funeral, 179; builder 199
Romney, Laura Eccles. *See* Eccles, Laura
Rupert, Idaho, 246
Ryberg, Bill, 128
Ryberg, Eric, 127-28

- S -

Saint Joseph, Missouri, 23, 52
Saints. *See* Church of Jesus Christ of Latter-day Saints, The
Salem, Oregon, 36
Salisbury, H. H., 225
Salt Lake City, Utah: observes Eccles' death, 1; teamsters to, 24; Eccleses move from, 27; railroads to, 108, 251, 252; Eccles girls visited, 164
Salt Lake, Los Angeles, and San Pedro Railroad, 232
Salt Lake Tabernacle, 54
Salt Lake Theater, 143
Salt Lake Tribune, 182, 184, 189
Salt Lake Valley, 54
San Francisco, California, 35
San Pedro, Los Angeles, and Salt Lake Railroad, 107
Savage, Ray T., 145
Savage, Vida Eccles. *See* Eccles, Vida
Sayre, Art, 92
Schaub, K. C., 271
Schrans, H. C., 172
School of the Prophets, 42
Scofield, Utah: mills at, 59, 84, 212, 213; store at, 59, 71; lumber attached, 85
Scotland: industrial revolution in, 2-3; liquor consumption in, 5; LDS Church grows in, 14; S. Eccles on mission to, 59; J. Stoddard from, 63; Eccles visits, 117, 168-69; Eccles' upbringing in, 130-32, 197. *See also* Paisley
Scott, Sir Walter, 168
Scowcroft, Heber: organizes coal company, 267
Scowcroft, Joseph, 145, 241, 243, 246, 268
Scowcroft, Vivian Eccles. *See* Eccles, Vivian

Sears, S. W., 257
Sharp, James, 261
Sharp, John, 257
Sharp, William G., 267
Shepard, J. I., 270, 271
Sherman, J. S., 223
Shockley, A. S., 222
Shockley and McMurran Lumber Company, 222
Shoshone Indians, 31
Shupe, Daniel W., 250
Shupe-Williams Candy Company, 122, 249-50
Shurtliff, F. M., 229, 255
Shurtliff, L. W., 178
Singleton, M. E., 238
Slusser, C. R., 271
Smith, Elias A., 261
Smith, George Albert, 266
Smith, Hyrum, 13
Smith, John Henry, 262, 269
Smith, Joseph, 12, 13
Smith, Joseph F., 164, 175, 179-80, 231, 269
Smith, Julina, 164
Smith Valley, Nevada, 236
Smithfield, Utah, 116
Snake Indian War, 31
Snake River, Idaho, 32
Snake River Valley, Idaho, 116
Snow, Eliza R., 28, 38
Snow, Frank F., 269
Snow, George A., 269
Snow, Lorenzo, 107, 137
Snow, O. G., 260
South America, 109, 239
Sparks, John (governor), 118, 253
Spaulding, J. E., 251
Spencer, D. S., 271
Spencer, Hiram H.: Eccles' associate, 61, 62; lumber interests of, 84, 214, 215, 221; finances building, 217; in furniture company, 270, sugar interests of, 241, 243, 246; with Ogden waterworks, 265
Spencer, Idaho, 214
Spencer, Ramsey, and Hall, 84, 205, 216
Sprague, H. B., 172
Sprowl, Andrew, 11-12, 12n, 14
Stanley, C. A., 223
Stanley, F. S., 223
Stanley, L. C., 223
State Bank of Brigham City, 122, 260
State Bank of Richmond, 260-61
Stayner, Arthur: horticulturist, 100
Stevens and Stone Mill, 249

Stoddard and Son Lumber Company, 215
Stoddard Brothers Lumber Company, 222
Stoddard, D. I., 224
Stoddard, E. I., 224
Stoddard, Elizabeth Yates: marries John Stoddard, 64
Stoddard, Ellen, 62, 64, 65
Stoddard, Emily Kershaw, 63-64
Stoddard, Emma Eckersley, 63-64, 86
Stoddard, George E.: manages mill, 219, 222, 223, 224; moves to Michigan, 223; with Oregon Sugar, 242, Amalgamated Sugar director, 243, 246
Stoddard, Henry: moved to Oregon, 86
Stoddard, Jessie, 86
Stoddard, John: Eccles associate, 62, 222, 229; in Beaver Canyon, 62, 213; marries, 64; family of, 65; in Ogden, 65; imprisoned, 66; in Oregon, 71, 83, 86, 154, 215; buys lumberyard, 215; finances building, 217
Stoddard, Joseph, 222, 224
Stoddard Lumber Company, 205, 222, 224
Stoddard, Sarah Yates, 64
Stoddard, William, 86
Stohl, Oleen N., 263
Stone, W. S., 249
Stratford, Egbert, 270
Stuart, David, 19, 21, 30
Sugarbeets, *See* Sugar industry
Sugar House, Utah, 100
Sugar industry: early Utah disasters in, 100; history of, 101n; to meet industrial needs, 102; Eccles expands in, 105; Eccles' companies amalgamated, 115-16; prospers in West, 116; cane sugar, 117; Eccles refineries, 208, 240-246; affected by beet leafhopper, 246; candy business, 249-50. *See also* individual companies as given in Appendixes 1 and 2
Sugar Trust, 244, 245. *See also* American Sugar Refining Company
Sumpter, Oregon: gold rush, 228, 229
Sumpter Valley, Oregon, 87, 217
Sumpter Valley Railroad Company, 128, 205, 228-30. *See also* Sumpter Valley Railway
Sumpter Valley Railway: founded, 2; backed by Union Pacific, 87-88; legend of, 88; mills on, 92, 220; planned, 217-18, 228; opens road, 222
Swan Land and Livestock Company, 232
Sweet, Fred A., 267

- T -

Tanner, Nathan, Jr., 79
Taylor, Armstrong and Romney Company, 217
Taylor, James, 248
Taylor, John, 249, 257
Taylor Mills, 249
Telluride, Colorado, 270-71
Telocaset, Oregon, 84, 216
Thailand, 109
Thatcher, Aaron, 258
Thatcher Brother's Banking Company of Logan, 128, 175, 206, 256, 258-29, 261
Thatcher, John, 258
Thatcher, Moses, 258, 260, 269
Thomstorff, Bertha Eccles. *See* Eccles, Bertha Olivia (daughter)
Timber and Stone Act (1878), 214, 219-220; prohibits shipping, 83, 215; circumvented, 93
Timber Cutting Act (1878), 93
Tithing, 135-36, 137
Toponce, Alexander, 264
Tracy, Joseph, 30
Transcontinental Railroad, 39, 68
Treadwell, Nora Stoddard Eccles. *See* Eccles, Nora Stoddard
Tribe, George H., 267
Tri-State Yards, 227
Twin Falls, Idaho, 246

- U -

Uinta, Utah, 251
Uncommercial Traveler (Dickens), 18
Union Opera House, 271
Union Pacific Railroad: Eccles at mine of, 44; line to North Platte, 52; buys Eccles' line, 107; incorporated in Utah, 183; supports Sumpter railway, 87-88, 218, 228; at Milford, 230; to complete California line, 232; granted land, 263
United Order Manufacturing and Building Company, 205, 226, 254-55
United States Department of Justice, 246
United States, Government of: timber regulations of, 85, 93; indicts Eccles, 94; against polygamy, 154, 187; harasses lumbermen, 213, 225; land policies of, 219-20, 263
United States Forest Service, 220
United States Fuel Company, 118, 267
United States Smelting, Refining and Mining, 267
United States Supreme Court, 94, 186, 187

INDEX / 293

University of Michigan, 146
Unlawful cohabitation, 72. *See also* Plural marriage
Upper Snake River, 61
Utah: political history of, 67; bi-faith organization in, 74; attains statehood, 79; timber regulations in, 85; inheritance tax in, 182, 183, 184, 188-89; territorial legislature of, 186-87, 188; settlers move to Oregon, 220; railroad from, to California, 230
Utah and Colorado Canning Company, 248
Utah and Northern Railroad, 61, 213, 218, 258
Utah and Pacific Railroad, 107, 205, 230-32
Utah Canning Company, 122, 248
Utah Central Railroad, 251
Utah Condensed Milk Company, 122, 206, 247-48, 260
Utah Construction Company: organized, 2, 108, 205, 231; branches interests, 109, 194, 236; Eccles holdings in, 186; history of, 251-54. *See also* Utah International, Inc.
Utah-Idaho Central Railroad, 206, 226, 236-39
Utah-Idaho Sugar Company, 122, 171, 240-41, 244, 265-66
Utah Implement Company, 122
Utah International, Inc., 157, 190, 254. *See also* Utah Construction Company and Eccles Investment Company
Utah Loan and Trust Building, 110, 118-19
Utah Loan and Trust Company, 255, 260
Utah Lumber Company, 122
Utah, Nevada, and California Railway Company: organized, 231
Utah Packing Company, 248
Utah Power and Light Company, 270, 271
Utah Public Service Commission, 238
Utah Rapid Transit, 233, 238
Utah State Agricultural College, 156-57, 237
Utah State University, 259. *See also* Utah State Agricultural College
Utah Sugar Company, Lehi: incorporated, 101; Eccles directs, 102; history of, 240-41; sells stock, 245-46; land holdings of, 265
Utah Supreme Court: on distributing estates, 186, 187
Uvada, Nevada, 107, 230, 231

- V -

VanNoy, W. T.: manages mill, 46, 48, 49, 211; sells interest, 57, 211; in Beaver Canyon, 62, 213
Viento, Oregon, 84, 92, 217, 221, 234
Vineyard Land and Livestock Company, 118, 206, 253. *See also* Utah Construction Company

- W -

W. H. Eccles Lumber Company, 122, 206, 220, 225
Wabuska, Nevada, 236
Wallace, William, 168
Washington. *See* Chenowith, Puget Sound
Watson, E. W., 248
Watson, James, 21
Watson, John, 134, 137, 215, 255; Ogden ZCMI manages, 60; speaks at Eccles' funeral, 179
Wattis Edmund O., 108, 251-52, 268
Wattis, William H., 108, 194, 251-52, 268
Webber, Thomas G., 262
Weber Academy (Weber State College), 134-77
Weber Club, 116, 177, 255
Weber Mill, 249
Weber Valley, Utah, 94, 220
Wells, Melvin D., 269
Wells Fargo Bank of San Francisco, 103, 240
Wellsville, Utah, 62, 63, 237
West, Joseph A., 75, 229, 230
West, Chauncey W., 249
Western Pacific Railroad, 108, 252
Whalen, Thomas, 184
Wheeler Creek, 43
White, Barnard, 49, 211, 269
Whitney, H. G., 171, 173, 199
Whitney, Oregon, 229
Willamette River, 34
William Eccles and Company, 84, 205, 216
Williams, William R., 249-50
Winder, John R., 241
Wisconsin, 223
Wisconsin and Oregon Lumber Company, 225
Wolf Creek, Oregon, 222
Wood, J. D., 236
Wood River, Idaho, 192, 212
Woodruff, Abraham O., 244
Woodruff, Wilford, 101, 104, 107

World's Columbian Exposition in Chicago, 168
World War I, 237
World War II, 227, 238, 269
Wright, A. T., 70
Wright, Arthur, 145
Wright, Bertha Eccles. *See* Eccles, Bertha (daughter)
Wright, Gilbert G., 269
Wright, J. M., 254
Wyoming, 25, 42, 44, 65, 117-18, 215, 251, 268
Wyoming Coal Company, 117
Wyoming Sugar Company, 145

- Y -

Yerington, Nevada, 235
Young, Brigham: promise to W. Eccles, 31; criticized, 37, urges cooperation, 41, 42; attempts sugar refining, 100; home of, 164; Eccles like, 196; bank president, 256; daughters of, 258
Young, Hyrum S., 164, 215, 217, 257

- Z -

ZCMI, 41, 257
Zion, 12, 15, 22, 28
Zion's Central Board of Trade, 74

Soc
HC
102.5
E2
A77

DATE DUE	